T0316931

Supra-National Integration and Domestic Economic Growth

Labour, Education & Society

Edited by György Széll,
Heinz Sünker, Anne Inga Hilsen
and Francesco Garibaldo

Volume 28

PETER LANG

Frankfurt am Main · Berlin · Bern · Bruxelles · New York · Oxford · Wien

Simone Selva

Supra-National Integration and Domestic Economic Growth

The United States and Italy
in the Western Bloc Rearmament
Programs 1945-1955

translation by Filippo del Lucchese,
revision by Simone Selva

PETER LANG
Internationaler Verlag der Wissenschaften

Bibliographic Information published by the Deutsche Nationalbibliothek
The Deutsche Nationalbibliothek lists this publication in the Deutsche Nationalbibliografie; detailed bibliographic data is available in the internet at http://dnb.d-nb.de.

The translation of this work has been funded by SEPS
Segretariato Europeo per le Pubblicazioni Scientifiche

Via Val d'Aposa 7
40123 Bologna - Italy
E-Mail: seps@seps.it
www.seps.it

Original Edition:
Simone Selva: Integrazione internazionale e sviluppo interno. Stati Uniti e Italia nei programmi di riarmo del blocco atlantico (1945-1955).
Carocci, Rome 2009, ISBN: 978-88-430-5253-0

Library of Congress Cataloging-in-Publication Data

Selva, Simone.
[Integrazione internazionale e sviluppo interno. English]
Supra-national integration and domestic economic growth : the United States and Italy in the Western Bloc Rearmament Programs 1945-1955 / Simone Selva ; translation by Filippo del Lucchese ; revision by Simone Selva.

p. cm.
Includes index.
ISBN 978-3-631-60579-0
1. Italy--Economic conditions--1945-1976. 2. Italy--Defenses--Economic aspects.
3. Italy--Military relations--United States. 4. United States--Military relations--Italy.
5. Military assistance, American--Italy. 6. North Atlantic Treaty Organization--Italy.
I. Title.
HC305.S46813 2012
355'.032409045--dc23
                          2012030559

ISSN 1861-647X
ISBN 978-3-631-60579-0
© Peter Lang GmbH
Internationaler Verlag der Wissenschaften
Frankfurt am Main 2012
All rights reserved.

www.peterlang.de

For my parents, and their tried patience
For Mari, and our past together

Table of contents

8

Introduction

Supra-national economic integration and the Cold War. The Atlantic bloc countries amidst domestic growth and external equilibrium

A widely-held interpretation of American foreign policy after World War II views the transition between the Marshall Plan and security policies initiated under the shadow of the Atlantic Alliance at the turn of the 1950s as a watershed in the events of those years. One of the major questions facing me when I undertook this work concerned the effectiveness of this reading, which identified this shift as a turning point in the history of Euro-Atlantic relations in the early Cold War[1]. The least convincing aspect was that the entire US strategy of building membership of Western Europe could have changed in such a short time, between the gestation of the Western alliance and the Korean crisis[2]. The approach favored by the protagonists of the Marshall Plan aimed at building social cohesion by facilitating the process of reconstruction of European economies using both economic and cultural means. The idea that this tactic had been so swiftly and so entirely abandoned to make room for an armed defense of the free world based on strategic military defense policies seemed to be too mechanical and linear. Had this been the case, the consequence of American choices in a continent like Europe, particularly in areas where national communist parties and workers' movements were enjoying increasing consensus, would have been two-fold. Firstly, the institutional role of the infant Atlantic Pact would have been completely taken over by security and military issues, thus influencing the whole meaning of the Western alliance and of what membership of it

---

1 D.Yergin, *Shattered Peace. The Origins of the Cold War and the National Security State*, Houghton Mifflin, Boston, 1978; M.Leffler, *A Preponderance of Power. National Security, the Truman Administration, and the Cold War*, Stanford University Press, Stanford, 1992; B.Cumings, *The Origins of the Korean War, vol. 2, the Roaring of the Cataract 1947-50*, Princeton University Press, Princeton, 1990; J.L.Gaddis, *Strategies of Containment. A Critical Appraisal of Postwar American National Security Policy*, Oxford University Press, Oxford, 1982; R.Pollard, *Economic Security and the Origins of the Cold War 1945-1950*, Cambridge University Press, Cambridge, 1985; W.Stueck, *The Korean War. An International History*, Princeton University Press, Princeton, 1995; M.Trachtenberg, *A Constructed Peace. The Making of the European Settlement, 1945-1963*, Princeton University Press, Princeton, 1999; J.L.Gaddis, *The Cold War. A New History*, Penguin, New York, 2005; see also some authoritative contributions in the first volume of M.P.Leffler, O.A.Westad (eds), *The Cambridge History of the Cold War*, Cambridge University Press, New York, 2010;

2 for a slightly different and more balanced interpretation of the changing US strategies to stabilize Europe and confront rising Soviet power at the dawn of the Cold War see the recent book by J.L.Harper, *The Cold War*, Oxford University Press, Oxford, 2011, particularly chapter 4;

entailed. Secondly, it would have resulted in an abrupt change of course in law enforcement strategies and containment of the communist presence in those European societies emerging from the conflict, in contrast with the objectives of social integration of the lower classes hitherto pursued by the European Recovery Program (ERP) with its aimed impetus for national economic systems. If membership of the Atlantic Alliance was built on the defense of young European democracies from both external threats and internal ones through security measures, then in countries like Italy and France where internal instability was most apparent, the answer could only be two-fold: on the one hand, a military build-up at both a domestic level and of the national armed forces of the member countries of the Pact developed according to a geo-strategic logic conceived in Washington and in NATO's high command; on the other hand, the continued marginalization of the Left with a range of tactics, from propaganda to legislation on internal security and from action against trade unions to covert operations.

In the 1990s, this broad interpretative framework regarding the shift from the Marshall Plan to the Atlantic Alliance was widely accepted in the historiography on post-World War II international and transatlantic relations. At the time, the historical debate on the economic and political relations between Italy and the United States, which form the bulk of this book, adhered to this view on the history of the foreign economic policy of the United States in the early 1950s. In Italy, in the closing years of the twentieth century, a series of scholarly reconstructions on the history of the Italian Republic in the first post war decade, focused on a wide range of specific research issues that shared this perspective[3]. They ranged from the country's diplomatic relations at the very beginning of the Atlantic Alliance to the early steps in the process of European economic integration. Some of these works on the interweaving between the early Cold War years and the history of the newborn Italian Republic, though more interested in delving into the interplay between the Cold War and the issue of economic stabilization and development, limited their view to the Truman Administration and its initiatives all across Western Europe. Korean rearmament was thus linked to the next page in the history of US hegemony in Europe and the struggle to ensure political stability and alliance to the West by promoting economic growth and social cohesion[4]. Nevertheless, even this literature does not

---

3 M.Del Pero, *L'alleato scomodo. Gli Usa e la DC negli anni del centrismo (1948-1955)*, Carocci, Roma, 2001; R.Gualtieri, *La politica economica del centrismo e il quadro internazionale*, in U.De Siervo, S.Guerrieri, A.Varsori (eds), *La prima legislatura repubblicana, Vol. II, Continuità e discontinuità nell'azione delle istituzioni. Atti del convegno*, Roma 17-18 October 2002, vol. I, Carocci, Roma, 2004; id., *L'Italia dal 1943 al 1992. DC e PCI nella storia della repubblica*, Carocci, Roma, 2006;

4 C.Spagnolo, *La stabilizzazione incompiuta. Il Piano Marshall in Italia 1947-1952*, Carocci, Roma, 2001; M.Campus, *L'Italia, gli Stati Uniti e il Piano Marshall 1947-1951*, Laterza, Roma and Bari, 2008. In the framework of a recently renewed public interest in the historical and contemporary meaning of the Marshall Plan, some fresh historical contributions to the post-World War II economic history of Western Europe focus on the European Recovery Program without no link to the successive economic implication of the American military assistance under the aegis of the Atlantic Pact, see F.Fauri,

12

go beyond the earlier assessment, in fact it actually states that this balance and coexistence between economic aid and military assistance was soon to be upset by the rocketing in public spending fueled by the Korean crisis. This happened just when Washington had decided to distribute contracts for military production among European economies with a view to strengthening political ties between the two areas. According to these scholarly interpretations, the US government decided to use military contracts as a bargaining tool to persuade Rome to combat communism in the workplace and in factories[5].

Therefore, this historiography considers military containment and the break-up of the antifascist alliance between the Catholics and left-wing political parties and working class movement, that had led to the drafting and approval of the Italian Constitution prior to the launch of the Marshall Plan, as the twin pillar for the country's admission not only to the Atlantic Alliance, but also to the political community of countries opposed to the Soviet-dominated East European bloc. Furthermore, admission to the Atlantic community required a certain relinquishing of national sovereignty which in the case of Italy meant a compulsory commitment to confront and tame the Italian Communist Party and its fellow-travelers. This must-do anti-communist policy was in return for military assistance and economic aid in the form of defense procurement to the Italian industrial system[6]. Accordingly, the country's readmission to the international community after its war defeat would come about through a combination of economic stabilization and the enforcement of defense and security policies aimed to protect it from both external aggression and internal threats. This new approach was to distance the Italian working class movement from Italy's mainstream politics[7]

During the late 1990s a significant wave of scholarship was devoted to the study and research of the development policies that the post war economic and political elites of Italy undertook to raise the living standards of the less well-off sector of the population, mainly located in the South, and thus focused their attention on programs to industrialize the Southern regions of

---

P.Tedeschi (eds), *Novel Outlooks on the Marshall Plan. American Aid and European Re-Industrialization*, Peter Lang, Bruxelles, 2011;

5 M.Del Pero, *The United States and Psychological Warfare in Italy 1948-1955*, in "Journal of American history", n. 187 (2001), pp. 130-1334;

6 M.Del Pero, L'Italia e la comunità atlantica, in U.De Siervo, S.Guerrieri, A.Varsori (eds), *La prima legislature repubblicana,* vol. 2, pp. 211-215; id., *Containing containment: rethinking Italy's experience during the Cold War*, in "Journal of Modern Italian Studies", n. 4, (2003), pp. 536-537; see also id., *When the High Seas Finally Reached Italian shores. Italy's Inclusion in the Atlantic Communitas*, in M.Mariano (ed.), *Defining the Atlantic Community. Culture, Intellectuals and Policies in the Mid-Twentieth Century*, Routledge, London, 2010, pp. 161-173;

7 F.De Felice, *Nazione e sviluppo: un nodo non sciolto*, in *Storia dell'Italia repubblicana, Vol. 1, La trasformazione dell'Italia: sviluppo e squilibri, tome 1, Politica, economia, società*, Einaudi, Torino, 1995, pp. 816-834; M.G.Rossi, *Una democrazia a rischio. Politica e conflitto sociale negli anni della guerra fredda*, in *Storia dell'Italia repubblicana, vol. 1, La costruzione della democrazia*, Einaudi, Torino, 1994, pp. 915 ff.;

the country with a view to levering internal aggregate demand[8]. Although innovative from a methodological point of view, these studies were consistent with the leading school of historical studies of the decade in that their research focused on development and an industrial policy implemented from the early 1950s onwards, and was rather limited to the South of the country. South of Rome, in fact, the constituency of the Italian left-wing was much weaker and less organized than in its strongholds in the Central-Northern regions.

After long and careful reflection on this scholarship, several doubts and compelling questions remained on whether, and how, the security and defense policy of NATO were the only way the government of Washington pursued the build-up of the Western bloc after the demise of the Marshall Plan. I wondered whether, in fact, the Atlantic Alliance and the United States devised and implemented these defense and security policies as a complement to the economic assistance programs of the ERP, whose duration through 1951 was considered not long enough to warrant the Atlantic membership of Italy in the long term.

The hypothesis I formulated was that the Atlantic Pact actually contained a dual strategy whereby it sought to meet the challenges of the emerging bipolarity by combining the economic and security issues of its European partners.

This theme was not new in itself either in the field of Italian or international historiography. Indeed, the debate that had developed from the late sixties through to the nineties had advanced along three lines of investigation. A first school of enquiry focused on the transatlantic side of the problem and targeted, mainly from an international point of view, the model of international economic integration that the United States pursued through the military assistance programs promoted under the umbrella of NATO. This model was based on both the growth of exchange of consumer and instrumental goods between the countries of the Western bloc, and a positive balance of payments in the individual economies of its member states[9]. A second wave of works pinpointed the impact of this combination between economic reorganization and restructuring of the military posture in the war-torn European societies. This approach was dictated by the neo mercantilist model of industrialization, germane to the historical experience of the European nation-states that the liberal and social democratic cul-

---

8 S.Battilossi, *L'Italia nel sistema economico internazionale. Il management dell'integrazione: finanza, industria, istituzioni 1945-1955*, FrancoAngeli, Milano, 1996; M.Salvati, *Amministrazione pubblica e partiti di fronte alla politica industriale*, in *Storia dell'Italia repubblicana*, Vol. 1, pp. 413-534; C.Spagnolo, *La polemica sul 'country study', il fondo lire e la dimensione internazionale del Piano Marshall*, in "Studi Storici", n. 1 (1996), pp. 93-144; F.Barca (ed.), *Il capitalismo italiano dal dopoguerra ad oggi*, Donzelli, Roma, 1997; R.Gualtieri, *Piano Marshall, commercio estero e sviluppo in Italia: alle origini dell'europeismo centrista*, in "Studi Storici", n. 3 (1998), pp. 853 ff.;

9 R.N.Cooper, *The Economics of Interdependence: Economic Policy in the Atlantic Community*, McGraw-Hill, New York-London, 1968, particularly introduction, pp. 234 ff.; R.N.Rosecrance, *The Rise of the Trading State. Commerce and Conquest in the Modern World*, Basic Books, New York, 1986;

tures had shared. This second line of enquiry, dominated by German and British historiographies, aimed to understand to what extent the virtuous circle between *sicherheit* and *wirtschaft* was relevant in Europe in the early Cold War period and to what extent the transition to a free-trade model of internal growth driven by increasing demand for consumer goods and capital investment was important. According to this perspective the West German economy of the 1950s (at the time a flourishing mass consumer market) dictated the success of this model, widely known in the literature as libero-scambism[10]. In fact, Germany's importance was highly significant in the continental economic integration framework not only because the country was at the epicenter of this development, but also because her initial exclusion from the Western alliance delayed the process of the country's rearming. This meant that in the early fifties the Federal Republic of Germany was free, after selling her raw materials and capital goods, to dedicate the country's resources to the development of the civilian market whereas the Atlantic partners were called on by NATO to contribute to the industrial effort required by its defense policy.

Finally we should consider the perspective which, following the political and cultural watershed of 1989, opened up the debate on the political destinies of the European post war societies and especially the alternative between politics of inclusion and policies of militarization. This alternative was particularly imperative in Italy, where the closer we came to the Cold War, the more urgent it was to combine the reorganization of political consensus with the country's foreign policy constraints[11]. The latest crop of studies, which concentrates on the origins and development of mass consumer society, assumes that the rules and forces of free-market economics shaped and dominated government-citizen relationships in post war Italy[12].

---

10 W.Abelschauser, *Wirtschaft und Rüstung in den Fünfziger Jahren. Anfänge westdeutscher Sicherheitspolitik 1945-1956*, edited by the Militärgeschichtliches Forschungsamt, Vol. 4/1, Oldenbourg, Munich, 1997; A.Milward, *Different Securities?* in G.Schmidt (ed.), *A History of NATO. The First Fifty Years,* Vol. 1, Palgrave Macmillan, New York, 2001; L.Paggi, *Strategie politiche e modelli di società nel rapporto USA-Europa 1930-1950*, in id., (ed.), *Americanismo e riformismo. La socialdemocrazia europea nell'economia mondiale aperta*, Einaudi, Torino, 1989; the most outstanding and relatively recent work that showed up in the American economic historiography to date is B.Eichengreen, *The European Economy since 1945. Coordinated Capitalism and Beyond*, Princeton University Press, Princeton (N.J.), 2007. According to this author the combining between a mass consumption model based on private consumer goods, an impressive expansion in public spending, and extensive trade liberalization let the West European countries to keep competitive in the post-World War II international economy.

11 F.De Felice, *Nazione e sviluppo*; id., *Nazione e crisi: le linee di frattura*, in *Storia dell'Italia repubblicana,* Vol. 3, *L'Italia nella crisi mondiale. L'ultimo ventennio.* Tome 1, Economia e società, Einaudi, Torino, 1996, pp. 7-130.; L.Paggi, foreword to F.De Felice, *La questione della nazione repubblicana*, Laterza, Roma-Bari, 1999;

12 in this respect the Italian historiography is a remarkable case in point in the framework of a broader European historical trend. Over the last ten years an impressive amount of studies on this topic turned

This research perspective maintains that the Italian postwar mass consumption model was a growth-biased policy based on mass production of consumer durable goods for private consumption.

In contrast to this last wave of scholarship, this book attempts to retrieve a more classical economic and political history discourse by approaching the history of the Italian economic policy since the birth of the Republic from the vantage point of its continuity and discontinuity with the past. In addition, this research identifies post war Italian economic policymaking as a combination between expansionary economic policy initiatives to get the Italian labor movement involved in material reconstruction and economic growth and anti-communist inspired strategies which aimed to reassure the United States governments, and the Western bloc countries at large.

Thus the general thesis of this research is that between the end of the European Recovery Program and the mid-1950s a mix of security policies and economic growth initiatives was the fly-wheel for most West European countries' political and economic supra-national integration, involving both internal growth and international market integration. Through the case study of the military assistance programs of NATO to Italy between the birth of the Atlantic pact and the implementation of comprehensive economic growth programs by the Christian Democrat-led economic and political elites of Italy, I aim to pinpoint a set of connections that linked the shaping of domestic economic policy and the country's foreign policy ties. The negotiations between Italy and its Western allies on the military assistance programs cut across all those economic policy issues that arose from the interplay between internal choices and supra-national integration of the West European economies. They ranged from trade policy to the post-Marshall Plan need to ease the pressures on the balance of payments that were generated after the end of the capital inflows provided by the ERP programs. Moreover, military aid negotiations influenced the fiscal policies formulated in the West European member states of NATO to match the re-launch of industrial investments and aggregate demand with a requirement to cool off public debt and restore balanced public finances as well as influencing the debate on which public spending model should be adopted to pump the internal market successfully. The United States and Italy continued to be involved in bilateral negotiations on the military assistance programs to the Peninsula until the very end of 1950. Subsequently this bargaining process took place against the background of supranational economic and defense institutions such as NATO, the OEEC and then later, IBRD. Consequently, this book provides a detailed reconstruction of these negotiations in order to explore this interdependence and

---

up. Among the most authoritative works it is worth mentioning E.Scarpellini, *Comprare all'americana*, Il Mulino, Bologna, 2001; A.Arviddson, *Marketing modernity: Italian Advertising from Fascism to Postmodernity*, Routledge, London, 2003; P.Capuzzo (ed.), *Genere, generazione, consumi. L'Italia degli anni Sessanta*, Carocci, Roma, 2003; E.Papadia, *La Rinascente*, Il Mulino, Bologna 2005; P.Capuzzo, *Culture del consumo*, Il Mulino, Bologna, 2006; E.Scarpellini, *L'Italia dei consumi*, Laterza, Roma-Bari, 2008;

offers a case study that spans all the transatlantic, European and national research perspectives.

This case study is of paramount importance for researching and reconstructing this two-fold strategy by the US that combined economic and military assistance due to America's post war concern that Italy might become communist. Moreover, as we move from the reconstruction years to the development assistance programs launched in Washington by the mid-1950s to help the country join the community of Western industrial democracies this research perspective becomes ever more significant. This interpretative framework does not in any way intend to underestimate the anti-communist bias and the striking contrast between the birth of democracy and the harsh violence and social conflict that overshadowed the early stages of the Italian Republic[13]. On the contrary, from the perspective of international economic relations, the very nature and objective of this work is to re-interpret the American presence in postwar Italy as balanced between strategies to broaden its western-oriented constituency and moves to make the communist issue a national test of loyalty to the Atlantic Alliance. In this respect, the two-pronged American struggle to both expand the Italian domestic market and its total aggregate demand through the impact that economic mobilization for rearmament could have on the civil sectors, and to influence and shape the dynamics and nature of this expansion in civilian demand and manufacturing, is a remarkable case in point. As a matter of fact, against a background of supra-national interdependence in both goods and capitals typical of the post-World war II American-run capitalist development, the US authorities exploited the military assistance programs implemented under the umbrella of NATO to pursue both an anti-communist means to secure Italy to the Atlantic bloc, and a tidy policy to combine Cold War politics and economic growth[14]. Therefore, according to the research conducted in this work, the widespread and wide-reaching anti-communist bias that swept Italy in the early Cold War

---

13 L.Paggi, *Violenza e democrazia nella storia della Repubblica*, in "Studi Storici", n. 4 (1998), pp. 935-952; L.Baldissara, *Democrazia e conflitto. Gli anni cinquanta come storia*, in id. (ed.), *Democrazia e conflitto. Il sindacato e il consolidamento della democrazia negli anni Cinquanta (Italia, Emilia Romagna)*, FrancoAngeli, Milano, 2006, pp. 13-66; G.Marino, *La repubblica della forza. Mario Scelba e le passioni del suo tempo*, FrancoAngeli, Milano, 1995; M.G.Rossi, *Una democrazia a rischio*. From a different perspective, another cohort of historical literature investigated through the initiatives under way in the Italian and European left since the birth of the Atlantic Pact onward to hamper Italy's military build-up. Astonishingly, this scholarship miss the point and does not place its reconstruction against this post war harsh social conflict between Western oriented forces and pro-Soviet Italian labor movement. In this respect see for example M.Lodevole, *The Western Communists and the European Military Build-up 1949-50: a Preventive Strategy*, in "Cold War History", Vol. 10, n. 2, (2010), pp. 203-228.

14 Both in general and with specific respect to the Italian case see Mutual Security Agency, Office of Assistant Director for Europe, 'Developments in NATO', 6 February 1953, in NARA, RG469, Mission to Italy, Office of the Director, Subject Files (Central Files) 1948-1957, b. 25,. fold. 6 (Evaluation Team);

years, mirrors a time in the history of Italian democracy when attempts to disregard the working class movement, and strategies that aimed for its inclusion in the core of western constituency, co-existed.

An historical inquiry into the military assistance programs as a case study for the reconstruction of the intertwining between domestic and foreign economic policy, internal choices and international constraints that constitutes the common denominator of the three historiographical perspectives briefly outlined above, reveals three significant issues. First and foremost the political economic governance of internal development as a patchwork of policies clearly aimed to build up and cement a stable and loyal social constituency. This perspective provides scholars with the enviable opportunity to assess the political economy of rearmament. Its broad scope, which ranges from foreign economic policy to the economic cultures underpinning the postwar shape of state-market relationships, not to mention the key industrial policy issue revolving around the reorganization of the internal manufacturing system after the demise of Fascism, means it offers a wealth of historical paraphernalia which allows us to reappraise the Italian postwar economic growth model as narrated so far by historians[15].

The second perspective pertains to that development of diplomatic relations between Italy and the United States that was clearly linked to the rearmament programs. Bilateral negotiations on military assistance went way beyond both the economic implications of rearmament for Italy and its economy, and the debate on which policies were worth undertaking to confront them. In fact, the military assistance programs touch upon a variety of political issues of great importance in the history of postwar diplomatic relations between the two countries, such as the revision of the Italian Peace Treaty and the final solution to the international political clash over the North-Eastern city of Trieste and its repositioning between the American and the Soviet spheres of influence on the European theater[16].

Therefore, political relations and economic diplomacy are bound together in the history of the military assistance programs. As a matter of fact, this research clearly shows how both Rome and Washington took advantage of their bargaining on the so called off-shore procurement programs to trade off economic and political targets respectively. Accordingly, the off-shore procurement contracts that are extensively examined in this book, were negotiated against the background of the wider economic confrontation of the US in its trade war against the Soviet

---

15 for a sample of the historiography so far available on the subject see S.Battilossi, *L'Italia nel sistema economico internazionale*; F.Petrini, *Il liberismo a una dimensione. La Confindustria e l'integrazione europea 1947-1957*, FrancoAngeli, Milano, 2005; L.Segreto, *The Importance of the Foreign Constraint: Debates about a New Social and Economic Order in Italy, 1945-1955*, in D.Geppert (ed.), *The Postwar Challenge. Cultural, Social, and Political Change in Western Europe, 1945-58* , Oxford University Press, Oxford, 2003;
16 As widely known to those familiar with this literature, either of these diplomatic issues were key to let Italy move in the international community after its defeat in World War II.

bloc throughout the 1950s. This commercial war was intended to undermine the strength of the communist parties and their trade union fellow-travelers in Western Europe.

The third research issue that stems from a comprehensive reconstruction of the military assistance programs to Western Europe involves both internal policymaking and foreign economic policies and sheds light on the economic cultures of the Italian elites at the very beginning of the international economic integration process that characterized the post war era. The position of these elites and the debate over the military assistance programs is a vantage point from which to reconstruct which were their preferred policy options for opening up the Italian economy and making Italy a stable international trading and manufacturing partner for the West. It emerges that the Italian economic and political elites clashed over the best viable way to ensure goods, capital and monetary integration in the European market. On the one hand we find the economic elites mentoring the Christian Democratic Party in power at the time, on the other, a significant array of economic interests linked to the export sectors and the value of the currency on the foreign exchange markets. My interpretation of this situation clashes with most historical that contend that there was a striking contrast between politics and economics, i.e. between the De Gasperi-led governments and the leading economic institutions of Italy, from the Central Bank to Confindustria, the nation-level association of entrepreneurs. The aim is to account, in as detailed a way as possible, for the variety of approaches and proposals that both sides of the Italian ruling class adopted. The central theme was the debate on the best viable way to open up the national economy to the supra-national market integration in the making at the time. Two very different options came up: one proposed tying the Italian trade and monetary area to the dollar market, while the other preferred to attempt to make Italy part of a truly integrated and interdependent European trade and currency market based on the interlocking exchange of durables and investment goods across the continent. The latter solution envisaged that the German consumer market would drive a continent-wide market integration serving as the fly-wheel which would permit each single European economy to progress over a reasonable period of time.

My own perspective on the mix between anti-communist bias and economic stabilization strategies that influenced the American presence in postwar Europe following the end of postwar economic reconstruction and the Marshall Plan owes much to both the historiography of modern Italy, but also to a number of authoritative studies that advanced and reshaped the international debate on the early Cold War. These studies are in some cases broad-based and at others very specific. In this respect, Victoria De Grazia's image of a *White Atlantic* leading American cultural hegemony in Europe throughout the twentieth century comes with implications broader than her specific research area on the making of a mass consumer culture and market across the old continent. According to De Grazia, by the time American-style mass democracy was at its most successful on the European continent, the very nature and the historical meaning of the Cold War had already undergone a major change. By the late 1950s, in fact, the Cold War as a military confrontation had definitely come of age. By the time of the world famous ‹‹kitchen debate›› exchanges between Soviet Premier Nikita S. Khrushchev and

American Vice President Richard M. Nixon, the Cold War was already an economic competition between the two superpowers[17]. Charles S. Maier identified the fulfilling of material needs as crucial in the early Cold War years, according to a logic whereby economic growth and defense would lead to internal cohesion and the protection of territory[18]. This interpretation of the key role played by public spending and rearmament would endure throughout the period of post war stabilization through to the mid-1950s. This watershed in the historiography on the Cold War is bound to the concept of American freedom that emerged in the United States. As Eric Foner put it, the combination of freedom from fear and freedom from need had been at the basis of US international economic policies from the time of the New Deal in the 1940s[19].

Although the historiography of twentieth century Europe increasingly stresses how the cultures and ideas of war fell apart even as the concept of citizenship became central to the contemporary European parlance, it also pays attention to the interplay between security and prosperity[20]. Furthermore, several studies focus on the relationship between the significant improvement in the average living standards and the aftermath of a mass consumer society as the key pair to reinterpret post war Europe and the 1950s from a social and economic history perspective[21]. The fact that the Italian case study merits particular attention is highlighted by a recent group of studies that have concentrated on the postwar economic development in Southern Italy against the background of Italy's international economic role and relations in the early Cold War years. Although these studies offer different perspectives, all of them attempt to examine the interweaving between the structure of society in Italy as the American economic intervention shaped it and the anticommunist bias as a specific asset to the US intervention in Italy in the early Cold War years[22]. Overall, the aim of this book is to advance

---

17 V.De Grazia, *Irresistible Empire. America's Advance Through Twentieth Century Europe*, Belknap Press, Cambridge (Mass.), 2005; R.Oldenziel, K.Zachmann (eds), *Cold War Kitchen. Americanization, Technology, and European Users*, The MIT Press, Cambridge (Mass.), 2009;

18 C.S.Maier, *Among Empires. American Ascendancy and its Predecessors*, Harvard University Press, Cambridge (Mass.), 2006;

19 E.Foner, *The Story of American Freedom*, W.W.Norton & Company, New York, 1998;

20 J.J.Sheehan, *Where Have all the Soldiers Gone? The Transformation of Modern Europe*, Houghton Mifflin Company, Boston and New York, 2008, Chapters 7 and 8, and particularly pp. 193-160; T.Judt, *Postwar. A History of Europe since 1945*, The Penguin Press, New York, 2005, pp. 242 ff.; see also, M.Mazower, *Dark Continent. Europe's Twentieth Century*, Vintage Books, New York, 1998;

21 S. Cavazza, E.Scarpellini (eds), *La rivoluzione dei consumi. Società di massa e benessere in Europa 1945-2000*, Il Mulino, Bologna, 2010; R.J.Pulju, *Women and Mass Consumer Society in Postwar France*, Cambridge University Press, New York, 2011;

22 E.Bernardi, *La riforma agraria in Italia e gli Stati Uniti. Guerra fredda, Piano Marshall e interventi per il Mezzogiorno negli anni del centrismo degasperiano*, Il Mulino, Bologna, 2006; M.Campus, *L'Italia, gli Stati Uniti e il piano Marshall*; M. Gesummaria, *Piano Marshall e Mezzogiorno*, Mephite Edizioni, Napoli, 2003; L.Pellé, *Il Piano Marshall e la Ricostruzione in Puglia 1947-*

20

this line of investigation on post war Italian politics and economics against the country's transatlantic constraints. It is a research perspective launched at the turn of the 1980s by leading scholars of economic and international history[23], and later expanded further by a cohort of younger historians working between these two historical disciplines[24]. More recently it was revamped by works specifically devoted to furthering knowledge on the role of the Italian business community and the country's economic policymakers and entrepreneurial elites in the construction of a modern industrial democracy and a stable partner of the Atlantic bloc international economy[25]. Finally, this approach takes advantage of the broader debate on the meaning and nature of international economic aid from 1945 to the 1960s. This viewpoint, which is mostly concerned with interpreting US foreign economic policy and the economic aid programs furthered by international economic institutions such as the IBRD it backed, has

52, Piero Lacaita, Manduria-Bari-Roma, 2004; C. Villani, *Il Prezzo della stabilità. Gli aiuti americani all'Italia 1953-1961*, Progedit, Bari, 2007; R.Forlenza, *A Party for the Mezzogiorno. The Christian Democratic Party, Agrarian Reform and the Government of Italy*, in "Contemporary European History", Vol. 19, n. 4 (2010), pp. 331-349; E.Bernardi, *Riforme e democrazia. Manlio Rossi Doria dal fascismo al centro sinistra*, Rubbettino, Soveria Mannelli, 2011;

23 V.Zamagni, *Betting on the Future: the Reconstruction of Italian Industry 1946-1952*, in J.Becker, F.Knipping (eds), *Power in Europe? Great Britain, France, Italy and Germany in a Postwar World 1945-1950*, vol. 1, Walter de Gruyter, Berlin and New York, 1986; J.L.Harper, *America and the Reconstruction of Italy 1945-1948*, Cambridge University Press, Cambridge, 1986; J.Miller, *The United States and Italy. The Politics and Diplomacy of Stabilization 1940-1950*, The University of North Carolina Press, Chapell Hill, 1986; P.P.d'Attorre, *Il Piano Marshall in Italia: politica, economia, relazioni internazionali nella ricostruzione italiana*, in E.Di Nolfo, R.Rainero, B.Vigezzi (eds), *L'Italia e la politica di potenza in Europa 1945-1950*, Marzorati, Milano, 1990; F.Romero, *The United States and the European Trade Union Movement 1944-1951*, The University of North Carolina Press, Chapell Hill, 1993;

24 L.Segreto, *Finanza, industria e relazioni internazionali nella Ricostruzione italiana. Il prestito dell'Eximbank all'Italia 1947-1955*, in "Passato e Presente", n. 51 (2000); Id., *The Impact of US Productivity Philosophy in Italy after the Second World War*, in D.Barjot (ed.), *Catching up with America. Productivity Missions and the Diffusion of American Economic and Technological Influence after the Second World War*, PUF-LA Sorbonne, Paris, 2002; B.Curli, *Ricostruzione e sviluppo. La Banca Mondiale e l'economia Italiana 1947-1951*, in "Archivi e Imprese", Vol. 8, n. 15, (1997), pp. 33-71; F.Fauri, *Il Piano Marshall e l'Italia*, Il Mulino, Bologna, 2009;

25 F.Petrini, *Il liberismo a una dimensione*; id., *Americanismo e privatismo. La Confindustria e il Piano Marshall*, in "Ventunesimo secolo", n. 2 (2007); A.Rapini, *La nazionalizzazione a due ruote*, Il Mulino, Bologna, 2007; in this respect see also, among others, F.Ricciardi, *Il 'Management' del 'governo della scarsità': L'Iri e i Piani di ricostruzione economica*, in "Studi Storici", n. 1 (2005), pp. 127-154; S.Nocentini, *L'Ice e la distribuzione degli aiuti postbellici in Italia (1943-1950)*, idem, pp. 155-186; I.Napoli, *La Deltec e la ricostruzione italiana 1944-1953*, id., pp. 187-218;

recently contended that even from late-1940 these international economic aid programs aimed both to target economic growth and development, and to fight a war on poverty and scarcity[26].

Methodology and Structure

Most of the studies on the economic implications of rearmament in post-World War II Europe continue to work on the so-called burden-sharing stake, that is to say the ratio of national public spending to the common defense effort established under the umbrella of NATO to finance its coordinated rearmament programs at national level. This approach led the vast majority of historical reconstructions to work on the changing ratio of defense spending to the total balance sheet in each European member state of the Atlantic Alliance. In pursuing this research endeavor, most historians assume that each country was to expand its defense spending in proportion to its GDP and resorted to the national account statistics methodology to carry out this type of investigation[27]. This approach is indeed of paramount importance to my own work in so far as it sheds light on the ratio of rearmament to the reorganization of civilian production and consumption in war torn European economies. The impact of rearmament on the process of economic recovery has been touched upon by a significant number of studies. In the case of Italy, Formigoni's book can be considered at the forefront of this scholarship: his *La Democrazia Cristiana e l'alleanza occidentale* convincingly argues that on this point a series of striking contradictions emerged both between the Christian Democrats and the national economic policymaking elites and within the Christian Democratic Party itself[28].

However, this perspective does not allow us to make a comparison with the years preceding this post war period, when the newborn democratic governments of Italy were provided with the weapons, military spare parts and machine tools necessary for the reorganization of the national army firstly by the United Kingdom and then by the United States.

My own perspective throws light on the implications on Italy's foreign trade and monetary equilibrium of the post war military assistance it received. The stabilization policies pursued through the ERP, in fact, had been clearly aimed to restructure monetary stability and the foreign exchange equilibrium in the European countries. This was particularly the case for the foreign exchange rate of the European currencies and the European countries' trade balance against the dollar area and its commodity markets. This research perspective on the economic implications of military assistance after the end of the Marshall Plan is therefore a viable basis

---

26 M.Alacevich, *The World Bank and the Politics of Productivity: the Debate on Economic Growth, Poverty and Living Standards in the 1950s*, in "Journal of Global History", n. 6 (2011), pp. 53-74;

27 in this respect it is a paramount study T.Geiger, *Britain and the Economic Problem of the Cold War. The Political Economy and the Economic Impact of the British Defence Effort 1945-1955*, Aldershot, Ashgate, 2004;

28 G.Formigoni, *La Democrazia cristiana e l'alleanza occidentale 1943-1953*, Il Mulino, Bologna, 1996;

from which to compare the American stabilization policies from the European Recovery Program to the Atlantic Alliance rearmament programs.

From the time of the Marshall Plan, American policymakers had to tackle the problem of how to couple domestic economic stabilization and industrial recovery with supranational integration of the European economies into the wider postwar international economy without imperiling their external monetary and trade equilibrium. The early post-1945 resurrecting of the intra-European commodity market by means of bilateral trade agreements in Europe did not satisfy the American objective to integrate the European economies in a multilateral commercial and currency setting. The 1947 bilateral trade and payment agreements among the West European countries raised liquidity problems across the continent: some countries suffered from imbalances, other accrued an excess of currency liquidity. This asymmetry in monetary equilibrium among the European economies brought the reorganization of a continent-wide trade area to a stalemate. Very soon thereafter, between 1947 and 1950, the foundation of a multilateral trade and payments system was laid down in three successive steps. First the Bank for International Settlements provided the European economies with a multilateral monetary set-off to balance bilateral trade exchanges. Thereafter, the OEEC was to run a share of the ERP funds to offset disequilibrium in the balance of payments arising out of either the intra-European trade, or between the European currency areas and the dollar markets. In this respect the OEEC resorted to the so-called special drawing rights to ease pressure on the European monetary areas suffering from trade imbalances with the dollar area. Finally, the setting-up of the European Payments Union (EPU) offered the European countries a viable way to finance imports in national currency up to an amount not exceeding their own share of the EPU fund.

The US commitment to redress the balance of payments of the West European countries can be better appreciated by closely examining the Marshall Plan support for this process that led to the creation of an international trade and payments system. During the 1950/1951 fiscal year, for instance, the ERP financed EPU for as much as 600 million US dollars. Meanwhile, the US Congress increasingly made the point that the creation of a single European economic area could be achieved not only by raising industrial productivity, the employment rate and market competitiveness across the European economies, but also by means of «dismantling quota and quantitative trade restrictions, as well as barriers on labor migration across Europe»[29].

Therefore, currency liquidity and capital investments to fund imports were at the foreground of American foreign economic policy way before industrial mobilization in the wake of the Korean War stimulated domestic demand for the import of military spare parts and investment goods for the European defense and military industrial complex all across the European

---

29 A.Tarchiani to Ministero degli Esteri, 'Piano Marshall e Punto IV' [original manuscript in Italian, our own translation from Italian to English], 25 May 1950, in ASBI, Carte Caffè, pratt., n. 50, fold. 1;

member states of NATO. This liquidity issue was all the more significant in Italy, where the country's economy suffered from a very narrow money and investments market. Here, a sudden industrial reconversion to the war effort was likely to trigger leapfrogging inflation.

During this period, the interweaving between economic growth and defense economics became a crucial foreign policy issue even in Washington. As I will outline briefly in the first chapter, between 1948 and 1950 the search for a balance between these two cornerstones of Washington's foreign economic policy raised concerns and produced conflicts right across the American political system. Particularly, during this period several leading policymakers raised concerns in Washington regarding the impact that sharp appropriation cuts on ERP and the reworking of public finance determined by war mobilization might have on the critical process of economic recovery and stabilization in Europe. These concerns led to conflict on whether or not the West European allies should be rearmed to such an extent as to provide the Italian industrial system with autonomous production capacity. A further argument against combining economic growth and rearmament as a feasible way to forge US policy toward Western Europe was a widespread fear that the reorganization of the European military-industrial complex on a stable basis might impair the American war industry and its profits.

Over the following two years, even as bilateral assistance programs addressed the European defense requirements through the so-called Mutual Defense Assistance Program, the Truman Administration engaged in lengthy discussions on how an expansion in military production could continue alongside a steady rise in the average living standards and aggregate demand of civilians. Washington thus focused on how to finance the rearmament of its European partners without impairing their foreign trade equilibrium and the ongoing recovery in their balance of payments. Therefore, in order to target the economic strategies underpinning the US defense assistance programs over the postwar era it is worthwhile to investigate both the coupling between rearmament and economic recovery, and the interplay between rearmament and the early steps toward trade integration and currency convertibility among the European economies.

In many respects, the 1951 Mutual Security Act summed up this debate: the passing of this law led the US Congress to launch the new system of multilateral off-shore procurements with which the United States intended to recover foreign monetary equilibrium and internal economic and social stability in the framework of Korean War mobilization.

The entire first chapter therefore addresses two historiographical issues. Firstly, I aim to compare the economic assistance programs promoted under the umbrella of the ERP and the subsequent military aid initiatives in order to understand how the US trade and monetary policies changed from the late 1940s to the early 1950s; secondly, I investigate how the Korean War reshaped the Truman administration approach to the process of economic reconstruction in Western Europe. In this respect, the objective is to offer a snapshot of all the differing views within the US government. In order to achieve this two-fold goal I will give as detailed a reconstruction as possible of the shift from bilateral military aid to the implementation of military assistance programs in a multilateral setting, where NATO played a key role in distributing the new off-shore procurement contracts. I will contend that this new role of the Atlantic Alliance met with resistance from both the US government and the Washington policymaking elites previously involved in drafting and allotting most of the bilateral military assistance aid packages.

After outlining this shift, the second chapter moves on to investigate how the American authorities resorted to the off-shore procurement programs both to continue their support to the European partners' domestic industrial investments and foreign exchange equilibrium offered under the Marshall Plan, and to connect these objectives to future internal economic growth in those countries. This process came about against the background of the early European economic integration process that shaped a continent-wide market of durables, investment and capital goods. This chapter then focuses on the Italian economic elites to offer a case study on the European governments' response to the American goal to provide them with military assistance to stimulate capital investments at home and stabilize the balance of payments. As neither of these goals aimed to reshape capital investments and international trade, this market oriented perspective clashed with the European governments' views and policies on this issue. The Italian economic policymakers proved to be reluctant to make use of the American funds in US dollars to finance the Italian importers and the balance of payments' current account. On the other hand, their position was in line with the Italian stance during the Marshall Plan years, when the Rome government struggled to use the US financial assistance to back the Italian public debt. The Italians pursued this policy regardless of whether the military assistance programs had a bilateral or multilateral structure. Within this framework I therefore investigate the ways in which the Italian political and economic elites linked the industrial mobilization that the rearmament programs stimulated to the twin intra-European and transatlantic supranational economic integration dynamics.

The resurrecting of Italy's foreign exchange equilibrium, with particular reference to its balance of payments, and the country's launching of domestic development policies to allow its economy to sort out post war material reconstruction and undertake development is discussed in the following chapters from the vantage point of the US and NATO military assistance programs to the Italian aeronautical industry and those mechanical and metalworking manufacturing sectors involved in this industrial mobilization. In so doing, the aim is to figure out to what extent this was linked to economic and political variables crucial to the post war Italian and European nation-building process, from the role of national business communities to the political and diplomatic relations with the other Atlantic bloc countries. The broader objective is to get a comprehensive perspective regarding the influence and impact of the off-shore procurement programs on the international economic relations system following the folding of ERP. In fact, I point out that the OSP had a substantial impact on a variety of problems germane to the period. From the issue of the much-discussed theme of the red scare, to the relevance of the national account statistics on the reinterpretation of the process of nation-building and supranational economic integration in Europe, up to the debate on the best feasible economic policies to manage the historical shift from the post war reconstruction years to the economic take-off that characterized the late 1950s, the multilateral rearmament of Italy and Western Europe at large affected a variety of crucial issues. All of these cut across and re-aligned both the national political and economic elites and the country's foreign economic policy in relation to its counterparts in Washington.

Chapter 1

The economic implications of early military assistance to Western Europe under the Truman Administration, 1949-1951

1.1 Introduction

Both Italian and international historiography view the year 1950 as a watershed in post World War II US foreign policy. In particular, the year allegedly marked a shift in US foreign aid policy from economic assistance programs such as the Marshall Plan to a series of initiatives aimed at providing the free world with both security and well being. This objective was pursued through a set of military assistance programs wherever the Soviet threat appeared likely to turn into an attack on Western bloc countries. The outbreak of the Korean War on June 25, 1950, is often regarded as the point when Soviet threats gained momentum. Indeed, during the months before hostilities began in the Far East, the West and its leaders had been anxiously viewing events such as the Soviet development of atomic devices and the Communist takeover in China. Within this overall shift from an economics-oriented to a security-minded model of foreign assistance policy, historians note particularly both the signing of the North Atlantic Treaty in April 1949 and the subsequent approval by the US Congress of an impressive military assistance program to the Western European countries, the Mutual Defense Assistance Program (MDAP). These two events more than any others, according to the literature, account for the ongoing transformation that marked US policy toward Western Europe from the late 1940s through the early 1950s.

The two most important historiographical interpretations of the nature and meaning of US foreign policy shortly after the end of World War II are that American policy was led either by economic intervention or by a focus on security aspects of the transatlantic alliance. Most scholars concerned with this distinction have concentrated their attention and research efforts on these two options, which faced the US government throughout the postwar era. On the one hand, some historians and political scientists view the Truman Doctrine and the two-year period from 1947 to 1948 as the turning point when US policy shifted from economic to military containment of the Soviet Union. This process was seen as culminating with the endorsement in Washington of the National Security Council's Policy Paper 68[30]. On the other hand, many scholars are convinced that this shift came about sometime later, with the outbreak of hostilities in Korea[31].

Among the impressive number of studies and accounts of these events based on this twofold approach are the two most important works on the Korean War. According to William Stueck,

> the Korean war played a pivotal role in the rearming of the West and in expanding US military commitments on a global scale.
> US aid to foreign countries, which before June 1950 had been more economic than military, shifted decisively to the latter category[32].

To Bruce Cumings, in contrast, this conflict on the Far East stage of the Cold War should be regarded only as one of the most important steps in the building of a world-scale American hegemony based far more on military and ideological containment of the enemy than on economic assistance. Cumings observed, «much of the security program established in early 1947 was a ratification and public airing of previous decisions.»[33]

Studies of the European Recovery Program (ERP) and the Atlantic Pact have produced conflicting interpretations of post World War II US foreign policy. Within this historical discourse, it is noteworthy that some interpretations do not focus on the distinction between economic assistance and military aid on the part of the United States. Those studies come from completely different disciplines and theoretical perspectives, which view US foreign policy after World War II as the last chapter of a long-term policy that began in the early twentieth century and post World War I era.

Thus, scholars such as Frank Ninkovich see US foreign assistance policy after 1945 as the latest chapter in the history of Woodrow Wilson's internationalism, which led Franklin Roosevelt to intervene against Germany and its allies during World War II. From that per-

---

30 D.Yergin, *Shattered Peace*; D.Ellwood, *Rebuilding Europe. Western Europe, America and Postwar Reconstruction*, Longman, London and New York, 1992, chapter 7; M.Leffler, *A Preponderance of Power*; B.Cumings, *The Origins of the Korean War*, vol. 2;

31 J.L.Gaddis, *Strategies of Containment*, chapter 2; R.Pollard, *The National Security State Reconsidered: Truman And Economic Containment, 1945-1950*, in M.J.Lacey (ed.), *The Truman Presidency*, Cambridge University Press, New York, 1989, pp.205-34; see particularly pp. 207, 214-20; R.Pollard, *Economic Security and the Origins of the Cold War*; W.Stueck, *The Korean War*, introduction and chapter 10; M.J.Hogan, *A Cross of Iron: Harry S. Truman and the Origins of the National Security State, 1945-1954*, Cambridge University Press, New York, 1998; M.Trachtenberg, *A Constructed Peace*, pp. 86-88, 100-101, 111; J.L.Gaddis, *The Cold War. A New History*;

32 W.Stueck, *The Korean War*, p.5; his more recent work is *Rethinking the Korean War: A New Diplomatic and Strategic History*, Princeton University Press, Princeton (N.J.), 2002;

33 B. Cumings, *The Origins of the Korean War*;

spective, modern international politics is based on a strict interdependence among world powers, economic centers, and nations. What matters is the building of a free and stable international order, whether the means to achieve it are based on security or prosperity[34].

From yet another perspective, Charles S. Maier interprets post World War II US foreign economic policy as Washington's attempts to deal with a worldwide economic and social crisis to both stabilize American society at home and to promote international economic integration. To Maier, this was Washington's way of coping with international slumps throughout the twentieth century, from the post World War I period through the world economic crisis in the 1970s. Foreign policies such as containment and productivity were used to stabilize an economically unstable and politically weak and insecure international relations system[35].

Turning from studies aimed at providing long-term interpretations to focus on the late 1940s, we can see that the Truman Administration was sensitive to the security aspects of the intensifying Cold War even before 1950 and the onset of war in Korea. The launching of the Brussels Pact as early as 1948 and the ensuing Washington talks to set up a mili-

---

34 F.Ninkovich, *Modernity and Power: A History of the Domino Theory in the Twentieth Century*, The University of Chicago Press, Chicago, 1994; id., *The Wilsonian Century: US Foreign Policy since 1900*, The University of Chicago Press, Chicago, 1999; see also, consistent with this interpretation, A.Stephanson, *Liberty or Death: The Cold War as US Ideology*, in O.A.Westad (ed.), *Reviewing The Cold War: Approaches, Interpretations, and Theory*, London, 2000, pp. 81-100; A.Stephanson, *Quattordici note sul concetto di Guerra fredda*, in "Novecento: Rivista di storia contemporanea", n.2 (2000), pp. 67-87; W.F. Kimball, *The Juggler: Franklin Roosevelt as Wartime Statesman*, Princeton University Press, Princeton (N.J.), 1991; a reworking and appraisal of the literature aimed at account-ing for US policy in Europe after 1945 through the nexus between Wilsonism and bipolarism can be found in F.Romero, *Il Wilsonismo*, in "Parolechiave", n. 29 (2003), particularly pp. 182-84; a test of this historiography focused on the Italian case, and containment pursued by Washington from 1948 onward can be found in the excellent and concise M.Del Pero, *L'Italia e la comunità atlantica*, pp. 207-19;

35 See the following works by C.S.Maier: *The Politics of Productivity: Foundations of American In-ternational Economic Policy After World War II*, in P.J. Katzenstein (ed.), *Between Power and Plenty: the Foreign Economic Policies of Advanced Industrial States*, University of Wisconsin Press, Madison (Wisc.), 1978, pp. 23-49; id., *The Two Postwar Eras and the Conditions for Stability in Twentieth-Century Western Europe*, in id.(ed.), *In Search of Stability: Explorations in Historical Political Econ-omy*, Cambridge University Press, New York, 1987, pp. 153-84; id., *Consigning the Twentieth Centu-ry to History: Alternative Narratives for the Modern Era*, in "American Historical Review", n.105, (2000), pp. 807-31; id., *Due grandi crisi del XX secolo: Alcuni cenni su anni Trenta e anni Settanta*, in L.Baldissara (ed.), *Le radici della crisi. L'Italia tra gli anni Sessanta e Settanta*, Carocci, Roma, 2001, pp. 37-56. For an in-depth reflection on the complementarity between growth and security pur-sued in Western Europe by American leaders after World War II, see C.S.Maier, *Alliance and Auton-omy: European Identity and US Foreign Policy Objectives in the Truman Years*, in M.J. Lacey (ed.), *The Truman Presidency*, pp. 277-83;

tary alliance to provide the United States and its West European allies with peace and security make clear the extent to which a divided Europe determined the military and strategic policies of the Western bloc countries as a whole and of the US government in particular. Peace and stability became increasingly important to security in the late 1940s. In 1948 there was a breakthrough: whether we view the United States as answering the French and British call for US military involvement across the Old Continent[36], or as the Truman Administration undertaking a free and independent foreign policy decision, it represented a real watershed in US foreign aid policy.

This turning point is clearly shown by testimonials such as that of John Ohly, Special Assistant to the Secretary of Defense in the late 1940s, and Deputy Director for the MDAP at the Department of State between 1949 and 1950:

> Except in the cases of Greece, Turkey, and China I have no recollection of any proposals for large-scale military assistance to any area as far back as early 1947. However, by the end of 1947, the possibility of providing some military assistance to Western Europe was already under consideration in both the National Military Establishment and the Department of State and, in early 1948, very serious consideration was given to the addition to the then proposed Foreign Assistance Act of 1948 (authorizing economic aid to Europe and other aid programs), of a new separate Title VI that would authorize military assistance on a large scale to any country that the President might find required[37].

In March, the Western bloc governments began talks and summits to set up a transatlantic security system. At the beginning of summer 1948 the US Senate passed the so-called Vandenberg Resolution, which committed the White House to support the creation of a series of local security systems «based on a lasting and real self-help and mutual aid.» Then it endorsed a National Security Council directive suggesting that the Truman Administration shape the new Atlantic community as both a military and an industrial alliance. US intelligence promoted the creation of a large-scale transatlantic security system based on close cooperation and coordination among the Atlantic Pact countries to make their respective

---

36 G.Lundestad, *Empire by Invitation? The United States and Western Europe, 1945-52*, in "Journal of Peace Research", n. 23 (1986), pp. 263-77; id., *The American 'Empire' and Other Studies of US Foreign Policy in a Comparative Perspective*, Oxford University Press, New York, 1990; recently this thesis has been reappraised and framed within a long-term perspective by the same author in G.Lundestand, *Empire by Invitation: The United States and Western Europe: Past, Present and Future*, in A.Giovagnoli, L.Tosi (eds), *Un ponte sull'Atlantico: L'alleanza occidentale 1949-1999*, Guerini e Associati, Milano, 2003, pp. 21-48; id., *The Rise and Decline of the American 'Empire'. Power and Its Limits in Comparative Perspective*, Oxford University Press, Oxford, 2012;

37 John H. Ohly oral interview, 30 November 1971, p. 24, in HSTPL, Oral History Interviews;

defense productions work together. This was supposed to match the security objectives of the North Atlantic Treaty Organization (NATO)[38].

Thus it is indisputable that even shortly after the launch of the European Recovery Program in spring 1948 we cannot identify US assistance policies toward Western Europe only with economic assistance and reconstruction aid. Indeed, in Washington it was agreed that the Marshall Plan was not enough to secure the European allies from Soviet threats. On the contrary, both in Congress and within the Truman Administration, many policymakers and politicians were convinced that it was necessary to do much more, as President Truman recalled only a few years later[39]. Following the signing of the North Atlantic Treaty, the US president had shown his sensitivity to the close relationship between security and prosperity and their importance to US policy toward the Atlantic Pact countries: «the security and welfare of each member of this community depends upon the security and welfare of all. None of us alone can achieve economic prosperity or military security. None of us can assure the continuance of freedom.»[40] Clearly, the idea that it was necessary to balance the Atlantic bloc countries' military security and economic stability was widely shared in Washington.

The idea of security within the context of transatlantic relationships in the late 1940s is crucial to understanding Washington's European policies at that time: the organization of treaties and defense pacts aimed at securing the most exposed Western bloc areas against the Soviet threat led the White House to provide its partners with either military or financial aid. Nonetheless, the rearmament-oriented support became extensive only after 1949. In fact, throughout the second half of the 1940s, rearmament was not at the core of Washington foreign policy. As a result of legislative obstacles, the recent war experience, and the ever-changing diplomatic relations between the United States and the Soviet Union before the onset of the Cold War, military assistance was not the top priority of Washington's foreign economic policy, which was clearly led by the European Recovery Program and its stabilization policies. According to the Truman Administration, before the birth of the Atlantic Alliance a US-centered international relations system set among the Western bloc countries could be achieved only through economic reconstruction and growth, as well as trade cooperation and integration among their economies, whereas the security of borders and nations was regarded as a secondary policy priority. In this context, it can be understood why in summer 1948 the Brussels Pact military establishment had to ask that the United States grant military assistance to the European member states.

---

38 NSC 14/1, 1 July 1948 in *FRUS, 1948*, vol. 1: *General: United Nations*, part 2, Government Printing Office, Washington D.C., 1976;

39 H.S.Truman, *Memoirs*, vol. 2, *Years of Trial and Hope*, Doubleday & Co., New York, 1955, pp. 240 ff.;

40 Harry S. Truman, Press Release, 12 April 1949, in HSTPL, Development and Ratification of NATO Collection;

But security increased in importance to Washington with the establishment of defense pacts and their coupling with financial and military assistance to the recovering West European economies. Within a few years US international economic policy was interwoven with the early years of NATO. The process gained momentum with congressional enactment of the Mutual Security Program in late 1951. With this foreign aid legislation the Truman Administration merged economic and military assistance and for the first time centered all its foreign aid policy on the military.

Therefore, if we view rearmament within the narrower framework of Truman's international economic policy rather than that of late 1940s US foreign policy, we can see that the Truman presidency did not propose the increased defense budgets necessary to provide NATO and its member countries with military assistance to Congress until the early 1950s. In this context, 1949 and 1950 can be regarded as watershed years, as has often been suggested in the historical literature. Before exploring this relationship between military spending for foreign aid purposes and the overall US foreign assistance policy in the early 1950s, it is necessary to examine the structure and evolution of American military assistance to friendly nations before the signing of the Atlantic Pact.

1.2 Dollars and weapons: The structure and organization of US military assistance after the Second World War

US military and security commitments abroad after the end of World War II are usually underestimated. There is an extensive and well-known literature concerning the post war demobilization of both the military and war industries undertaken by the Truman Administration shortly after 1945 through the late 1940s. Likewise, historians of American foreign relations and international political economy have examined the reconversion of the American military industrial complex to civilian production. Most works that view post World War II US foreign policy as a shift from economic assistance to security are based on only a few main arguments. They argue that the two-year period spanning 1948 and 1949 should be regarded as the starting point of this major reassessment of US policy in Europe, which often has been studied and reconstructed with regard to its effects on domestic politics and the US government. And the impressive rise of military spending after 1949 is well known. While between 1945 and 1947 the Pentagon budget was reduced from \$81 to \$13 million[41], between summer 1949 and winter 1951, by contrast, the defense budget nearly tripled, and rose from \$13.5 to \$45 billion. The Korean War alone cannot explain such an expansion[42].

If we set aside these arguments, however, and frame US military assistance within the broader framework of foreign aid rather than its impact on the defense budget, US military involvement in foreign affairs can be regarded as part of Washington's international economic policy and its history during the early 1950s. From this perspective, we find that military assistance initiatives anticipated the endorsement of the MDAP by the US Congress and the Atlantic Pact countries. It is unquestionable that military aid was expanded significantly only after the outbreak of war in Korea. Accounting for 8 and 48 per cent of total foreign assistance in 1947 and 1952, respectively, the proportion of foreign aid used for military purposes became impressive and significant only after the beginning of war in the Far East[43]. Nonetheless, the tendency dates back to the second half of the 1940s, when Washington had begun to support and protect its friendly nations militarily. After the end of World War II, the United States began to distribute some military surplus to the West European allies, though such transfers were not carried out according to any priority attached to military aid in US foreign policy directives. Yet this type of transfer continued during succeeding years for foreign policy purposes. For example, the Italian government of Alcide de Gasperi requested and received weapons, bazookas, and trucks before the 1948 elections[44]. US funds granted to other nations for military purposes were far more significant than a relatively less strategic and important country like Italy received from the Truman Administration. When the US president brought the Truman Doctrine before Congress, it allocated \$400 million to Greece and Turkey, which increased to \$ 670 million in 1949. These funds supported both the Turkish military and the right-wing monarchist political elites

---

41 M.S.Sherry, *Preparing for the Next War. American Plans for Postwar Defense 1941-45*, Yale University Press, New Haven (Conn.), 1977;

42 B.O. Fordham, *Building the Cold War Consensus. The Political Economy of US National Security*, The University of Michigan Press, Ann Arbor (Mich.), 1998. On the important debate within the Truman Administration on the Pentagon budgets and the feasibility of expanding them between 1949 and 1951, see M.Hogan, *A Cross of Iron*, chapter 7; F.L. Block, *The Origins of International Economic Disorder. A Study of United States International Monetary Policy from World War II to the Present*, The University of California Press, Berkeley (Ca), 1977, chapter 4; P.H. Nitze, *From Hiroshima to Glasnost: At the Center of the Decision: A Memoir*, Weidenfeld, New York, 1989, pp. 93-98;

43 For these data and statistics I drew on IMF, Western Hemisphere Department North American Division, 'Review of the United States Foreign Aid Program', May 15, 1953, in ASBI, Carte Caffè, pratt., n. 50, fold. 1;

44 C.J. Pach, *Arming the Free World. The Origins of the United States Military Assistance Program 1945-50*, The University of North Carolina Press, Chapel Hill (N.C.), 1991; L.Sebesta, *L'Europa indifesa: Sistema di sicurezza atlantico e caso italiano*, Ponte alle Grazie, Firenze, 1991, p. 149;

of Athens in their fight against the leftist Greek liberation movement[45]. In 1948, Washington also supported the Chinese nationalist government with $ 125 million to assist their fight against the Communists[46].

The attention paid to Turkey and Greece, as well as US concern about the future of Iran and Palestine, can be explained by the increasing importance of these countries to the Truman Administration's foreign policy in the Middle East. If such attention can be explained in Turkey's case by referring to the Soviet pressures on Ankara and Iran since about 1946, it can be less easily grasped in the case of Greece, which had not been pressured by Moscow.

President Truman knew that Turkey and Greece posed different problems of security and required different means to insure their western loyalty. In the Greek case it was a matter of providing the national military with what it needed «for their task of destroying the rebel guerilla forces and eliminating the Communist menace to the political stability and national integrity»; in the Turkish case, security meant being prepared to face external threats[47].

Furthermore, in both cases as well as all across the Mediterranean area, what made the US government grant military assistance was an ever-increasing need for energy resources, particularly oil[48]. This problem became especially crucial in the postwar years to the West European countries, which suffered following the division of Europe between the two superpowers and their blocs from a lack of the natural resources that has been supplied by

---

45 Indeed, the major military assistance initiatives to Middle Eastern countries indirectly involved a country like Italy, which at this time was still on the border between East and West and could not be rearmed before the national poll of 1948, which became a watershed in Italy's post–World War II history. Nonetheless, as early as 1947 the Americans understood that military aid, even if granted to third countries like Turkey or Greece, could be used to rebuild a war torn economy and its industrial system like the Italian one. In fact, shortly after the appropriation of funds to these two nations, the Americans approached the Italian government's representatives in Washington to offer military procurements for Italy's state-owned steel and mechanical industries. See 'La possibilità di concorso delle aziende IRI nella esecuzione del Piano Truman per l'assistenza alla Grecia e Turchia,' 6 July 1947, in ASIRI, Ufficio Tecnico Centrale (IRI Roma), b. Commesse belliche 1945-48, ID/611,6.

46 IMF, Western Hemisphere Department, North American Division, 'Review of the United States Foreign Aid Program,' p. 1; IMF, Western Hemisphere Department, North American Division, 'The Recent Pattern of United States Foreign Aid,' April 9, 1956, p. 1, in ACS, Ministero del Tesoro, Direzione Generale del Tesoro, Ispettorato Generale per i rapporti con l'estero (IRFE), b. 10; D.B. Kunz, *Butter and Guns: America's Cold War Economic Diplomacy*, The Free Press, New York, 1997, pp. 30-31. As for the appropriations to Greece and Turkey up to 1949, see also Harry S.Truman, Press Release, 12 April 1949, in HSTPL, Development and Ratification of NATO Collection;

47 Harry S. Truman, 'Final Draft of President Truman's third quarterly report on Greek-Turkish aid', 12 May 1948, in HSTPL, Truman Doctrine Study Collection, fold. 1;

48 With respect to the relation between oil and the Cold War see D.Painter, *Oil, Resources, and the Cold War 1945-1962*, in M.P.Leffler, O.A.Westad (eds), *The Cambridge History of the Cold War*, vol. 1, pp. 486-507;

the East European nations until the outbreak of the Cold War[49]. In the case of China, to which Washington granted both military and economic aid, the United States was interested not only in securing the country from internal threats, but also in shaping it as the key nation for the security of the Far East as a whole[50]. Even South America and its instability were to be dealt with through military deterrence: there, policy was set by the Rio de Janeiro Pact.

These military assistance programs demonstrate to what extent the United States was interested in providing its allies with political stability, as well as how they were implementing that policy. Even if these programs were not framed within an overall foreign aid policy like the broad and well-structured Marshall Plan, they had positive effects on the US economy and its postwar recovery. According to World Bank president Eugene Black, who later testified on these issues before an Eisenhower Presidential Commission, between 1946 and 1952 one-third of US exports (roughly $30 billion) had been funded and led by the assistance programs promoted by Washington abroad[51].

These early programs anticipated the two types of military assistance offered to the Western bloc allies and the NATO partners in the following years. In the first, Washington provided its partners with end-item materials and weapons from either US war surplus or obsolete and no longer used military stocks. In the second, the White House provided military assistance by sending dollars abroad. This way of supporting security through financial aid was aimed at letting the West European countries rearm themselves without

---

49 For an overall sketch of the geopolitical framework within which US military aid to the Middle East existed before the founding of the Atlantic Alliance, see B.R. Kuniholm, *The Origins of the Cold War in the Near East: Great Power Conflict and Diplomacy in Iran, Turkey and Greece*, Princeton University Press, Princeton (N.J.), 1980; and id., *The Near East Connection: Greece and Turkey in the Reconstruction and Security of Europe 1946-1952*, Holy Cross, Brookline (Mass.), 1984. For different policies carried out by the Union of Soviet Socialist Republics (USSR) in Greece and Turkey after the end of World War II, see particularly L.S.Wittner, *American Intervention in Greece 1943-1949*, Columbia University Press, New York, 1982; B.R. Kuniholm, *US Policy in the Near East: The Triumphs and Tribulations of The Truman Administration*, in M.J.Lacey(ed.), *The Truman Presidency*, pp. 299-338, especially pp. 302-5; for an interpretation of US military intervention in the Middle East affairs to control the raw materials in that key area, see B.Cumings, *The Origins of the Korean War*;

50 D.Acheson, *Present at the Creation: My Years in the State Department*, Norton & Co, New York, 1987, pp. 7-8, 303-7; J.W.Dower, *Occupied Japan and the Cold War in Asia*, in Lacey (ed.), *The Truman Presidency*, pp. 366-409, esp. p. 377;

51 IBRD, Statement of Mr. Black to the Randall Commission, 21 October 1953, in ASBI, Carte Caffé, pratt., n. 53, fold. 3; for a different interpretation of US foreign aid programs since 1945 based on the ratio between Cold War security concerns and domestic industrial policies, see J.Stein's *Running Steel, Running America: Race, Economic Policy and the Decline of Liberalism*, The University of North Carolina Press,Chapel Hill (N.C.), 1998, in which she argues that Washington's foreign assistance program, from the Marshall Plan to military aid, weakened American industry and made way for market-oriented industrial development without any state control over the economy;

undermining the recent improvements in their balance of payments deficits, particularly related to US currency: the European balance of payments dollar deficit had been cut through the anti-inflationary use of ERP funds. For this reason Washington chose to grant funds for both military and non-military purposes in US dollars[52]. All the military assistance projects scheduled under the 1949 MDAP were given either as material assistance or financial aid. Thus, US military assistance was organized much as the ERP was in both grants and loans. Weapons and end-user military supplies, components for European military production, and spare parts to be used in Europe were called, respectively, end items and machine tools, whereas US financial assistance was called defense support. This included both dollar inflows aimed at supporting the European balance of payments deficits and, in cases such as the Italian one, budgetary contributions that would decrease the impact of military spending on European budget deficits.

US opinion makers and the American public were aware that the military assistance program brought before the US Congress shortly after the signing of the North Atlantic Treaty in April 1949 was meant to provide friendly nations with both military items and financial support. During the first year of MDAP implementation, in autumn 1950, doubts and concerns raised by the American public and voiced by US commentators on the use of funds for military assistance focused on the distinction between «dollars» and «weapons», between which the $ 4 billion military appropriations for the next fiscal year were to be shared: many observers were concerned with the effects of military assistance on ERP appropriations[53].

1.3 Rearmament versus economic reconstruction: peculiarities and limits of the first military assistance program for Western Europe

As Lorenza Sebesta shows, the Truman Administration was hampered in drafting its postwar military assistance projects by the lack of any legislative instrument to appropriate funds to the Western bloc. Sometimes the White House was forced to rely on the Constitutional provision that allowed the president, as the supreme head of military forces, to bypass

---

52 US policy toward Italy demonstrates that the Truman Administration gave priority to balance of payments deficits in relation to US currency. Washington paid less attention to the Italian balance of payments deficit in relation to the British pound. See, for example, 'Memorandum by the Assistant Secretary of State for European Affairs (Perkins) to the Under Secretary of State (Webb)', Washington, 4 March 1951, in *FRUS 1951*, vol. 4, *Europe: Political and Economic Relations*, Government Printing Office, Washington D.C., 1985, p. 577;

53 See, for example, *The New York Times*, 15 October 1950;

Congress[54]. The most outstanding example of these difficulties can be found in the failure to implement the language of the National Security Council's policy paper NSC 14/1 of July 1948, pledging that the United States would defend its West European and Far Eastern allies both politically and militarily from the Soviet threat. In fact, Washington did not go beyond sending a representative to London to participate in the Brussels Pact conference called to set up a military alliance aimed at providing peace and stability to the Western bloc. On that occasion, the United States participated in the debate according to the principle that they would not cooperate directly in military operations, but reserved the right to be involved in European security issues.

Greater involvement would come about only when the Western powers and the United States began negotiations to set up the Atlantic Pact. This time Washington pledged to contribute on a permanent basis to European security. Above all, in article 3 of the Atlantic Treaty (which concerned the importance of mutual aid and self-help to the Atlantic community), the Atlantic Alliance committed the United States, as the Atlantic partner best armed and most sound financially, to an ongoing presence across Europe.

There were few other financial resources available to strengthen the weak European security system. In fact, even if the Atlantic Treaty did not force the United States to provide the allies with weapons and war materials, it was assumed that US military power and economic stability committed Washington to assist the Western alliance over the long term. This interpretation of the US commitment to the Atlantic community under the Treaty was clearly stated by Secretary of State Dean Acheson and widely agreed upon within the State Department[55]. When it was brought before the US Congress on July 25, 1949, the first MDAP was viewed by the Truman Administration as close to, and interwoven with, the US commitment to help its NATO partners, even though it was formulated before the signing of the North Atlantic Treaty. From the conception of the North Atlantic Treaty, US policymakers had been concerned about the balance between the newly established military aid program and the ongoing implementation of ERP. Would it be possible to appropriate funds for both military and civilian purposes without short-changing the latter? The Foreign Assistance Correlation Committee (FAAC) was one of many inter-ministerial boards created to study and plan feasible military assistance programs for Europe. It was composed of representatives from the Defense Department, the State Department, and the Economic

---

54 L.Sebesta, *L'Europa indifesa*, pp. 148-49.

55 Dean Acheson, 'Address to the Committee on Foreign Relations of the Senate', April 27, 1949; Summary of Telegrams by the Office of the Secretary of State to unspecified recipients, 10 May 1950, in HSTPL, NATO Collection, fold. North Atlantic Council; 'The North Atlantic Pact: Collective Defense and the Preservation of Peace, Security and Freedom in the North Atlantic Community', 20 March 1949, in *FRUS 1949*, vol. 4, *Western Europe*, Washington D.C., 1975, pp. 240-41; Department of State, 'Statement on the US Military Assistance Program', 22 May 1949, in *FRUS, idem*, pp. 299-300; see also Lord Ismay, *NATO: The First Five Years, 1949-1954*, Paris, 1954;

Cooperation Administration (ECA), the government agency charged with administering the Marshall Plan). In February 1949, the FAAC warned the White House not to sacrifice economic reconstruction in favor of rearmament and suggested that economic assistance be given top priority, so that rearmament funding would not weaken or delay economic reconstruction in Europe[56]. Even Secretary of Defense Louis Johnson was concerned about the effect of rearmament on reconstruction. He told the Senate Committee on Foreign Relations that the new military assistance program should not interfere with the implementation and accomplishment of ERP[57]. Dean Acheson repeatedly voiced his apprehension about the new program's possible repercussions on the Marshall Plan. He hoped to solve the problem and avoid that risk by coordinating and rationalizing the distribution of military supplies between the United States and the receiving countries as much as possible[58]. The search for financial sources to provide military assistance throughout Western Europe without impeding European budgetary stability led the American bureaucracy to produce a wide range of proposals. It can be argued, for example, that the replacement of bilateral military assistance between the US and each European ally provided for by MDAP with the multilateral principle and structure that underpinned the Mutual Security Program and its implementation in NATO answered the need not to weaken the budgetary stability that most European countries had barely reached during the postwar years.

During 1950, one idea of the Truman Administration was to provide the manufacturing NATO countries with German raw materials without charge. The German economy could provide NATO not only with raw materials and goods needed by military industries, but also end-user items and capital goods. The US Secretary of State was convinced that the German economy, though in poor repair, could provide immediate and continuous contributions in many sectors, including «steel, coal, non-ferrous metals fabrication, shipbuilding, antifriction bearings, fine mechanics and optics, machine tools, vehicles, chemicals, electrical equipment.»[59]

When he briefed the European governments on this idea, Acheson expressed his concern with the slowdown in economic reconstruction that the European countries might suffer if the United States could neither expand public spending nor find sources other than public finance for funding European rearmament. According to the Secretary of State, the problem was so pressing that even the military production necessary to provide the armies of the

---

56 'Basic Policies of the Military Assistance Program', 7 February 1949, in *FRUS 1949*, vol. 1, *National Security Affairs: Foreign Economic Policy*, Washington D.C., 1976, pp. 254-55;
57 L.Kaplan, *The Long Entanglement: NATO's First Fifty Years*, Praeger, Westport (Conn.), 1999, p. 46;
58 D.Acheson, *Present at the Creation*, p. 309;
59 'The Secretary of State to the United States High Commissioner for Germany McCloy', 18 October 1950, in *FRUS 1950*, vol. 3, *Western Europe*, Government Printing Office, Washington D.C., 1977, pp. 389-91;

European nations with basic materials and weapons could impede budgetary stability and cause monetary disequilibrium as well as a slowdown in foreign trade. «They do not possess -he wrote more or less when the MTDP was endorsed- the necessary industrial capacity without diversions from civilian production which would jeopardize economic recovery.»[60]

Thus we can see that both public and government circles worried that the cost of letting the European NATO partners purchase war material with US dollars could reduce appropriations administered under the European Recovery Program.

The simultaneous flow of military and civilian aid into Europe was certain to cause deeper and wider consequences than those forecast by the Truman Administration. Financial imbalances might occur in any European country's balance of payments: the more they depended on foreign markets to procure raw materials and capital goods, the more their balance of payments could worsen if not funded accordingly. The United Kingdom, for example, provided other West European countries and the United States with strategic materials through its colonies. In this case, however, rearmament was not likely to risk London's foreign accounts and public finance. In fact, in its supplier role, the Atlantic community's defense effort represented a chance for the United Kingdom to increase and multiply its dollar and gold reserve assets, which more than doubled within the pound currency area between summer 1949 and autumn 1950. This came about because some primary goods necessary for military production owned by the United Kingdom and its colonies led the pound currency area export; and shortly after the outbreak of war in Korea, those exports increased by 30 per cent[61]. Furthermore, when it was forced to import certain scarce raw materials from other currency areas, the United Kingdom was able to balance these pressures on its trade account through impressive capital inflow from the same raw material exporting countries. We can understand this trend if we think about Great Britain as a huge, well-structured banking system that attracted capital investments. Thus, even the countries with the scarcest materials reinvested their profits in the United Kingdom, which reduced its prospective

---

60 'The Secretary of State to the Embassy in the United Kingdom', in *FRUS 1950*, vol. 3, *Western Europe*, p. 32; for the idea of making the German economy pay for the monetary costs of European rearmament to avoid a slowdown in the reconstruction process throughout Europe, see also 'The Secretary of State to certain Diplomatic Offices', idem., p. 34; see National Advisory Council Minutes, Meeting n. 168, 26 December 1950, in NARA, RG56, NAC Papers, NAC Minutes, b. 2 (9 Feb. 1950-28 Dec. 1950); for an assessment of German productive capacity in 1950, see 'The Ambassador in the United Kingdom (Douglas) to the Secretary of State', in *FRUS 1950*, vol. 3, *Western Europe*, pp. 50-51;

61 H.Pelling, *Britain and the Marshall Plan*, MacMillan, London, 1988, p. 110. For a very different position -that the effects of rearmament on the British balance of payment were negative because of the fluctuations of raw materials prices exported by the United Kingdom in 1951- and use of this fact to account for British trade restrictions as implemented by the new British conservative government from that year forward, see G.Tullio, *Monete ed economie: Le relazioni anglo-italiane nel secondo dopoguerra*, Edizioni Scientifiche Italiane, Napoli, 2001, pp. 272-277;

balance of payment deficit by expanding its foreign debt[62]. In Federal Republic of Germany, on the contrary, imports of war materials were so expensive and their impact on Germany's balance of payments so remarkable that Western European countries established a special credit account to avoid a drop in imports and foreign trade for Germany. That prospect would threaten the entire process of intra-European trade liberalization[63].

Those charged with managing US foreign economic policy soon understood the extent to which rearmament was going to impede and delay the setting up of a balanced trade and money market among the West European countries pursued through ERP funds. American leaders were worried about both the British, who were strengthening their creditor role, and the Germans, for whom rearmament meant a drop in their trade account[64]. Germany's trade account deficit could bring about a long-term dependency on the American money market, a risk that led the Economic Cooperation Administration to oppose further US financial contributions to the European Payments Union[65].

One of the most feasible solutions to these problems and to the ERP effects on Western Europe would be to conceive and propose MDAP to the European allies as a warrant for public and private investments in Western European countries assisted and backed by the European Recovery Program. Basically, according to this school of thought, it was a matter of using the security policies promoted by Washington, its resources, and institutions (above all, the North Atlantic Alliance) to protect and stimulate the ongoing economic reconstruc-

---

62 Donato Menichella, 'Considerazioni finali, 1952,' in F.Cotula, C.O. Gelsomino, A.Gigliobianco (eds), *Donato Menichella: Stabilità e sviluppo dell'economia italiana, 1946-1960.* vol. 2, *Considerazioni finali all'assemblea della Banca d'Italia*, Laterza, Roma Bari, 1997, pp. 148-50;

63 J.J.Kaplan, G. Schleiminger, *The European Payment Union: Financial Diplomacy in the 1950s*, Clarendon Press, Oxford, 1990, pp. 97-111; T.Geiger, D.M.Ross, *Banks, Institutional Constraints, and the Limits of Central Banking: Monetary Policy in Britain and West Germany 1950-52*, in "Business History", n. 33 (1991), pp. 143-48; T.Geiger, L.Sebesta, *National Defense Policies and the Failure of Military Integration in NATO: American Military Assistance and Western European Rearmament 1949-1954*, in F.H.Heller, J.Gillingham(eds), *The United States and the Integration of Europe: Legacies of the Postwar Era*, St. Martin's Press, New York, 1996, p. 261;

64 Nonetheless, it is worth remarking that the Europeans did not share this pessimistic outlook, which in some cases (such as the Italian) regarded West Germany's economy as capable of achieving its defense effort without impairing its economic recovery. See, for example, 'Ambasciata d'Italia a Bonn a Ministero Affari Esteri', 29 February 1952, in ASMAE, DGAP, Germania, 1950-1957, b. 90, fold. Germ. I/3 (politica estera della Germania: riarmo e partecipazione all'esercito europeo CED);

65 In particular, the concern would be picked up by the experts on the National Advisory Council on International Monetary and Financial Problems (NAC), an inter ministerial body chaired by the Secretary of the Treasury and charged with coordinating the international economic policy carried out by the United States. See, for example, National Advisory Council Staff Committee, Minutes of Meeting, n. 275, 19 March 1951, and Minutes of Meeting, n. 280, 13 April 1951, both in NARA, RG 56, NAC Staff Committee Minutes 1945-59, b. 2;

tion[66]. Averell Harriman, US ambassador to Europe for Marshall Plan affairs between 1948 and 1950, was one of the most ardent supporters of this policy among the Washington leadership. In the interwar years, Harriman's experience and knowledge of European problems had matured during his service on the board of Directors of the International Chambers of Commerce. As a member of that important board, he frequently discussed the effects of trade restrictions on the expansion and economic growth of European markets. He came to the conclusion that in Europe full trade liberalization was not feasible without large-scale military cooperation across the Atlantic: «Because there wasn't a military understanding of some kind, every country, for its own security, demanded to be as autarkic as possible.»[67] Broadly speaking, we can understand this approach if we keep in mind that many policymakers within the Economic Cooperation Administration were not much concerned about the impact of NATO on the reconstruction of Europe. This viewpoint was clear, for example, from the recollections of Richard Bissell, Assistant Administrator for the ECA[68]. Unexpectedly, the approach was welcome and widely endorsed within both the State Department and the Pentagon, both of which supported the idea that the economic reconstruction of Europe and its related political stabilization could not be achieved if European citizens did not feel secure and protected from the «red scare».[69]

At the same time, the Keynesian enclave within the Truman Administration, led by Leon Keyserling, increasingly emphasized the benefits to the American economy of increasing war production. According to the head of the Council of Economic Advisors, an increase in defense expenditures and economic mobilization for purposes of rearmament could quickly create a surge in the domestic economy[70].

However, attempts to conceptualize a way to promote economic growth and military security at the same time represented a minority view within the Truman Administration. Most policymakers thought that the two goals could not be combined and that security concerns

---

66 'Basic Policies of the Military Assistance Program', 7 February 1949, in *FRUS 1949*, vol. 1, *National Security Affairs: Foreign Economic Policy*, pp.254-55; Harry S.Truman, 'Address to the Congress', 25 July 1949, in HSTPL, NATO Collection, fold. MAP. The European governments viewed the relationship between ERP and MDAP completely differently. In Italy, Piero Malvestiti thought that economic growth was a prerequisite to achieving whatever defense effort was planned. For Malvestiti, see for example *Il Mondo*, 7 April 1951;

67 A.Harriman oral interview, in HSTPL, Oral History interviews;

68 R.M.Bissell oral interview, 1971, pp. 48-49, inHSTPL, Oral History interviews;

69 J.Ohly oral interview, p. 33, in HSTPL, Oral History interviews; R.Pollard, *The National Security State Reconsidered*, p. 224;

70 L.Keyserling, memorandum 'The Economic Implications of the Proposed Programs', 8 December 1950, in *FRUS 1950*, vol. 1, *National Security Affairs: Foreign Economic Policy*, Washington D.C., 1977, pp. 430-31; L.Keyserling to H.Truman, 2 November 1951, in *FRUS 1951*, vol. 1, *National Security Affairs: Foreign Economic Policy*, Washington D.C., 1980, pp. 245-54; H.Q.Dearborn (Council of Economic Advisors) to NSC, 8 May 1950, in *FRUS 1950*, vol. 1, *National Security Affairs*, p. 309;

would impair the reconstruction process. Paul Nitze, then the deputy to the Assistant Secretary of State for Economic Affairs, was convinced that increased military spending in Western Europe would impede the European economy, where, far from expanding European markets, reductions in growth and consumption were needed. He based this opinion on long-term knowledge of European public opinion on the issues that rearmament posed, which he had extensive experience monitoring on behalf of the Department of State[71].

Indeed, even the National Advisory Council on International Monetary and Financial Problems targeted this array of problems, offering a somewhat more complex analysis with a country-by-country breakdown of the impact of the Korean War. The German and Italian economies would have suffered from rising inflation as a result of a wider home market brought about by military productions without any corresponding improvement in employees' standard of living. On the other hand, in countries where the average standard of living was higher and already good, employees would suffer from the war effort, where full or semi-full employment status would not let the war effort target any urgent employment problem[72]. Paul Hoffman, head of the ECA, thought that rearmament could not match economic growth and its requirements, and he saw the rise of military spending as a function of cuts in civilian investments[73]. John Ohly, who was not working shoulder-to-shoulder with Hoffman's agency, nevertheless perceived clearly that «there was a great concern in ECA about how the military assistance program could be related to the economic assistance and a fear that a military build up in Europe would divert resources desperately needed to support the economic recovery.»[74]

This viewpoint would be revised from 1950 onward, when the War Production Board experience received new attention and the Washington leadership focused on the ratio between defense economics and economic development. In the first half of the 1950s, the United States assumed that expansion of military production was the way to implement the so-called Keynesian multiplier. In other words, defense economics was supposed to depend on a model of economic expansion mainly based on private consumption and investments. Such an approach was likely to let the United States achieve two important objectives. On

---

71 'Memorandum by Paul Nitze, Deputy to the Assistant Secretary of State for Economic Affairs, to the Foreign Assistance Steering Committee', 31 January 1949, in *FRUS 1949*, vol. 4, *Western Europe*, p. 57; see also 'Minutes of Meeting n. 148 of the Policy Planning Staff', 11 October 1949, in *FRUS 1949*, vol. 1, *National Security Affairs*; P.Nitze, *From Hiroshima to Glasnost*, pp. 120-23;

72 National Advisory Council Meetings, Minutes of Meetings, Meeting n. 160, p. 2, in NARA, RG 56, NAC Papers, NAC Minutes, b. 2 (9 Feb. 1950-28 Dec. 1950);

73 P.Hoffman to A.Harriman, 9 January 1949, in *FRUS 1949*, vol. 4, *Western Europe*, p. 367; Hoffman probably was pessimistic because he was inclined to make a distinction between military aid and economic assistance programs. See P.Hoffman, oral interview, 1953, p. 23, in HSTPL, Oral History interviews;

74 J.Ohly, oral interview, p. 35, in HSTPL, Oral History interviews;

the one hand, it was feasible to promote economic growth without imposing any expansion of public finance to support the offer of goods. On the other hand, a vast array of government spending policies could be carried out without bringing about an anti-cyclical phase[75].

The military establishment stated repeatedly that European security should be built by military means. Therefore, the Defense Department regarded the new military assistance program merely as a way to strengthen European security against external or internal threats[76]. Their thinking was far removed from the idea that a collective security system linking the Western bloc countries could have implications well beyond the military. This somewhat narrow interpretation of military assistance by the Pentagon and the military establishment is all the more remarkable if we consider that in a few years the financial and industrial implications of defense efforts would be so widely accepted and shared in Washington that the economic impact of collective security was a cornerstone of the Mutual Security Program[77]. At the time, the American military elite, led by Paul Nitze, focused their attention on the very limited financial resources needed to fund the rearmament program during the 2.5 years before the end of ERP, rather than on the achievement of a military build- up suitable for an international relations system in the face of the intensifying Cold War[78].

Therefore, the military assistance legislation brought before Congress reflected the Truman Administration's primary concerns: the economic repercussions of such a program on the European economies and the objectives of close military and defense cooperation with the European partners that the United States was called upon to provide. For their part, the European governments did not conceive the American offer of aid merely as the provision of weapons, spare parts, and other military items. On March 16, 1949, the Western Union foreign ministers wrote to Lewis Douglas, the US ambassador to Great Britain, that Europe

---

75 US Department of Commerce, *Markets after the Defense Expansion*, Washington D.C., 1952; on defense economics as a means to stimulate private consumption, see the still eye-opening study by L.Paggi, *Strategie politiche e modelli di società nel rapporto USA-Europa 1930-1950*, in L.Paggi (ed.), *Americanismo e riformismo*, pp. 43-62; for an interpretation quite different from mine stressing that social spending could not be coupled with security, see M.Hogan, *Cross of Iron*;

76 L.Kaplan, *The Long Entanglement*, p. 38;

77 In order to understand how this approach was increasingly shared in the analysis and appraisals of the collective military build-up promoted by NATO, see, for example, Mutual Security Agency, Office of Assistant Director for Europe, 'Developments in NATO', 6 February 1953, in NARA, RG 469, Mission to Italy, Office of the Director, Subject Files (Central Files) 1948-57, b. 25, fold. 6 (Evaluation Team); the importance of the financial implications of rearmament had been perceived by the US Joint Chiefs of Staff since 1950. On this point, see JCS, Memorandum for Secretary of Defense Johnson, 13 July 1950, in HSTPL, NATO Collection, fold. Development of NATO as an Organization;

78 LOC, Manuscript Division, Paul Nitze Papers, Subject Files 1942-1989, b.131;

was assuming both military and financial support[79]. The day after the signing of the North Atlantic Treaty, when they officially asked Washington to help the European rearmament effort, the Brussels Pact five powers clearly referred to «financial and military assistance»[80]. The idea of US assistance was even more clearly expressed by the Italian Foreign Minister Carlo Sforza: «The Italian government, in order to increase its military production and the industrial capacity of Italy's war industry, due to the lack of dollars, will desperately need American aid to cover the costs in US dollars of its rearmament.»[81]

Early on, the US government seemed supportive of this interpretation of the European call for assistance. When Harriman discussed the issue with French Minister of Foreign Affairs Robert Schuman, he took it for granted that European partners were ready to sacrifice other economic and industrial sectors, but he was also aware that the United States should be prepared to cover some additional costs in US dollars[82]. Milton Katz, then Acting US Special Representative in Europe, had the same opinion; for example, he told Hoffman that the US government should fund the European dollar deficit, which was likely to worsen as a result of European procurement of raw materials and machinery from abroad. These purchases would have a negative impact on the European dollar deficit if subsumed under the ERP, because the small US dollar appropriations under the 1949-50 ERP were barely enough to maintain the European economic growth already achieved[83].

The MDAP, which for fiscal years 1949-50 and 1950-51 would be funded for as much as $6.5 billion, seemed consistent with the American policymakers' position. It resulted from the legislation presented before the US Congress on July 25, 1949[84]. The Truman Administration organized its military assistance into three types. Primarily, they wished to provide the European partners with weapons and war materials previously used by the American troops during the Second World War. Then, they wanted to grant financial assistance in US dollars to fund imports of consumer goods required either to implement European mili-

---

79 Summary of Telegrams by the Office of the Secretary of State to unspecified recipients, 5 April 1949, in HSTPL, NATO Collection, folder Mutual Assistance Program;

80 Ismay, *NATO: The First Five Years*, chapter 1;

81 «Il governo italiano, data la penuria di dollari, avrà bisogno -nel programma di accrescimento della produzione militare in Italia- di aiuto da parte degli Stati Uniti per quello che riguarda i costi in dollari di questo nuovo piano produttivo.» 'Nota dell'ambasciata italiana a Washington al Dipartimento di Stato', 8 marzo 1949, in C.Sforza, *Cinque anni a Palazzo Chigi: La politica estera italiana dal 1947 al 1951*, Atlante, Roma, 1952, pp. 244-45;

82 'Memorandum by Ambassadors Caffery and Harriman to the French Minister of Foreign Affairs (Schuman)', Paris, 3 March 1949, in *FRUS 1949*, vol. 4, *Western Europe*, p. 149;

83 'The Acting US Special Representative in Europe Under the Economic Assistance Act of 1948 (Katz) to the Administrator for Economic Cooperation (Hoffman)', Paris, 31 March 1949, in *FRUS 1949*, vol. 4, *Western Europe*, pp. 257-58;

84 Federico Caffè, Appunto per il signor governatore, 'Nuova organizzazione per la distribuzione degli aiuti americani', in ASBI, Carte Caffè, pratt., n. 48, fold. 1;

44

tary production or to build it up where it had been dismantled during the war. Finally, there was a reference to the provision of US military personnel to equip and train European troops[85].

Thus, US military and technical assistance within the broader context of a drive for productivity were by mid-1949 two long-term aspects of US foreign policy. Truman launched a vast program of financial and technical assistance to modernize the European industrial and financial systems in January 1949; from fiscal year 1950-51 technical assistance became one of the most relevant debit items in US foreign assistance programs, measured not so much by the size of the appropriations as by the importance given this program in Washington[86].

If we break down the aggregate amount appropriated for mutual assistance purposes into its main debit items, the nature of the program is straightforward, as is the extent to which the United States responded to rearmament's effects on European monetary stability. Of $1.45 billion in requests submitted to Congress by the White House, over $1 billion were for technical assistance, arms, and military equipment, while less than $300 million would provide US currency to fund expansion of military productions in Europe, and eventually the establishment of a continent-wide military industrial complex[87]. Americans realized from the beginning that supplying European imports of material needed to stimulate military production there via US markets could quickly generate an inflationary pressure on the US economy; this opinion was widely shared in Washington[88].

The Mutual Defense Assistance Act, as drafted by Congress in the summer of 1949 and enacted on October 6, shortly after the Soviets' first atomic explosion in September, was quite different from the legislation proposed by the White House. First, it was the result of divergent opinions within the Truman Administration, particularly between the Defense Department and the State Department, which disputed the nature and main features of the program. Acheson and the Pentagon disagreed about which government branch should head the program. That match would be won by the State Department, which prevailed over both the Defense Department and the proposal to establish a new agency like the Economic Cooperation Administration. Second, the two entities disputed the meaning of mutual

85 Harry S.Truman, Address to the Congress of the United States, 25 July 1949; L.Kaplan, *The Long Entanglement*; p. 48; L.Sebesta, *I programmi di aiuto militare nella politica americana per l'Europa: L'esperienza italiana 1948-1955*, in"Italia contemporanea", n. 173 (1988), pp. 43-63;

86 A.Tarchiani to Ministero degli Esteri, telespresso, 25 May 1950, in ASBI, Carte Caffè, pratt., n. 50, fold. 1;

87 This proportional distribution of the three kinds of aid provided by the MDAP was constant throughout the following two fiscal years. See Record of the Under Secretary's Meeting, Department of State, 22 June 1951, 'Progress Report on MDAP', in *FRUS 1951*, vol. 1, *National Security Affairs, Foreign Economic Policy*, pp. 326-27; Harry S.Truman, Report to Congress on the Mutual Defense Assistance Program, Washington D.C., 1950-52; this presidential report covers the period from October 1949 through October 1951;

88 R.Bissell, Oral History interview, pp. 23-24, in HSTPL, Oral History interviews;

assistance[89]. Finally, they debated the structure and organization of aid: should it be a bilateral or a multilateral assistance program?

Even ignoring these problems within the Truman Administration, there were many other changes in the law passed by Congress from the proposal Truman brought before it. China was added to the list of nations eligible to receive assistance, and Congress limited the power of the president in the program. As for the amount of money appropriated and how it was to be spent, the aggregate sum was reduced to $1 billion; $900 million would be used later on to support a collective defense plan approved at the NATO level and endorsed by the North Atlantic Alliance Defense Committee[90]. Furthermore, the act increased the disproportion between «dollars» and «arms». In fact, it is noteworthy that since the previous winter US support for the creation of a collective defense structure in Europe had been sketched as a grant-in-aid program based on equipment and arms supplied from the American military to modernize and update the old European military equipment as quickly as possible. This was even more necessary considering that the time needed to plan defense procurements with the American defense industry was likely to delay the delivery of consumer goods and end items to the Europeans. On the other hand, Washington had viewed the financial assistance as specifically covering additional US dollar costs created in the European military-industrial complex by an increase in European military production[91]. In other words, the American leaders did not conceive aid in dollars to cover European monetary system deficits that would accrue through increased expenditures on imports.

Even if the Truman Administration had wanted such limited stimulation of European military production, there was widespread concern in Congress about the effects that it could have on the American military-industrial complex. This further weakened support for the principle that the United States should support European industry in order to set up a standing army across Western Europe. This issue surfaced during debate on the legislation when Senator Arthur Vandenberg, and then John Vorys, proposed removing any expenditures for expanding European military production[92]. When the law was passed, the 16 per cent of the total aid that had been requested for this purpose became, rather than a fixed sum, a share of the total annual appropriation for foreign military assistance. The funding of European imports was not aimed at further expanding European industry, but at supporting a general updating of European plants. Thus, the United States intended the influx of dollars to stimulate the existing European war industry and maintain its production levels. The United States was committed to letting the Europeans purchase updated machinery and consumer goods. This

---

89 L. Kaplan, *The Long Entanglement*, pp. 40-41;

90 'Statement by the President upon using Order Providing for the Administration of the MDAA', 27 January 1950, (http://www.trumanlibrary.org/publicpapers/)

91 'Memorandum by Ambassadors Caffery and Harriman to the French Minister of Foreign Affairs (Schuman)', March 3, 1949, in *FRUS 1949*, vol. 4, *Western Europe*, pp. 148-149;

92 L.Kaplan, *The Long Entanglement*, p. 51;

Congressional reappraisal of mutual security produced a program called Additional Military Production, whose negative impact on European defense economics is ascribable not only to the poor functioning of the program, but also to the limits imposed by Congress's view of mutual security on the development of military production in Europe.

The US Congress severely limited the usefulness of the equipment and arms sent to Europe to stimulate European industry by mandating that equipment be sent only for replacing and updating existing European industry.

We can thus grasp the meaning of the distinction between «arms» and «dollars». In fact, as mutual assistance divided military aid into these two categories, there was a clear distinction between the military and strategic side of rearmament and its implications in the financial and monetary realm. Even an impressive transfer of machinery and military end-items could not mitigate the impact on European trade and balance of payments deficits, as aid in US dollars was meant to fund the Europeans' balance of payments deficits rather than their defense budgets.

1.4 Conclusion

In this first chapter my goal was to clarify the main features of a mutual security program that marked a watershed in the history of US foreign military assistance. One of its most distinctive characteristics was the attempt to set every military assistance initiative promoted since the end of World War II into a broad framework. The mutual security legislation endorsed by the US Congress marked a major repositioning of military assistance away from providing the allies with equipment and weapons intended to be used for the domestic purposes of producing peace and stability within every Western bloc country. The new aim was to secure Western Europe from external threats; military assistance was aimed much more toward protecting allies from foreign threats than from internal insurgency. The new law let the Truman Administration implement the rearmament of the West more quickly than had previously been possible.

Despite the features that shaped the MDAP as a landmark of full multilateralization of Western rearmament, the military assistance program produced by this appropriations bill lacked some of the characteristics destined to influence the West European countries' domestic economies and the European trade integration openly supported by Washington; these were built up only during the years that followed. Above all, what was missing was a close coordination of arms trade among the European NATO members and the establishment of bodies specifically aimed at bridging the European balance of payments disequilibrium caused by rearmament, which during the Korean War was still managed by the European Payments

Union[93]. The Temporary Council Committee likely became the most important NATO body charged with this task and the overall balance between national defense efforts and economic stability. Furthermore, the US government still conceived mutual assistance strictly as part of bilateral diplomatic and international relations between the United States and each European partner[94]. Intra-European trade of arms and consumer goods for military production purposes was a major feature as early as 1949, when the Western Union powers and the US diplomatic representative in Europe considered the possibility of using US military aid to promote European economic integration. By that time, US Ambassador to London Douglas's open-minded approach to building a multilateral rearmament program was broken off by Washington, which accounts for the early obsolescence of the MDAP[95]. In fact, in the years following 1950, the US reappraised their approach to, and solution for, Europe's dollar gap problem.

Improvement of Europe's balance of payments deficit against US currency by funding European imports through the US market, as the European Recovery Program had done, came into question.

Many American policymakers suggested that Washington help its European partners through less rigid trade policies rather than through an influx of dollars into Europe[96]. This prevented the MDAP from letting the European economies earn dollars through the rearmament program, and opened up a discussion in Washington on the role of military assistance in producing financial stability across Western Europe. Such an achievement could

---

93 On the TCC, the most recent account is H.R. Hammerich, *Jeder fur sich und Amerika gegen alle? Die Lastentailung der NATO am Beispiel des Temporary Council Committee 1949 bis 1954*, Oldenbourg, Munich, 2003. See also J.Hoffenaar, *Military Wishes and Economic Realities: The NATO Temporary Council Committee and the Build up of the Dutch Armed Forces 1951-1952*, paper presented at the 30th International Conference of Military History, Rabat, Morocco, 1-7 August 2004;

94 L.Kaplan, *NATO Divided, NATO United: The Evolution of an Alliance* , Praeger, Westport (Conn.), 2004, p. 6;

95 L.Douglas to D.Acheson, 26 March 1949, telegram, in *FRUS 1949*, vol. 4, *Western Europe*, pp. 250 ff.; see also S.Chillé, *Gli Stati Uniti e l'integrazione europea 1946-1957*, in R.H.Rainero (ed.), *Storia dell'integrazione europea*, vol. 1, *L'integrazione europea dalle origini alla nascita della Cee*, Marzorati, Milano, 1997, pp. 463-523;

96 In 1950 and 1951, two US government advisory bodies charged with studying and reappraising US international economic policy and its problems (one chaired by Gordon Gray, the other by Nelson Rockefeller) produced reports. Both suggested that the Truman Administration end aid to friendly nations through programs like ERP. Rather, Washington should cope with the European balance of payments and monetary difficulties through open trade and tariff policies. For a comparison of these two documents, see B.Kaufman, *Trade and Aid: Eisenhower's Foreign Economic Policy 1953-1961*, The Johns Hopkins University Press, Baltimore (Md.), 1982. See also Gordon Gray, *Report to the President on Foreign Economic Policies*, Washington D.C., 1950; US Congress, Senate, Committee on Appropriations, Special Subcommittee on Foreign Economic Cooperation, *Analysis of the Gray Report*, 82d Cong., 1st session, 1951, Washington D.C., 1951;

not be accomplished by the MDAP; it was fully targeted on military aid only a couple of years later by the off- shore procurement programs signed and implemented under the broader umbrella of the Mutual Security Program (MSP).

Policies for the rearmament of Western Europe, drafted and pursued through the 1949 MDAP and the 1950 MSP, were aimed at strengthening every European partner within a security framework agreed upon at the NATO level, but they did not cope with the European dollar shortage problem and the structural problems of the Intra-European payments system. Thanks to MSP, the European Payments Union was relieved of dealing with the impact of rearmament on the European dollar deficit. In late 1951, a new NATO common fund was created to alleviate the pressure of rearmament on European currencies and trade balances.

Chapter 2

The mutilateralization of rearmament between US dollar and European markets:
domestic growth and external equilibrium in the early years of transatlantic economic
integration

2.1 From bilateral transatlantic relations to multilateralism: the inception of rearmament before the off-shore procurement programs 1950-1952

It is interesting to note that the MDAP came up with two new features that were path-breaking when compared to overall US foreign policy. Firstly, this new program reunified and rationalized all the military assistance initiatives carried out previously. In fact, such reorganization was a required condition both to implement a continent-wide coordination of military production, and to promote self-sufficient industrial capacity. Secondly, by contrast with the previous reorganization of national armies across Europe that had been geared to targeting internal subversion and strengthening homeland security, with the launch of the MDAP the aim of Washington was to finance a military build-up which would provide its West European allies with a defense posture against external military threats[97]. Moreover, this aid permitted the Truman Administration to speed up the process of rearmament that in the first two years after World War II had aimed to provide Western Europe with the minimum required military defense[98].

Yet the MDAP essentially remained a bilateral assistance program to provide the West European countries with bilateral military aid. As such, it could not serve the US objectives to make up the so called *dollar shortage* in Europe and to promote intra-European trade and monetary integration in Western Europe. In fact, at that time these objectives were being pursued through the EPU and the ERP's counterpart funds[99]. Moreover, this bilateral structure prevented Washington from using its military aid programs to further the continent-level co-ordination of raw materials, industrial infrastructures and manpower that an early supra-

---

97 See, for example 'Memorandum of Conversation General MacArthur-A.W.Harriman', 6 August 1950, in CU, MD, papers of A.Harriman, b. 5, fold. Far East Trip 1946;

98 with reference to the debate on the nature and objectives of rearmament within the Truman Administration prior to the birth of the Atlantic Alliance see CU, MD, papers of A.Harriman, bb. 2-5;

99 H.R.Hammerich, *Jeder für sich und Amerika gegen alle? Die Lastenteilung der NATO am Beispiel des Temporary Council Committee 1949 bis 1954*, pp. 31-35; to get a better understanding of how the United States resorted to the counterpart funds to promote intra-European trade and monetary integration see T.Voorhees, 'A proposal for strengthening defense without increasing appropriations', 5 April 1950, in *FRUS 1950*, Vol. 3, *Western Europe*, pp. 45-48;

national economic institution such as the OEEC pursued. On the other hand, the organization of the MDAP was different from the multilateral structure and organization that NATO adopted in the early 1950s[100].

In contrast to the MDAP, the off-shore procurement programs launched under the umbrella of the Mutual Security Program effected a multilateralization of rearmament that was closely linked to the financial and monetary stabilization of intra-European trade and payments and helped Europeans to recover from the dollar shortage[101].

During the two years prior to the beginning of the OSP, American military assistance lacked these twin features because there was both a widespread fear that rearmament might imperil economic recovery in Europe, and fierce opposition from the US business community to the expansion of the European military industrial complex, as well as to the financial scope and impact of the MDAP. In fact, the size of the MDAP was limited after lengthy clashes between the influential Bureau of the Budget on the one hand and the Departments of Defense and State on the other[102]. Furthermore, against the background of the early Cold War American concerns for the fate of Western Europe, through 1951 the goal of military assistance was to resurrect the war torn armies of these nations and their industrial capacity «to build the necessary level of military strength to discourage aggression, without undermining the economic strength which is fundamental to long-run security»[103]. Both the MDAP and the MTDP, the

---

100 In particular, after 1951 the government of the United States supported close cooperation between NATO and OEEC to push forward industrial and trade integration among the West European economies. See Psychological Strategic Board, Office of Coordination, 'ECA-Economic Aid and Defense of Free World', 3 October 1951, in HSTPL, Records of the Psychological Strategic Board (the document is also available from the DDRS); Confindustria, n.a., 'Costituzione di un Comitato economico e Finanziario. Proposta del sostituto degli Stati Uniti', 15 March 1951, in ASC, CED, b. 49.1/2 (Commesse alle Forze armate degli Stati Uniti), fold. Commesse. Promemoria del dottor Mattei-Targiani-Campilli, s.f. Relazioni varie sui lavori del DPB-NATO. In this regard, see also D.Krüger, *Sicherheit durch integration? Die wirtschaftliche und politische Zusammenarbeit Westeuropas 1947 bis 1957-58*, Oldenbourg Verlag, München, 2003, pp. 97-157. Kruger maintains this argument consistently and convincingly;

101 'The Mutual Security Program. Report Prepared by the Office of the Director for Mutual Security', 30 June 1953, pp. 20-25, in DDRS; The Eisenhower Administration conceived the OSP contracts as a fly-wheel to promote trade and monetary cooperation between the dollar markets and the European economies. I deal more in detail with this point in the following chapters. The following document is revealing in this respect, Confindustria, Appunto informativo, 'L'industria italiana e le commesse americane', 13 December 1952, in ASC, CED, b. 49.1/2 (Commesse alle Forze armate degli Stati Uniti), fold. Circolari. Appunti. Sgravi fiscali sulle commesse off-shore. Indagine sulla situazione delle commesse estere, s.f. Commesse off-shore. Trattamento fiscale;

102 J.Ohly, Memorandum for the files, '1951 MDAP Budget', 5 December 1949, in DDRS; J.Ohly to Mr. Bell, 1 December 1949, in DDRS;

103 H.S.Truman to the Congress, 1 June 1950, in Public Papers of the United States. Harry S.Truman (http://www.trumanlibrary.org/publicpapers/index.php);

military aid program which was launched in 1950, shared these limits to their finances, organization and scope. However, the Mutual Security Program was to overcome these constraints in later years.

Despite these significant limits, it is useful to begin any inquiry into the off-shore procurement programs by making some remarks on these early military assistance programs. In so doing, the aim is to reconstruct the debate that led the US government and NATO to turn bilateral military assistance into a set of multilateral programs that intended to address both defense and security targets, and monetary stabilization and trade integration among the Western bloc economies. As a matter of fact, although the MDAP was above all a first-aid program, from as early as 1949 up to 16 per cent of its total appropriations were reserved for financing the expansion of self-sufficient industrial capacity in Europe. The American aim was to build up a European military industry that would provide the European partners with self-sufficient manufacturing capacity of military spare parts, machine tools and end items. In turn, this self-sufficiency in manufacturing would raise demand for raw material and investment goods on the international commodity markets bound to both the sterling and dollar currency areas[104]. This leap in demand for raw material and investment goods was closely linked to the problem of coping with a shrinking current account in the balance of payments of the European countries involved in the rearmament process. This problem arose as early as 1950, and prior to the beginning of the OSP programs, as a result of the inflationary spiral that saw raw material and commodity prices rise during the Korean War[105].

Indeed, from the outset of Washington's planning of the MTDP, the Truman Administration was concerned about the impact that a significant involvement of the European military industrial complex in the war mobilization might have on civilian consumptions and aggregate demand. This concern led some American policymakers to argue in favor of financing European imports to prevent the process of rearmament from imperiling the monetary and financial stabilization pursued through the Marshall Plan. Averell Harriman, director at the time of the Economic Cooperation Administration, maintained that the US government should provide its West European allies with both strategic material and financial assistance in US dollars to stimulate rapid growth in European military industrial output. In striking contrast to the position of the Washington-based American policymakers[106], Harriman argued that it was worth starting up new production lines in Western Europe[107]. This policy was based on the

---

104 ECA, Office of the US Special Representative in Europe, 'OSR Review for Period of September 9 through 22, 1951', in NARA, RG59, Lot File 52-26, Records of the Mutual Defense Assistance Program, Subject File relating to Programme Management (Bell Rowe File) 1949-1952, b. 2;

105 National Advisory Council Meetings, Minutes of Meetings, Meeting n. 160, 2 August 1950, in NARA, RG56, NAC papers, NAC Minutes, b.2 (February 9, 1950-December 28, 1950);

106 D.Krüger, *Sicherheit durch Integration?*, pp. 71-72;

107 L.Sebesta, *L'Europa indifesa*, p. 153; on Harriman's position, see also LOC, MD, Averell W. Harriman papers, Special Files: Public Service 1918-1986, b. 271;

theoretical assumption that the defense industry was likely to raise living standards in Western Europe and also deemed necessary as part of the ideological race against the USSR[108].

In the course of 1950 Harriman found himself ever less isolated within the Truman Administration, as a growing number of policymakers became convinced that economic assistance and security policies could co-exist, and that rearmament posed no danger to the process of economic recovery. Indeed, Harriman's view gained ground within both the US Administration and NATO[109]. A short time after the outbreak of war in Korea, during lengthy discussions held in Washington regarding both the need and feasibility for an expansion of industrial output in Europe, it emerged that a wide range of government agencies and policymakers shared two leading principles that would determine the implementation of the military assistance programs in the future. Within the National Advisory Council on International Monetary and Financial Problems, there was widespread consensus among government members regarding two policy principles. Firstly, they argued that financial appropriations destined for the stimulation of industrial output in European economies should not be plowed back into national reserves or used to complete the postwar monetary stabilization. Indeed, while the ECA was more inclined to let the Europeans use the MDAP in this way[110], the US Secretary of State, Acheson, stubbornly insisted that both financial assistance appropriated to Western Europe under the umbrella of the MDAP, as well as the counterpart funds generated within the ERP and held at the European Central Banks, be used to finance imports related to defense production and internal industrial investments[111].

Secondly, they stressed that military aid should help European countries «to contribute toward their own defense, and that we were not requesting the Congress for funds to provide aid except insofar as it was necessary to carry out rearmament without an unacceptable and ex-

---

108 'Summary of Hearings on the Mutual Security Program Before the House Committee on Foreign Affairs, Testimony by A.W.Harriman, Special Assistant to the President', 3 July 1951, in NARA, RG 469, Mission To Italy, Office of the Director, Subject Files (Central Files) 1948-57, b. 18, fold. 2 (Congress Hearings);
109 In this respect the testimony by Milton Katz, between 1950 and 1951 at the head of the Defense Financial and Economic Committee of NATO should be noted: «I did not, as some people did, regard NATO as a diversion from the Marshall Plan objectives. I regarded it as a recognition that one of the requirements for achieving the Marshall Plan objective of restoring the economies, political independence and cultural vitality of a self-sustaining and self-regenerating Europe was a sense of military security.» Milton Katz interview, p. 121, in HSTPL, Oral History interviews;
110 D.E.Bell to J.H.Ohly, 'Report of Activity, December 26-29', p. 6, 30 December 1950, in DDRS;
111 NAC Minutes of Meetings n. 160, 2 August 1950, in NARA, RG56, NAC papers, NAC Minutes, b. 2 (February 9, 1950-December 28, 1950), pp. 3-4; in this perspective, with reference to the American view on Italy, see the Defense Department's approach reported in Foreign Military Assistance Coordinating Committee, 'Current Situation in Italy', 17 April 1950, in DDRS;

cessive deterioration in their own economies›› [112]. In the United States during 1950 there were two opposing views: on the one hand the American business community still maintained that it would not be feasible to combine war mobilization and economic growth [113]; on the other hand, from as early as spring 1950, and especially among the high ranking experts on security-related economic policy problems, a growing number of people put forward the opposite argument. According to Tracy Voorhees, who represented the Eisenhower Administration on the economic and financial bodies of NATO involved in the multilateral negotiations on the OSP during the 1950s, the rearming of Western Europe was to serve as a fly-wheel to jump-start the aggregate demand for civilian consumer goods [114]. In May 1950 at the Atlantic Council (the inter-ministerial Committee of NATO made up of the Foreign, Defense and Finance Ministries from the member countries) the Secretary of State, Acheson, maintained that the defense effort in the European economies should be coupled with an expansionary economic policy to permit growth of the European domestic markets and raise the employment rate [115]. It is worth stressing that we can only understand the feasibility of this predominant American view by considering it within a comparative European perspective. In fact, in 1950 the European economies varied greatly. Some of these countries had a high rate of underemployed manpower that could be usefully employed in new production lines. In fact, the Department of the Treasury stressed that Italy was just such a case. Hence, rearmament in Italy was both to expand industrial output and to open new production lines, and thus to improve the living standards of the Italian population by stimulating the re-employment of labor and by increasing the average weekly working hours of the working population. On the contrary, some other West European nations with higher rates of economic growth came into a very different category. For example, the United Kingdom, the Netherlands and Denmark already had full utilization of industrial plants and manpower at the time and thus in these economies the rearmament effort would generate a severe internal economic downturn [116]. The only way to avoid a drop in civilian demand was to raise finance and imports for consumer goods.

During 1950, the government of the United States combined these two policy guidelines within a strict policy on European national defense expenditure. The US pressured their partners to increase the ratio of the defense budget against total state expenditures. In American eyes, this policy would both expand the annual Budget of the Defense Ministries, and generate ex-

112 NAC Minutes of Meetings n. 168, 26 December 1950, in NARA, RG56, NAC papers, NAC Minutes, b. 2 (February 9, 1950-December 28, 1950);

113 *The Journal of Commerce*, 2 October 1950;

114 Memorandum by T.Voorhees to G.Gray, 10 April 1950, in FRUS 1950, Vol. 3; H.Hammerich, *Jeder für sich und Amerika gegen alle?*, p. 34;

115 Summary of Telegrams by State Department to unspecified recipients, 10 May 1950, in HSTPL, NATO collection, fold. NAC;

116 National Advisory Council Meetings, Minutes of Meetings, Meeting n. 160, 2 August 1950, in NARA, RG56, NAC papers, NAC Minutes, b. 2 (February 9, 1950-December 28, 1950);

traordinary defense appropriations. This American insistence was consistent with the Atlantic Alliance Medium Term Defense Program. This program had been established to coordinate the rearmament programs according to the requirements laid down on defense and security targets for each NATO member state[117]. Repeated calls for broader defense appropriation were made to London from the summer of 1950 through January 1951[118]. The Americans extended the same requests to most West European countries, including Italy[119]. The pressure exerted by the US clearly shows the impact that the ongoing reorganization of rearmament was having on European countries in 1950; in short, they were to expand their budget appropriations both to strengthen their national armies, and to stimulate industrial output through the financing of imports and domestic industrial investments.

Therefore, in the period between the Atlantic Council meeting held in London and the beginning of the off-shore procurement programs in early 1952, the rearmament programs had become a process that would involve both industrial integration, and trade partnership and balance of payments equilibrium, as well as budgetary and monetary stability. The multilateral production program implemented through the off-shore procurements was thus a combination of these elements.

2.2 Sharing the burden of rearmament. The birth of the OSP in the push towards industrial integration, foreign exchange equilibrium and internal monetary stability

Despite the fact that a high number of top-ranking politicians within the Truman Administration and the US Congress maintained that ‹‹in many of these countries an increase of budgetary expenditures would significantly retard recovery progress››[120], for the whole of 1952 the US political system made no effort to force the Europeans to increase their national defense budgets in order to ease the costs to the US taxpayer of both the ordinary balance sheet and the extra budgetary military appropriations. Despite this insistence on the budgetary issue, the

---

117 Some easily accessed archival material pertaining to the MTDP has been published in *FRUS 1951*, Vol. 3, *European Security and the German Question*, Part 1, Government Printing Office, Washington DC, 1951, pp. 1 ff.; regarding the defense requirements that the MDAP posed on each member state, see H.R.Hammerich, *Jeder Für sich und Amerika gegen alle?* , pp. 72-74;

118 The UK Secretary of State (E.Bevin) to Her Majesty Ambassador at Washington (O.Franks), 2 September 1950, in *DBPO*, Series 2, vol. 3, *German Rearmament September-December 1950*, Her Majesty's Stationery Office, London 1989, pp. 1-3; Memorandum by the Secretary of State for Foreign Affairs and the Chancellor of the Exchequer, London, 23 October 1950, *idem*, pp. 195-96;

119 Record of a conversation held at Mr. Harriman's house in Washington (Attlee-O.Franks-E.Plowden-D.Acheson), 7 December 1950, in DBPO, Series 2, Vol. 3, German Rearmament, pp.353-354; T. Geiger, *Britain and the Economics of the North Atlantic Alliance 1949-1959*, pp. 7-10;

120 J.Ohly (Deputy Director for Mutual Defense Assistant), Memorandum for Major General L.L.Lemnitzer (Department of Defense), 'Covering Letter for Guidance for Reprogramming Fiscal Year 1950 Country Programs', p. 1, in *DDRS*;

implementation of the MTDP adopted at the North-Atlantic Council meeting of London aimed to balance war mobilization and the foreign exchange equilibrium in every NATO member country involved in the war effort. NATO strove to activate the European industrial capacity required to meet with military build-up without impairing the balance of payments of each European member country. Therefore, the MTDP was to coordinate the NATO economies in order to balance existing industrial capacity, national defense budget, and foreign exchange equilibrium[121]. Thus, the North Atlantic Council endorsed a call by the Atlantic Alliance's Defense Committee to promote ‹‹an examination of the financial and economic potentialities of the treaty nations to support military expenditures for the defense of the North Atlantic area››[122]. Throughout 1950, NATO and the United States government pursued this effort to engineer a multi-level coordination of the Western bloc economies that would integrate their budgetary, industrial and monetary assets. In order to reach this objective the Defense Production Board (DPB), a ‹‹technical committee deemed to plan and list which war material was likely to be produced by the West European defense industry››[123] was established within NATO. In addition, NATO set up the Defense Economic and Financial Committee (DEFC) in London, where the Finance Ministries of the Atlantic Alliance's member countries were to meet periodically[124]. It is revealing to note that according to the US Department of State the DPB was to fix the ratio of the existing industrial capacity to the defense and budgetary appropriations required in each country for the defense effort that had been negotiated and defined within NATO[125].

The aim of this consistent effort to coordinate the economies of NATO was to set up and improve economies of scale among the European countries[126]. This process was intended to promote a continent-wide trade exchange of raw materials, instrumental goods, spare parts and end item weapons. The final objective was the rationalization of production and the elimination of duplicates. The launch of this coordinated production program among the West European economies and the American economy led to lengthy discussions within NATO and its operating bureaus to improve the exploitation and coordination of raw material, investment

---

121 'Off-the-Record statement in regard to size and duration of MSP programs for Europe', 28 September 1951, in DDRS;

122 quoted in Acheson to Webb (Undersecretary of State for Economic Affairs), to pass to President H.S. Truman, Telegram, 19 May 1950, in HSTPL, NATO collection, fold. NAC;

123 L.Targiani, 'Pro-memoria. Impressioni riportate da Londra in merito alle commesse-15-17 gennaio 1952', p. 1, 23/1/1952, in ASC, CED, b. 49.1/2, fold. Commesse. Promemoria del dottor Mattei-Targiani-Campilli, s.f. 1952. Promemoria Targiani-Campilli-commesse; original quotation in Italian, my own translation into English;

124 For a different interpretation of the role and function of the DPB, see L.Segreto, *L'OTAN entre contraintes militaires et enjeux économiques et financieres*, p. 176;

125 T.Geiger, *The British Warfare and the Challenge of Americanisation of Western Defence*, p. 20;

126 The Secretary of State (Acheson) to the Acting Secretary of State, 18 May 1950, in *FRUS 1950*, Vol. 3, pp. 119-120;

56

goods, and manpower and manufacturing firms among these economies. These lengthy debates lasted throughout 1951. The head of the DPB, the American-born Herod, interpreted the role of the DPB in this perspective[127]. In fact, he instructed this bureau of NATO to estimate each West European economy's overall manufacturing capacity as well as its ratio to the overall national defense effort, in order to respect NATO build-up targets. Furthermore, the DPB was to pinpoint whether or not each European economy had a surplus industrial output of either manufacturing capacity or manpower that could be used on behalf of NATO and other member countries to meet the build-up objectives that had been set at NATO level. In addition, each NATO member state was expected to estimate its financial limits for the importing of weapons and military components produced in other countries under the Atlantic Alliance procurements policy[128].

Therefore, from as early as spring 1951, Washington and NATO were committed to identifying each European economy's manufacturing strength and the balance of payments threshold beyond which imbalances on the foreign exchange equilibrium would be caused by the defense effort. By fall of 1951 it was clear that NATO aimed to link the payment of future offshore procurements allotted to the NATO member states to the funding of imports and investment required by the industrial mobilization. In other words, this policy was designed to deal with the impact of war mobilization on the European balance of payments against both the US dollar currency area, as well as the intra-European currency disequilibrium that rearmament might trigger[129]. As a matter of fact, in late 1951 NATO launched an initial program of military procurements divided among the European economies. These orders were produced

---

127 ASF, Minutes of the board of directors, session of January 1952, p. 152 . Some specific projects aimed to set up co-production programs involving the economies of France and Italy to place orders with Fiat to supply the French military and rewarded in US dollars. These plans clearly illustrate the aim of rearmament to ease the pressure on the Italian balance of payments towards the US currency. With respect to this see L.Targiani, Pro-memoria, 'Impressioni riportate da Londra in merito alle commesse 15-17 gennaio 1952', 23 January 1952, in ASC, CED, b. 49.1/2, fold. Commesse. Promemoria del dottor Mattei-Targiani-Campilli, s.f. 1952. Promemoria Targiani-Campilli-commesse;

128 'IV Riunione del Comitato permanente affari economici', 19 April 1951, in ASC, Comitati Permanenti, b. 30.1/1 (Comitato permanente per gli affari economici. Biennio 1951/52), fold. 151 (IV Riunione del 19 aprile 1951. Questioni industriali relative al riarmo dei paesi occidentali. Esame delle questioni inerenti ai pools merceologici); n.a. (probably Rossi Longhi), 'Situazione attuale DPB-NATO', 16 April 1951; 'North Atlantic Defense Production Board' (minutes of meeting), 6 March 1951, both documents are in ASC, CED, b. 49.1/2 (Commesse alle forze armate degli Stati Uniti), fold. Commesse. Promemoria del dottor Mattei-Targiani-Campilli, s.f. Relazioni varie sui lavori del DPB-NATO;

129 Rossi Longhi to MAE, telegramma segreto, 12 February 1952, in ASMAE, Cassaforte, b. 16, Posizione Cassaforte 500/51, fold. NATO: Temporary Council Committee TCC; Rappresentanza italiana presso l'OECE-Parigi,Ufficio del delegato italiano al TCC a Pella, 'Esame del programma militare in seno all'Ufficio Esecutivo del TCC', 17 November 1951, in ASMAE, Cassaforte, year 1951, b. 15, Posizione Cassaforte 500/19, fold. 10 (NATO: Consiglio Nord Atlantico Ottawa-Settembre 1951);

in Europe and allotted to the West European NATO member states but paid off in US dollars out of the United States' federal balance sheet[130]. Hence, it was the US taxpayer who bore the financial burden of these rearmament programs. Right from the beginning of this multilateral production program, the Italian and German economies were considered by the United States to be the ideal manufacturing countries. From the first half of 1951 the Italian business community was well aware of this opportunity. Confindustria, the Italian Employers' Federation went out of its way to confirm that Italian firms were ready to work on military procurements for other member states of the Atlantic Alliance. Furthermore, the Italian entrepreneurs called for rewards in US dollars in order to import raw and strategic material to be used by the steel, mechanical and metalworking sectors involved in the military production programs. Vittorio Valletta, the director general of Fiat, recommended that the Italian firms refuse to work on military procurements if not rewarded in US dollars[131].

This military production program implemented in the second half of 1951 charged NATO and its operating bureaus with fixing production capacities and defense requirements in each West European member state of the Atlantic Alliance. In this respect, NATO was to serve as a sort of filter between the producing economies, the importing countries, and the United States government[132]. Although this program marked a step forward for the enforcement of production coordination and financial equilibrium within the Western bloc, payments for military procurements was still an issue. Provisionally, this program could finance them in US dollars because the United States government recorded them as US military end items transferred to West European national armies. In fact, they were worked in Europe and their financial burden was borne by the US taxpayer. Several high ranking policy makers within the Truman Administration focused their attention on this problem in an attempt to resolve it once and for all. Bissell, pro-tempore director of ECA, tackled the problem of how the multilateral military production programs would be financed and paid for in the future. He suggested that each member state of NATO should share this financial burden as far as possible. In calling for this

---

130 Confindustria, n.a. (authored by Targiani), 'Promemoria', 2 January 1952, in ASC, CED, b. 49.1/2, fold. Commesse. Promemoria del dottor Mattei-Targiani-Campilli, s.f. 1952. Promemoria Targiani-Campilli-commesse;

131 Appunto per il segretario generale, 'Comitato Permanente per gli affari economici-II Riunione', 9 March 1951, in ASC, Comitati permanenti, b. 30.1/1 (Comitato permanete per gli Affari economici. Biennio 1951/52), fold. 149 (II Riunione dell'8/3/1951-distribuzione internazionale delle materie prime critiche e relativa politica economica interna ed esterna. Problemi industriali del riarmo occidentale. Commesse e relativi finanziamenti);

132 ISAC, 'Memorandum of Understanding Between the Departments of State and Defense and the Economic Cooperation Administration on Relationships and Organization of United States Representatives and Certain North Atlantic Treaty bodies in European Production and Economic Aid Programs', 6 March 1951, in DDRS;

approach, he anticipated what would become the so-called "burden-sharing" principle[133]. The French Prime minister, Pleven, adopted the same approach. During 1950 he recommended that a sort of common financial fund should be established among the NATO member states. He believed that each state should contribute to this fund in proportion to their annual national income[134]. During winter 1950 many hypotheses were elaborated within the Atlantic community regarding which institution should administer this common fund[135]. Eventually, in early 1952, a common budgetary fund was set up within the Atlantic Alliance. Each member state was called on to share its budget appropriations in proportion to their national income. This principle meant that the United States was to pay the largest amount into this common fund. The government of the United States took the lead because of its twofold aim to finance the European public finances on the one side, and the balance of payments of both the Sterling area and the EPU member currency areas on the other[136]. This twofold objective is distinctive of the burden-sharing principle underpinning the Atlantic Alliance's common fund established that year[137]. Until now most of the economic and historical literature on the subject has

---

133 Magistrati(Delegazione italiana presso OECE) to Vittorio Zoppi (Segretario Generale MAE), secret, 19 November 1951, p. 8, in ASMAE, Cassaforte, b. 16, Posizione Cassaforte 500/51, fold. NATO: Temporary Council Committee;

134 Summary of Telegrams by State Department to unspecified recipients, 31 July 1950, HSTL, NATO collection, fold. NAC. Regarding the Italian liquidity contribution to the common budgetary fund of NATO see Ministero del Tesoro, Direz. Gen. del Tesoro, IRFE to MAE-DGCI, 'Procedure bancarie per il versamento delle contribuzioni ai bilanci NATO. Garanzie di cambio', 9 April 1952, in ASBI, Carte Caffè, pratt., n. 50, fold. 1;

135 NAC Minutes, Minutes of Meeting n. 190, 13 March 1952, in NARA, RG56, NAC papers , NAC Minutes, b. 2; L.Targiani, Pro-memoria, 'Perché ritardano le commesse e come si potrebbero accelerare', 7 January 1952; Confindustria, n.a. (probably Targiani), Promemoria, 2 January 1952, both documents can be found in ASC, CED, b. 49.1/2, fold. Commesse. Promemoria del Dottor Mattei-Targiani-Campilli, s.f. 1952. Promemoria Targiani-Campilli-commesse;

136 the State Department and ECA maintained that sharing out the financial burden of rearmament called for the United States to drive for «cutting the Gordian Knot which had prevented real progress in military planning.» 'Proposed Fiscal Year 1952 Foreign Aid Program, Title I, Europe', in NARA, RG 59, Lot File 52-26, Bell Rowe File, b. 3, p. 70 ff..; according to the Joint Chiefs of Staff «The creation of the forces necessary to make the NATO Medium Term Plan effective, will add materially to the security of the United States. It seems necessary and just therefore that the United States should bear not only the increased cost in its own military establishment but also should aid in closing in the gap between what the other NATO countries will be required to do and what they will be able to do». Joint Chiefs of Staff, Memorandum for Secretary Johnson, 13 July 1950, in HSTPL, NATO collection, fold., Development of NATO as an Organisation;

137 with respect to the international relations system of the twentieth century, for a theoretical definition of burden-sharing as a way of sharing out the economic burden engendered by international partnerships in the system of international relations in the twentieth century, the text of reference is: M.Chalmers, *Sharing Security: The Political Economy of Burdensharing*, St.Martin's Press, New

maintained that the budgetary sharing of rearmament costs aimed to concentrate the pressure of the defense effort on public finances. The majority of scholarly works have focused on the role of the United States in introducing a burden-sharing principle within the Atlantic community, and even those that underline the importance of the OEEC's European economic elites in enacting it, share this approach[138]. By contrast, I contend that the establishment of a NATO common fund and a collective defense budget of the Atlantic Alliance aimed to resolve not only the need to provide the European countries' balance-sheets with monetary liquidity to finance their defense effort, but also to stabilize their balance of payments to offset the strain of rearmament-induced industrial mobilization[139]. Within the Mutual Security Program the so-called *defense support* allotments were intended to target this twofold financial objective underpinning the creation of a collective defense budget by NATO. Every fiscal year a portion of the Mutual Security Program indexed as *defense support* was to be used as both reward for military procurements produced and transferred among the West European member states of NATO, or used for the strengthening of the American military force stationed in Europe, and to finance raw and strategic material imports as well as domestic industrial and capital investments generated by industrial mobilization[140].

The early military assistance program was negotiated against the backdrop of this multilateral evolution of the rearmament programs. When it got underway, in the course of 1951, it was a

---

York 2000. According to the author, irrespective of peace time or war, the international partnership among nations came with costs whose budgetary burden was shared by each country;

138 it is worth mentioning with respect to either of these perspectives, on the one hand, C.S.Maier, *Finance and Defense: Implications of Military integration*; id., *The Making of 'Pax Americana': Formative Movements of United States Ascendancy*, in R. Ahmann, A.M. Birke, and M. Howard (eds), *The Quest for Stability: Problems of West European Security 1918-1957*, Oxford University Press, Oxford 1993; on the other, T.Geiger, *Sistemi di analisi o modelli di crescita? L'influenza americana nell'elaborazione delle statistiche europee sulla crescita economica dopo la seconda guerra mondiale*, in "Nuova civiltà delle macchine", n. 3 (1999), pp. 34-35;

139 A.Rossi Longhi to MAE-Servizio OA, telegramma segreto, 12 February 1952, in ASMAE, Cassaforte, b. 16, Posizione Cassaforte 500/51. NATO: Temporary Council Committee.1952;

140 Mutual Security Agency, 'FY 1954 Title I (Europe) Defense Support Program. Italy. Developmental Aid for Fiscal Year 1954', 30 October 1952; State Department, 'State Department Comments on MSA Proposed Fiscal Year 54 Program for Italy. MSA Aid to Italy in Fiscal Year 1954', 31 October 1952, both in NARA, RG59, Records of the Office of the Special Assistant for Mutual Security Coordination, Office of the Undersecretary 1952-59, b. 25, fold. MAP-Italy (fiscal Year 1952-54); The Secretary of State to the Embassy in Italy, 'Finance Fiscal Year 1953', 17 March 1952; Dayton (MSA Rome) to the Secretary of State, Finance FY 1953', 20 March 1952, both in NARA, RG469, Mission to Italy, Office of the Director, Subject Files (Central Files) 1948-1957, b. 21, fold. 4 (Defense: Funds-Counterparts); Operations Coordinating Board, 'Progress Report on US Policy toward Italy (NSC5411/2)', 3 September 1957, p. 3, 'Financial Annex to Italy Progress Report (Military Aid and Offshore procurement)', in NARA, RG273, Records of the National Security Council, Policy Papers, b. 30;

first step towards integration of the manufacturing capacities and resources of the European nations in the Atlantic Alliance, and it bound this industrial interdependence to a truly intra-European trade area. In my view, this was the most distinctive feature of the off-shore procurement programs. In the years following the end of the OSP programs, the Pentagon played an ever-increasing role in this mechanism as it paid for investment goods and military end items produced and traded among the West European countries of NATO[141]. In this respect, the Aeronautical sector was an exemplary case. In the mid-1950s the US dollar was still the currency of rearmament. In fact, as the off-shore procurement programs were endorsed by the US Congress and NATO every year throughout the decade, the corollary of trade and payments were mostly rewarded in US dollars.

If we wish to sum up the nature of the OSP, we should note that their added value was their ability to exploit European industrial capacity to the full and to stabilize European currencies on the foreign exchange market as well as aiding European countries to achieve internal monetary stability, thus tackling three issues in one go.

2.3 The birth of multilateral military contracts and domestic economic development in Western Europe: the case of Italy with regard to the domestic market, foreign exchange equilibrium and public finances

The Italian economy, and the role it assumed within the Atlantic Alliance, make it an exemplary case for the reconstruction of the multi-level multilateralization of rearmament which took place between the 1951 off-shore procurement program discussed above and the setting up of a common budgetary fund within NATO soon after. We have already stressed how Washington identified Italy as an ideal manufacturing supply economy early on because of the country's unutilized industrial capacity and oversupply of labor. In fact, Italy started producing semi-manufactured goods and end-items prior to the formulation of the coordinated multilateral production programs laid down by the DPB studies and policy guidelines. These early orders to the Italian economy, followed shortly afterwards in 1951 by a number of military procurement contracts for the expansion of the Italian army's military strength, were

---

141 In this perspective the case of the F86D all-weather fighters, produced in 1953 by Fiat to supply either the Italian air force or other NATO member countries is revealing. The US Air Force financed the Italian plants and paid for the end items that Fiat was to sell. C.H.Shuff (Deputy for Mutual Security Assistance Affairs) to Ortona (consigliere ambasciata italiana in Washington), 15 May 1953; Kindelberger (North American Aviation)-Valletta(Fiat)-Tolino(Ministero Difesa-Aeronautica)-Tarchiani (Ambasciatore Italia in USA), 'Accordo per licenza e assistenza', 16 May 1953; 'Memorandum di accordo tra Governo degli Stati Uniti e governo italiano', 13 May 1953, all of these documents are in ASF, USA-Delibere, b. Contratto USAF-Governo italiano e licenza North American Aviation-Governo italiano-Fiat, year 1953;

combined with dollar aid to the Italian Ministry of Defense for the financing of the extra budgetary appropriations needed to expand Italian military land forces[142]. Italy is especially apt for illustrating the evolution of military assistance from bilateral industrial and budgetary aids to a multilateral manufacturing, trade and payments rearmament project based on burden-sharing of the defense effort among the partner countries. The suitability of the Italian case here is due to the fact that the early twofold military assistance, typical of the OSP programs, was launched in Italy even as the TCC was formulating it, and brought a truly multilateral military production program to the attention of the United States' government and to NATO. To better understand the situation we should examine how the Italian political and economic elites strove hard to accommodate Italy's new commitment to serve as production source for its NATO partners with the excess credit position of the Italian Lira within EPU. Italy's stubborn insistence on getting paid off in US dollars for working and exporting semi-manufactured weapons and end items stemmed from this early 1950s' currency glut against the other EPU currencies. Accordingly, during 1951 Italy engaged to pursue this twin objective. In the spring, Vittorio Valletta underlined how important it was for Italy's firms to sustain the burden of the first off-shore procurement program in return for the offsetting of payments in US dollars. Later on in the same year the seventh De Gasperi Cabinet again emphasized the Italian position by calling for a larger dollar inflow in return for committing the Italian entrepreneurial system to serve as a manufacturing source for the Atlantic Alliance. For example, the Italian Minister Campilli, instructed Italian manufacturers on how to select and accept military procurement contracts on order from foreign state-owned concerns or public administrations. Campilli recommended that the mechanical and electro-mechanical firms take into account which European currency areas these orders came from and their respective exchange rate against the Italian Lira[143]. On the other hand, however, Italy's commitment to supply manufactured goods under the early OSP program meant Rome had to deal with the issue of extra-budgetary defense appropriations. The DPB outline of military force requirements for Italy had specified the need for twelve new land forces. This meant that the Defense Ministry had to expand its budget appropriations to recruit new military personnel and

---

142 Mutual Security Agency, Special Mission to Italy for Economic Cooperation, 'Status of the Italian Military Production Program', 29 February 1952, in NARA, RG469, Mission to Italy, Office of the Director, Subject files (Central Files) 1948-57, b. 22, fold. 2 (Defense, Osp Program: contracts, Production); 'Aid-Memoire Minutes of Meeting held March 5, 1951, by the Deputies' Joint Committee' [Memorandum of conversation Malvestiti-Malagodi-Magistrati-Ferrari Aggradi-Jacobs-Dayton-Barnett-Chenery], in NARA, RG469, Mission to Italy, Office of the Director, Subject Files (Central Files) 1948-57, b. 39, fold. 4;
143 Appunto per il Segretario Generale, 'Rilevazione delle commesse di Stato', 20 October 1951; P.Campilli to A.Costa, 4 October 1951, both in ASC, CED, b. 49.1/2 (Commesse alle Forze Armate degli Stati Uniti), fold. Commesse. Promemoria del Dottor Mattei-Targiani-Campilli, s.f. Commesse per le Forze Armate americane. Circolari. Appunti;

equipment. At the same time the Italian Defense Ministry had to meet a set of orders to Italian mechanical firms for the purchase of military trucks and vehicles in line with the targets nego-tiated within NATO. The combination of these two budget expenses was a strain on the Ital-ian Defense Ministry Budget and accounted for the Italian government's decision early in 1952 to temporarily cancel a series of military procurements to Fiat to supply the country's land forces with trucks[144]. This decision stemmed from the De Gasperi Cabinet choice to shift budget appropriations away from these contracts to finance the establishment of twelve new military land divisions according to the DPB force requirements. This major concern for the impact that the OSP might have on the country's public finances sheds light on the implica-tions that the rearmament programs had on Italian economic policy at large. Furthermore, this budget-minded approach to the build-up exercise came from a De Gasperi government that was openly committed to targeting the issue of social stability, employment and economic growth[145].

The cancellation of orders to Fiat for the production of trucks for the Italian Army highlights the fact that the Italian public finances were unable to support multiple extra-budgetary de-fense appropriations. The problem of how to mitigate the impact of rearmament on public spending and accommodate extra-budgetary defense appropriations into the annual balance-sheet had been the subject of lengthy discussions and studies between the Italian Confindustria (Italian Employers' Federation) and the government from the summer of 1951, yet by early 1952 it had still not been resolved. When Italy went before the TCC to present its projected output to meet the 1952-53 off-shore production programs, the Italian government and Confindustria asked NATO to include the orders from the Italian Defense Ministry to the Italian manufacturers within the off-shore procurement contracts allotted to Italy to supply the national armies of NATO partners. Thus, military procurements worked in Italy to meet Ital-ian Defense force requirements were to be paid for in US dollars by the US government[146]. This approach would save these contracts without exerting pressure on Italian public finances and liabilities. The Italian proposal, formulated and brought before the TCC between Decem-ber 1951 and January 1952, had been to some extent anticipated by the Rome Cabinet on the FEB in July 1951. On that occasion, the Italian Minister for Foreign Affairs, Carlo Sforza, and the Italian government on the whole endorsed it with conviction. Even the Treasury Min-ister, Giuseppe Pella, well known in the literature for his firm monetarist approach to the management of the Italian economy, limited his criticism of this plan. He did cast some doubts on the plan according to the theoretical concept that an expansionary program involv-

---

144 ASF, Minutes of the board of directors, session of January 1952;

145 P.Craveri, *De Gasperi*, Il Mulino, Bologna 2006, pp. 473-474; R.Gualtieri, *La politica economica del centrismo e il quadro internazionale*, pp. 109-110; id., *L'Italia dal 1943 al 1992*, pp. 123-124;

146 for a very different perspective from mine, see C.Villani, *Il prezzo della stabilità*, pp. 37-39. Ac-cording to this author the Italian initiative to obtain a substantial amount of OSP contracts aimed only at working on orders placed with the Italian industry to supply other NATO partners.

ing a wide range of manufacturing sectors working with the defense industry was likely to trigger an expansion in the aggregate demand and hence a leap in the employment rate which would exceed growth in supply[147]. According to this rather Keynesian argument, a commitment to production for both the Italian armies and other NATO partner countries would trigger an imbalance between supply and demand in the sector of civilian consumer goods and durables. This imbalance, unless mitigated by monetary policy interventions on the discount rate to expand currency in circulation, would generate an inflationary trend caused by excess in aggregate demand on supply[148]. The Italian manufacturers supported the Italian proposal to the TCC through their own representative to NATO[149]. According to the representatives of Italian business, this solution would resolve all three of the problems that were delaying the allotment of OSP contracts to Italy. Moreover, they believed that this solution would increase international demand for Italian processed goods. Hitherto, Italy's share of the international export of manufactured goods had been stalled by the Italian economy's fiscal policy which was unsuited to its exporters' requirements. In fact, state taxes on exporters were much higher than in most other West European countries and this limited both the defense industry and the mechanical and metalworking sectors involved in defense procurements in their must-do pursuit for competitive price bidding on foreign markets[150]. This problem was also to imperil the allotment of a first off-shore contract to Fiat to assemble some 350 military trucks worth up to one and a half million US dollars[151]. On the other hand, the Italian government's proposal at

---

147 On this point, see also P.Craveri, *De Gasperi*, p. 457;

148 MAE, Servizio OA (Zoppi) to Ministero del Tesoro, Gab., 'Lavori del FEB: Proposta Italiana per il finanziamento dei Programmi di produzione integrata dal DPB', 23 July 1951, secret, in ASC, CED, b. 49.1/2 (Commesse alle Forze armate degli Stati Uniti), fold. Commesse. Promemoria del Dottor Mattei-Targiani-Campilli, s.f. Relazioni varie sui lavori del DPB-NATO;

149 'Comitato permanente affari economici, IX riunione', 8 January 1952, in ASC, Comitati permanenti, b. 30.1/2 (Comitato permanente per gli affari economici. Biennio 1951/52), fold. 156 (IX riunione a Milano dell'8/1/1952- Esame delle varie questioni connesse al NATO ed al PAM);

150 Confindustria, Appunto informativo n. 573, 'La riunione del Comitato Nazionale per la Piccola Industria', 26 February 1952, in ASC, Comitati permanenti, b. 30.1/1(Comitato permanente per gli Affari economici. Biennio 1951/52), fold. 149 (II Riunione dell'8 marzo 1951- Distribuzione internazionale delle materie prime critiche e relativa politica economica interna ed esterna. Problemi industriali del riarmo occidentale. Commesse e relativi finanziamenti); see also ASF, Minutes of the board of directors, meeting held on 1 August 1952, pp. 51 ff.; with reference to the Italian Employers Federation's concern with tax-related issues as a problem common to all the Italian exporters, and the pressures that the Federation made on the economic ministries to exert tax rebates and tax cutting measures on exports, see J.Carmassi, *Angelo Costa e l'integrazione europea*, in F.Fauri, V.Zamagni (eds), *Angelo Costa. Un ritratto a più dimensioni*, Il Mulino, Bologna 2007, pp. 251-252;

151 Appunto per il Segretario Generale, 'Commesse PAM-restituzione oneri fiscali settore autoveicoli', 22 April 1952; Appunto per il Segretario Generale, 'Commesse PAM- Restituzione oneri fiscali', 16/4/1952, both in ASC, CED, b. 49.1/2 (Commesse alle Forze armate degli Stati Uniti), fold. Circolari. Appunti. Sgravi fiscali sulle commesse off-shore. Indagine sulla situazione delle commesse

the TCC to involve the US taxpayer in sharing the financial burden of those orders worked in Italy in order to permit the country's military forces to respect the Atlantic Pact's defense requirements was also to target the problem of standardization in manufacturing. The issue at stake was the United States' insistence that the European defense industry adopt American-style production methods and models, especially in the European automobile and aeronautical industries. The aim of the United States was to facilitate the maintenance of vehicles used by the American troops stationed in Europe and ensure production of spare parts for vehicles produced in the US, as well as permitting trucks and vehicles discarded by the US military to be overhauled and transferred to the European armies[152]. Furthermore, Washington intended to introduce American-style manufacturing models in the European firms working on full production of spare parts of vehicles and trucks produced in the US[153]. The Confindustria fully backed the Italian proposal to the TCC in order to cope with the rising imbalance between the balance sheet of the three Italian defense armies and the force requirements negotiated by Italy within the DPB. If the TCC were to approve the Italian proposal, then the supply of military vehicles and equipment to the Italian land forces, air force and navy would be indexed as NATO end items and would not strain liabilities in the balance-sheet of the Ministry of Defense[154].

The Italian proposal to the TCC was widely welcomed by the Italian mechanical and metal-working firms and was the official Italian policy at the TCC throughout the fall of 1951 as presented by the Italian delegate to the TCC, Giovanni Malagodi[155]. The reaction of the Unit-

---

estere, s.f. Commesse off-shore-Trattamento fiscale; this set of orders to assemble military trucks was eventually allotted in April following the approval of tax rebates measures by the Italian Ministry for Finance. Prior to the approval of these tax rebates on the exported goods the Italian Ministry for Industry, the managing director of Fiat, Valletta and the representative of the Italian Employers Federation representative to NATO had worked hard to sponsor the passing of such a foreign trade policy by the Rome Cabinet;

152 Italian Embassy at RFT, Trade Advisory Office to Foreign Trade Ministry -DG Tarde Agreements, 'Acquisti delle Forze Armate Aeronautiche americane in Europa', 13 February 1952, in ASC, CED, b. 49.1/2 (commesse alle forze armate degli Stati Uniti), fold. Circolari, Appunti, Sgravi fiscali sulle commesse 'off-shore'; indagine sulla situazione delle commesse estere, s.f. Indagine sulla situazione delle commesse estere;

153 Pro-memoria, 'Presentazione al TCC della richiesta di commesse off-shore', 23 January 1952, in ASC, CED, b. 49.1/2, fold. Commesse. Promemoria del dottor Mattei-Targiani-Campilli, s.f. 1952. Promemoria Targiani-Campilli-commesse; L.Targiani, Promemoria, 'Considerazioni pratiche sulle commesse', 1 January 1952, idem; Mutual Assistance Advisory Committee, 'Minutes', 29 October 1952, in DDRS;

154 L.Targiani, Pro-memoria, 'Perchè ritardano le commesse e come si potrebbero accelerare', 7 January 1952, in ASC, CED, b. 49.1/2, fold. Commesse. Promemoria del dottor Mattei-Targiani-Campilli, s.f. 1952. Promemoria Targiani-Campilli-commesse;

155 Malagodi to Pella and Marras, 5 December 1951, Cattani to MAE-Servizio OA, telegramma, secret, not for circulation 5 December 1951; Malagodi to Pella, telegramma, secret, 31 January 1952;

ed States was clear and coherent. Harriman, with the assistance of the American economic experts based at the OSR in Paris and those working on the ECA Mission to Rome, took a lead in this respect and suggested that Italy change its fiscal policy to increase the internal revenue. At bilateral meetings with Pella, Malagodi and Marras, a high ranking military official in the Italian land forces, Harriman suggested that Italy reform its fiscal policy with a twofold objective: firstly, to ease pressure on low-income consumers and on the mass-production manufacturing firms working on mass goods and standardized durables; secondly, to raise tax revenues from cars, vehicles and broadly-defined luxury goods, including luxury residential homes[156]. This revision of domestic fiscal policy would aim to redress the balance of tax revenues between low wage earners and the upper classes, while also improving the state balance sheet to finance the country's defense effort[157]. The United States strove to introduce this strategy to finance the extra-budgetary defense appropriations required to meet the DPB force requirement in both Italy and in most of the other West European partners suffering from budgetary restraints. In fact, within the TCC Washington adopted this policy toward Rome, London and Paris[158].

Despite the line pursued by Washington in the second half of 1951 the Italian proposal was partially accepted. An analysis of American military assistance to the varying European countries, shows that a portion of any off-shore procurement contract allocated across Europe, and indexed as contracts registered on national balance-sheets, was indeed paid off in US dollars. Accordingly, the NATO common budgetary fund was to share the burden of these costs to strengthen the national armies according to the DPB force requirements. This compromise was the result of a clash within the US government on the possibility of forcing the Europeans to take significant extra budgetary defense appropriations[159]. The National Advisory Council on International Monetary and Financial Problems, for example, fiercely opposed NATO sharing the burden of national defense efforts especially in the case of France, which paradox-

---

G.Malagodi to E.Marras (Capo di Stato Maggiore Esercito), telegram, secret not for circulation, 6 February 1952, Cattani to MAE, Servizio OA, 6 February 1952, all of these documents are in ASMA-E, Cassaforte, b. 16, Posizione Cassaforte 500/51. NATO Temporary Council Committee 1952;

156 M.Magistrati (Delegazione Italiana per la Cooperazione Economica Europea) to V.Zoppi (Segretario Generale del Ministero degli Affari Esteri), secret, 19 November 1951, in ASMAE, Cassaforte, b. 16, Posizione Cassaforte 500/51. NATO: Temporary Council Committee;

157 Italian Representative at OEEC to De Gasperi, 'esame del programma politico-economico italiano in esame all'Ufficio Esecutivo del TCC', 17 November 1951, in ASMAE, Cassaforte, b. 16, Posizione Cassaforte 500/51. NATO: Temporary Council Committee TCC;

158 with reference to Harriman's consistency with the TCC recommendations to the member states of NATO see for example Steering Group on Preparations for Talks between the President and Prime Minister Churchill, Negotiating Paper, 'The Burden Sharing Aspects of the TCC Report', 5 January 1952, in DDRS;

159 NAC Minutes, Minutes of Meeting n. 168, 26 December 1950, in NARA, RG56, NAC Papers, NAC Minutes, b. 2 (February 9, 1950-December 28, 1950);

ically received huge amounts of financial aid[160]. A thorough break down of the months covered by the fiscal years 1952 and 1953 shows that out of total contracts for OSP of two billion and 225 million US dollars, the French Treasury alone received a 395 million budgetary contribution in US dollars to meet its extraordinary defense effort[161]. Most of these contracts were destined to strengthen the French military operations in the Indochinese war[162]. However, both Italy and the UK also received budgetary contributions in US dollars to support purchases of equipment and vehicles by their respective governments[163]. As far as the UK was concerned, monetary stability had long been a major American concern due to the high volume of industrial output that had started in the year preceding the mobilization for the Korean War[164]. The DPB's decision to choose Italy as a production source for the Atlantic Alliance rearmament programs meant that this country would receive a fair amount of off-shore procurement contracts to yield military end items[165]. Italy took advantage of this as NATO financed both the purchases of raw and strategic material and the industrial investments generated by the OSP programs. A comparison between the early OSP programs and this second fiscal year emphasizes the increasing influence in 1952-1953 of the OSP contracts on both Italy's foreign exchange equilibrium and domestic reserves[166]. Specifically, the aim of the second OSP program placed in Italy was to fill three gaps. First, it supplied the Italian Ministry for Defense with military equipment beyond this Ministry's ordinary balance-sheet. Secondly, it provided the US troops stationing in Europe with components and repairs. Thirdly,

---

160 NAC Minutes, Minutes of Meeting N. 168, 26 December 1950, in NARA, RG56, NAC Papers, NAC Minutes, b. 2 (February 9, 1950-December 28, 1950);

161 Office of the Director for Mutual Security, 'The Mutual Security Program', in 'NSC 161, Vol. I, Status of National Security Programs as of June 30, 1953', 30 June 1953, in DDEL, White House Office, Office of the Special Assistant for National Security Affairs (Robert Cutler, Dillon Anderson and Gordon Gray), Records 1952-1961, NSC Series, Status of Project Subseries, b. 3 (NSC 161, Vol. I, Status of National Security Programs as of June 30, 1953), fold. 3, p. 18;

162 Department of State, Committee on the Present Danger, 'Confidential Comment as to and for Particular Areas', n.d., in DDEL, J.F.Dulles Papers 1951-1959, Subject Series, b. 8 (Confidential Memos and Letters), fold. 1; Mutual Assistance Advisory Committee, 'Minutes of Meeting, February 16, 1952', 25 February 1952, in DDRS;

163 Memorandum for J.Ohly (Office of the Director for Mutual Security), 'NSC Action 720-C', 16 March 1953, in DDRS;

164 UK Government, 'Emergency Action by the US Government on Certain Raw Materials', 6 December 1950, in DDRS; NAC Minutes, Minutes of Meeting n. 168, December 26, 1950, in NARA, RG56, NAC Papers, NAC Minutes, b. 2 (February 9, 1950-December 28, 1950), p. 4;

165 A.Tarchiani to Ministero degli esteri, DGAE, 'Programma off-shore procurement 1952-53', 25 November 1952, in ASMAE, Cassaforte, b. 16, Posizione Cassaforte 500/51. NATO: Temporary Council Committee. 1952;

166 Comitato permanente per gli affari economici, IX riunione di Milano, 8 January 1952, in ASC, Comitati permanenti, b. 30.1/2 (Comitato permanente per gli affari economici. Biennio 1951/52), fold. 156 (IX riunione a Milano dell'8/1/1952. Esame delle varie questioni connesse al NATO ed al PAM);

this program funded the production and exchange of military goods across different West European countries[167].

2.4 The two Italian options to attain supranational economic integration and industrial modernization: dollar markets and intra-European trade exchanges

The Italian proposal at the TCC was presented at a time when there was widespread agreement among the European Finance Ministers and the US government's representatives in Europe on the need to oblige the North Atlantic Council to endorse the TCC guidelines on the build-up of the Atlantic Alliance, which involved a combination of the strengthening of defense and security targets and a rise in average living standards and the bettering of economic and social conditions in Europe on the whole[168]. However, within the Atlantic Alliance and the European countries themselves differences emerged as regards the most feasible way to create a truly interdependent trade and currency area. In particular, two very different proposals for the achievement of trade and monetary integration stand out. The first proposed the creation of a preferential transatlantic trade area that would include both the dollar and the British pound. This area was to promote the exchange of raw material, manpower and capital rewarded in US dollars in a currency and trade area smaller than the EPU itself. The idea of this project was that each European country would undertake bilateral trade relations with the dollar markets. The second proposal envisaged the strengthening of commercial and currency bonds among the European markets under the institutional umbrella of the OEEC with the German consumer market as the pillar of a truly intra-European trade and payments integration process aimed at creating European economic integration and currency convertibility[169].

---

167 Confindustria, n.a. (probably Targiani), Pro-memoria, 2 January 1952; Targiani, Pro-memoria, 'considerazioni pratiche sulle commesse', 1 February 1952, both in ASC, CED, b. 49.1/2 (commesse alle forze armate degli Stati Uniti), fold. Commesse. Promemoria del dottor Mattei-Targiani-Campilli, s.f. 1952. Promemoria Targiani-Campilli-commesse; Confindustria, Appunto informativo n. 635, 'A proposito di commesse', 17 June 1952, in ASC, CED, b. 49.1/2 (commesse alle forze armate degli Stati Uniti), fold. Circolari, appunti, sgravi fiscali sulle commesse "off-shore". Indagini sulla situazione delle commesse estere, s.f. Indagine sulla situazione delle commesse estere;
168 Malagodi to Pella, 31 January 1952; regarding the widespread agreement among the economic ministries of the European member states of NATO, see A.Rossi Longhi to MAE-Servizio OA, 12 February 1952, both in ASMAE, Cassaforte, b. 16, Posizione Cassaforte 500/51. NATO: Temporary Council Committee.1952;
169 Appunto, 'Prossima riunione del Comitato dei 5 (ACC). Progetto di agenda', 29 October 1951, in ASMAE, Cassaforte, b. 16, Posizione Cassaforte 500/51, fold. NATO: Temporary Council Committee 1952;

The compelling debate among NATO and its member countries on how to finance and pay for the off-shore procurement productions mirrors these two alternatives. In Italy the Malagodi proposal to the TCC embedded the transatlantic option, whereas some projects to supply the Italian Ministry for Defense with equipment and weapons produced by other European manufacturing economies and transferred to Italy were close to the second proposal. As long as the Italian proposal to the TCC was the official Italian stance within NATO, the transatlantic approach for supranational integration of the Italian economy prevailed. Accordingly, the government led by the Christian Democrats worked hard to both contain trade and payments with the European markets and, at the same time, to expand Italy's commercial and financial relations with the dollar area. In the eyes of the Italian political and economic elites headed by De Gasperi the off-shore procurement program was to further these aims. We can thus explain the Italian insistence, which I underlined earlier, on receiving payment in US dollars for the off-shore procurements worked in Italy, whether these were to meet the defense requirements of Italy or other west European countries. Therefore, I would argue that the Italian position within NATO and the TCC can be only partly explained by the surplus in the Italian balance of payments assets against some of the other European currencies. Thus, in line with the dominant policy, Italy both refrained from importing war materials from other EPU countries, and increased its exchange of raw materials and instrumental goods with the dollar area. The Italian balance of payments surplus arose with respect to the British Pound and the French Franc. This surplus position stemmed from the Italian exports of low capital intensive manufactured goods to the extra European markets belonging to either the Sterling or the Franc areas. As most of these markets were characterized by a low rate of domestic economic growth and industrialization they sparked the drive for an expanding international demand for Italian textile goods[170]. In the context of this ongoing trend on world markets, Italy's economic policymakers attempted to redress the Italian balance of payments against its European partners by both cutting quantitative trade restrictions, and offsetting payments for the OSP produced in Italy in US dollars in order to cool off its assets against the Sterling and franc markets[171]. With respect to the dollar-centered trade and currency areas, the Italian high-rank policymakers worked hard to expand the country's reserve assets. The approach by the Italian govern-

---

170 Banca d'Italia, *Relazione annuale per l'anno 1951*, Banca D'Italia, Roma, 1952;

171 it is worthwhile to remark that the position was strongly backed by the Italian Employers Federation. See in this respect, Comitato permanente affari economici, minutes of meeting held on 8 March 1951, in ASC, Comitati permanenti, b. 30.1/1(Comitato permanente per gli affari economici. Biennio 1951/1952), fold. 149 (II riunione dell'8/3/1951. Distribuzione internazionale delle materie prime critiche e relativa politica economica interna ed esterna. Problemi industriali del riarmo occidentale. Commesse e relativi finanziamenti); on the Italian inclination to cut exports towards the EPU markets to cool off Italy's assets against the Sterling and the Franc areas see F.Fauri, *Angelo Costa e la ricostruzione dell'economia italiana*, in F.Fauri, V.Zamagni (eds), *Angelo Costa. Un ritratto a più dimensioni*, p. 83;

ment involved a consistent economic policy to make any asset on the balance of payments that came from the defense effort or from the credit line for the financing of the rearmament on the bond market, convertible in US dollars.

These were the circumstances in which the fiscal policy of the Italian Minister for Finance, Ezio Vanoni, came into force in 1952. Throughout that year the Italian export industries were the beneficiaries of a substantial number of tax rebates on their exports[172]. Vanoni's ministerial decrees were specifically aimed at refunding taxes on the semi-manufactured and instrumental goods produced by Italian firms involved in the off-shore procurement contracts[173]. Furthermore, he took steps to make these refunds convertible in US dollars in order to redress the on-stream balance between the Italian Lira and the EPU member currencies[174]. The same strategy of linking the internationalization of the Italian economy to the dollar trade and currency areas underpinned the shaping of the Central Bank of Italy and the Treasury's credit policy towards the Italian banking system and the manufacturing system. The Italian authorities indexed all of the OSP produced in Italy as exports in order to permit the national bank system to give credit to the manufacturing firms involved in the OSP programs in US dollars. This mechanism meant that these credits were secured by the equipment and instrumental goods manufactured with the OSP themselves in US dollars[175]. The third initiative to ensure that the dollar trade and currency area was the pillar for the supra-national integration of the Italian economy was the foreign monetary policy adopted by the Italian policymakers in charge of addressing the economic implications of rearmament, even as rearmament was underway. In December 1950 Italy presented a Memorandum on the financial, budgetary and industrial problems raised by rearmament to the Atlantic Alliance in which Piero Malvestiti, economic advisor on rearmament to the Italian Prime Minister De Gasperi, argued that the Italian defense effort could not be implemented without targeting and reabsorbing the Italian

---

172 Confindustria, Appunto per il segretario generale, 'Commesse PAM-Restituzione oneri fiscali', 16 April 1952; Confindustria, Appunto per il segretario generale, 'Commesse PAM-restituzione oneri fiscali settore autoveicoli', 22 April 1952, both documents are in ASC, CED, b. 49.1/2 (Commesse alle forze armate degli Stati Uniti), fold. Circolari. Appunti. Sgravi fiscali sulle commesse off-shore. Indagine sulla situazione delle commesse estere, s.f. Commesse off-shore Trattamento fiscale;

173 F.Petrini, *Il liberismo a una dimensione*, pp. 220-221;

174 Costa alle associazioni nazionali di categoria, 'Restituzione dell'imposta generale sull'entrata per alcuni prodotti esportati', circolare urgentissima, October 1952, in ASC, CED, b. 49.1/2 (commesse alle Forze armate degli Stati Uniti), fold. Circolari. Appunti. Sgravi fiscali sulle commesse off-shore. Indagine sulla situazione delle commesse estere, s.f. Commesse off-shore. Trattamento fiscale;

175 Targiani, 'Pro-memoria Confidenziale', 23 April 1952, in ASC, CED, b. 49.1/2, fold. Commesse. Promemoria del dottor Mattei-Targiani-Campilli, s.f.. 1952. Promemoria Targiani-Campilli-commesse;

dollar gap[176]. Malvestiti called for a large amount of American dollar aid to buffer the impact of war mobilization on the balance of payments. In particular he argued that the industrial mobilization would expand domestic aggregate demand for civilian consumer goods that would, in turn, create a dramatic rise in imports thus placing the balance of payments under pressure[177]. The Italian Budget Minister, Giuseppe Pella emphasized this approach when he presented the Italian Defense effort program and the outlook for the country's industrial output for the months ahead in which he criticized the EPU. He viewed this international economic institution as a sort of medium-term credit institution which provided finance for the EPU member debtor countries instead of more rightly enabling creditor nations within EPU to convert their balance of payments surplus into US dollars. This policy would have prevented the inflationary spiral that typically beset creditor economies[178].

The last measure which was adopted to move closer to the dollar markets was to take all possible initiatives to expand the import-export trade with the dollar trade and currency areas. In this respect, the Italian entrepreneurs drove to use dollar earnings generated by equipment, semi-manufactured and end item military goods exported to other countries within the OSP program to import much needed civilian consumer goods from the United States. This measure was to increase the import-export trade with the dollar market and to tackle the potential danger of rising prices from the expansion in domestic aggregate demand induced by the rearmament programs. It was argued that the purchase of civilian consumer goods on the American markets might prevent price increases produced by the imbalance between supply and demand for consumer goods resulting from the defense effort[179].

According to the literature regarding Italy's foreign trade policy in the early 1950s, the then Minister for Foreign Trade, Ugo La Malfa, issued ministerial decrees to bring into force a substantial set of trade liberalizations that aimed to integrate the Italian economy within the

---

176 Italian Memorandum' (Memorandum Malvestiti), 19 December 1950, in NARA, RG469, Mission to Italy, Office of the Director, Subject Files (Central Files) 1948-1957, b. 36, fold. 6 (Italy Economic Problems);

177 ' "Aide-Memoire" Minutes of Meeting held March 5, 1951, by the Deputies' Joint Committee' [Memorandum of conversation Malvestiti-Magistrati-Malagodi-Ferrari Aggradi-Jacobs-Dayton-Barnett-Chenery], in NARA, RG469, Mission to Italy, Office of the Director, Subject Files (Central Files) 1948-1957, b. 39, fold. 4;

178 Rappresentanza italiana presso l'OECE, Ufficio del Delegato Italiano al TCC, 'Esame del programma militare in seno all'Ufficio Esecutivo del TCC', 17 November 1951, in ASC, CED, b. 49.1/2 (Commesse alle Forze armate degli Stati Uniti), fold. Commesse. Promemoria del dottor Mattei-Targiani-Campilli, s.f. Relazioni varie sui lavori del DPB-NATO; a slightly different version of the same manuscript can be consulted in ASMAE, Cassaforte, b. 16, Posizione Cassaforte 500/51. NATO Temporary Council Committee TCC;

179 s.a (probably authored by the Italian Employers Federation's representative to NATO Targiani), Pro-memoria, 2 January 1952, in ASC, CED, b. 49.1/2, fold. Commesse. Promemoria del dottor Mattei-Targiani-Campilli, s.f. 1952. Promemoria Targiani-Campilli-commesse;

European trade and monetary integration process. In particular, Italian historiography has hitherto interpreted La Malfa's sharp cut in import quotas, which was adopted in November 1951, as a tool to expand Italy's import-export trade in civilian investment goods and durables with the other West European economies. The historical literature affirms that this orientation was shared by both the Minister for Foreign Trade and the economic analysis units working within the Central Bank of Italy[180]. On the contrary, I would argue that if we place the relaxation of import quotas within the framework of the economic policy of rearmament, we can put forward a very different interpretation. In fact, in the context of rearmament it was advantageous to set the Italian economy within a broader process of international economic integration than the continent-wide European integration. The Italian Employers' Federation strongly adhered to this view. Historians have stressed that the Confindustria opposed the relaxation of import quotas and customs duties fiercely[181]. Indeed, two years after the adoption of trade liberalization the structure of Italy's balance of payments had changed substantially. By 1953 its position against most of the other EPU currencies had shifted from that of a creditor to that of a debtor. In order to deal with this situation Italian entrepreneurs favored an increase in purchases on the dollar markets and a cut in imports from the EPU member currencies in order to tackle the continuing imbalances[182]. Thus Malagodi, who was both a member of the De Gasperi government and a leading politician within the Italian Liberal Party (the government party that most closely represented Italian business), did everything he could to ensure that the off-shore procurements increased Italian import-export trade with the dollar trade areas[183].

---

180 R.Gualtieri, *L'Italia dal 1943 al 1992*, pp. 122-124; L.Mechi, *L'Europa di Ugo la Malfa. La via italiana alla modernizzazione 1942-1979*, FrancoAngeli, Milano, 2003, pp. 48-49, 57-59; L.Segreto, *The importance of the Foreign Constraint*, pp. 139, 145-46;

181 F.Petrini, *Il liberismo a una dimensione*, pp. 190-207; J.Carmassi, *Angelo Costa e l'integrazione europea*, pp. 244 ff.; F.Fauri, *La costruzione del MEC negli anni Cinquanta: atteggiamento e posizioni della Confindustria*, in "Rivista di politica economica", n. 2 (1996), pp. 89-134; id., *Struttura e orientamento del commercio estero italiano*, in "Studi storici", n. 1 (1997), p. 205;

182 Camera di Commercio industria e agricoltura di Milano, IV Convegno Nazionale per il Commercio Estero, 9-11 April 1954, Mozione Generale, in ASC, Comitati permanenti, b. 30.2/2, fold. 170 (IX riunione 25/6/1954. Liberalizzazione delle importazioni dall'area del dollaro. Avvenire del GATT. Scambi Est-Ovest), s.f. Verbali.Corrispondenza); in this specific respect see also, n.a. 'Liberalizzazione dall'area del dollaro', n.d. (probably 1954), in ASC, Comitati permanenti, b. 30.1/2 (Comitato permanente per gli affari economici. Biennio 1951/1952), fold. 158 (XI riunione del 21/2/1952. Esame delle possibilità di ripristino in Italia del mercato a termine della sterlina in connessione con la recente rielaborazione della disciplina valutaria in Gran Bretagna);

183 Comitato permanente per gli affari economici, Minutes Meeting held on 25 January 1955, in ASC, Comitati permanenti, b. 30.2/2, fold. Undicesima riunione del 25 gennaio 1955. Piano Vanoni. gatt. Disegno di legge per l'istituzione di un fondo di garanzia e integrazione delle indennità agli impiegati; with respect to the relations among the Italian Liberal Party and the Italian entrepreneurs, see G.Orsina, *Il sistema politico: lineamenti di un'interpretazione revisionistica*, in P.L.Ballini, S.Guerrieri, A.Varsori (eds), *Le istituzioni repubblicane dal centrismo al centro-sinistra 1953-1968*,

Moreover, La Malfa strove to align his foreign trade policy with this dollar-centered transatlantic perspective[184]. In this respect we should mention the foreign trade initiatives adopted by La Malfa in relation to the rearmament process. Firstly, at a series of NATO negotiations and meetings he proposed that the European economies that supplied raw and strategic material and imported manufactured items for their respective national armies should provide material and investment goods to manufacturing economies like Italy free of cost[185]. Secondly, the way that La Malfa reacted to the French and British protectionist measures in force at the time was quite telling, particularly his reaction to both the British and French refusal to adopt trade liberalization as significant as that implemented in Italy and to the dumping measures they posed on Italian exporters to protect their domestic producers[186]. La Malfa's threat to curtail Italy's recently implemented trade liberalizations further proves how far he was from supporting a foreign trade policy centered exclusively on the process of European economic integration[187].

Therefore I maintain that most of the Italian political elites and the country's big businesses shared this dollar-pegged transatlantic strategy for the internationalization of the Italian industrial system. Despite this convergence, however, they held two very different interpretations of this strategy. The Italian Employers' Federation struggled to push Italian exports toward the dollar markets as Italian entrepreneurs considered these markets as the first and most important area in which to have trade partners in the light of the imminent currency convertibility and full trade liberalization[188]. Furthermore, this move was justified as a close trade partnership with American markets held the potential of resurrecting the Italian foreign trade bal-

---

Carocci, Roma 2006, p. 320; D.Bruni, *La riorganizzazione del Pli*, G.Orsina, *Giovanni Malagodi e l'opposizione liberale al centrosinistra*, both in "Ventunesimo secolo", n. 1, (2008); for a general outlook, see also S.Lupo, *Partito e antipartito. Una storia politica della prima Repubblica 1946-78*, Donzelli, Roma, 2004, p. 125;

184 for an interpretation different from our own see L.Segreto, *The Importance of the Foreign Constraint* ;

185 'Situazione attuale DPB-NATO', 16 April 1951, in ASC, CED, b. 49.1/2 (Commesse alle forze armate degli Stati Uniti), fold. Commesse. Promemoria dottor Mattei-Targiani-Campilli, s.f. Relazioni varie sui lavori del DPB-NATO);

186 Corrias (Ministero Affari Esteri, DGAE), 'Appunto per S.E. il ministro', 21 September 1953, in ASMAE, DGAP, Ufficio I 1950/1957, b. 216 (politica estera americana in funzione economica), p. 6;

187 I deal with La Malfa's threat to curtail trade liberalization more extensively in chapter five:

188 'Appunti sui più urgenti provvedimenti in materia di scambi con l'estero', n.d. (probably 1952), in ASC, Comitati permanenti, b. 30.1/2 (Comitato permanente per gli affari economici. Biennio 1951/1952), fold. 158 (XI riunione del 21 February 1952. Esame delle possibilità di ripristino in Italia del mercato a termine della sterlina in connessione con la recente rielaborazione della disciplina valutaria in Gran Bretagna); P.Toscano, *Confindustria e Bretton Woods: la voce dei principali protagonisti*, in A.Cova (ed.), *Il dilemma dell'integrazione. L'inserimento dell'economia italiana nel sistema occidentale 1945-1957*, FrancoAngeli, Milano, 2008, pp. 296, 304;

ance[189]. In striking contrast with this business community view, the Italian economic policy-makers were convinced that a close trade partnership with the dollar market was to serve as a sort of fly-wheel to bring about a leap in the added value of the Italian manufacturing system. They believed that a rise in the import of investment goods and an increase in the import-export trade with the Unites States would trigger technological progress which would structurally reshape the Italian production chain[190]. Therefore, in the eyes of the Italian economic technocracies and the Italian Ministries, such a transatlantic oriented foreign trade policy was an essential part of an industrial policy geared to achieving significant technological advances in Italian industry. In fact, prior to the 1953 drop in the Italian surplus against the EPU currencies, Confindustria had opposed the full trade liberalization on imports from the dollar markets that the De Gasperi Cabinet had planned[191]. However, shortly after 1953 the Italian Employers' Federation came out in favor of freezing any increase in the imports on the EPU trade markets given that Italy's new position as a debtor meant that a close trade partnership with the European markets might imperil the Italian reserve assets[192]. On the other hand, high-rank economic policymakers, such as Malagodi, proposed a preferential commercial partnership with the US dollar and British pound trade areas and suggested intensifying the bilateral trade relations of each West European country with the American markets and a parallel curtailment of both imports and exports from the other European markets[193]. In other words, in

---

189 Confindustria, 'Pro-memoria', 2 January 1952, in ASC, CED, b. 49.1/2 (commesse alle Forze armate degli Stati Uniti), fold. Commesse. Promemoria del dottor Mattei-Targiani-Campilli, s.f. Relazioni varie sui lavori del DPB-NATO;

190 C.Antonelli, F.Barbiellini Amidei, *Innovazione tecnologica e mutamento strutturale dell'industria italiana nel secondo dopoguerra*, in AA.VV, *Innovazione tecnologica e sviluppo industriale nel secondo dopoguerra*, Laterza, Roma-Bari, 2007, pp. 168 ff.; A.Leonardi, *Il sistema bancario nella ricostruzione del paese: tra vecchi e nuovi equilibri*; L.Conte, *L'azione della Banca d'Italia (1948-1993)*. Both articles have been published in *Storia d'Italia, annali 23, La Banca*, Einaudi, Torino, 2008, at pages 617-619 and 662-664 respectively;

191 Comitato permanente per gli affari economici, 'Appunto per il segretario generale', 21 February 1952, in ASC, Comitati permanenti, b. 30.1/2 (Comitato permanente per gli affari economici. Biennio 1951/52), fold. 156 (IX riunione a Milano dell'8/1/1952- Esame delle varie questioni connesse al NATO ed al PAM);

192 Comitato sulle decisioni della Giunta esecutiva della Confindustria, 'Commercio con l'Estero', 23 July 1953, in ASC, Comitati permanenti, b. 30.1/2 (Comitato permanente per gli affari economici. Biennio 1951/1952), fold. 158 (XI riunione del 21/2/1952. Esame delle possibilità di ripristino in Italia del mercato a termine della sterlina in connessione con la recente rielaborazione della disciplina valutaria in Gran Bretagna);

193 Appunto, 'Prossima riunione del Comitato dei 5 (ACC). Progetto di agenda', 29 October 1951, in ASMAE, Cassaforte, b. 16, Posizione Cassaforte 500/51, fold. NATO: Temporary Council Committee 1952; on the Italian Treasury Ministry's opposition to an intra-European centered model of supranational economic integration such as the OEEC plan, see G.Pella, OCSE. *Dalla cooperazione europea alla cooperazione euro-americana*, Banco di Roma, Roma, 1961, pp. 40-45;

the view of Malagodi and other influential Italian economic policymakers, a closer trade partnership with the United States would be linked to a structural contraction in the import-export trade among the European currency areas.

This foreign trade policy, which had been formulated by the Italian political elites and backed by Italian big business and the manufacturing firms, was opposed by those who advocated making Italy part of a truly continent-wide trade integration process revolving around the German mass consumer markets and the Deutsch Mark currency area, under the institutional guidance of the OEEC. The Central Bank of Italy and a cohort of economists and economic elites headed by a leading figure, Guido Carli, formerly head of EPU and later Governor of the Italian Central Bank, made a firm case for this opposition[194].

We can thus see that the offsetting of trade exchanges in US dollars and the inflow of American dollar aid to finance internal industrial investments geared to the OSP programs influenced the Italian economy both as regards its foreign trade policy and its model of industrial modernization and development. In fact there was a clash of views within the Italian political and economic elites concerning the foreign trade and monetary policy and Italian industrial policy. Furthermore, the OSP highlighted not only the different strategies proposed for the strengthening of closer commercial relations among the West European economies and the creation of a truly intra-European trade and currency area, but also the different attitudes towards the interplay between European economic integration and the forging of a broader transatlantic economic area. In the early part of 1952 there was still widespread concern among high-ranking American government officials and bureaucrats over the impact that an intra-European market centered on the German economy, and financed through scores of American dollar aids, might have on the export-oriented American manufactures. Yet at the same time there was growing consensus that the European integration process and the broader transatlantic market linked to the American economy could co-exist and be interdependent[195]. Accordingly, the United States worked ever harder to promote cooperation between the OEEC and NATO. I believe that it is in this perspective that we should interpret the US initiatives to make payments for the OSP manufactured in Italy for transfer to other EPU member

---

194 Appunto per il segretario generale, 'Comitato Permanente per gli Affari Economici', 21 February 1952, in ASC, Comitati permanenti, b. 30.1/2 (Comitato Permanente per gli affari economici. Biennio 1951/52), fold. 156 (IX riunione a Milano dell'8/1/1952. Esame delle varie questioni connesse al NATO ed al PAM); The British government favored this option as they could take advantage of it to act as a go-between the Americans and the continental European countries. See on this Rossi Longhi to MAE, servizio OA, telegramma segreto, 12 February 1952, in ASMAE, Cassaforte, b. 16, Posizione Cassaforte 500/51. NATO: Temporary Council Committee.1952; see also G.Carli, *Cinquant'anni di vita italiana*, Laterza, Roma-Bari, 1993, pp. 99 ff.; and G.Di Taranto (ed.), *Guido Carli e le istituzioni economiche internazionali*, in *Scritti e discorsi di Guido Carli*, Bollati Boringhieri,Torino, 2009;

195 NAC Minutes, 'Minutes of Meeting n. 190', 13 March 1952, in NARA, RG56, NAC papers, NAC Minutes, b. 2;

economies in US dollars, as well as the pressure exercised on Italy to adopt full and compre-hensive trade liberalization[196]. This American stance brought to a halt the Italian plan of link-ing the internationalization of the Italian economy overwhelmingly to the dollar markets. The financial structure underpinning the OSP programs implemented over the following years further illustrates this American position. Over the following years, even though the NATO common budgetary fund was already fully operative, several OSP contracts were paid for by each of the importing European economies in their own currencies[197]. A remarkable example of this was the OSP contracts that Italy received to supply a number of F86K aircrafts to West Germany. These contracts, involving Fiat as the production source and the German Ministry for Defense as the beneficiary, were off set in Deutsche Marks and made transferable into dollars to finance the country's balance of payments assets on the American markets[198].

Therefore, as the Italian case study suggests, the OSP contracts were to promote the interna-tionalization of each European economy within the process of intra-European economic inte-gration. Despite this overt American objective, the Italian elites were to some extent able to negotiate their own ends. In fact, Malagodi and his fellow travelers were partially successful in making use of the off-shore procurements to launch significant technological advances across the Italian manufacturing sectors involved in the rearmament programs. The OSP pro-grams that the Atlantic Alliance placed in Italy between 1952 and 1954, to supply either the Italian Ministry for Defense or other European national armies, were just such a case. It is worth noting how throughout this period the highest added value manufacturing sectors in Italy were those involved in the off-shore procurement programs[199]. For example, the elec-tronic industry was to produce radars to supply the navy or the air force, whereas the car in-dustry was granted orders to manufacture military car and trucks. Moreover, the Italian me-chanical sectors worked either on producing components for air fighters, such as the turbo-charged jet engines for the Ghost model jet fighter, or on assembling the F86 all-weather fighters[200]. The off-shore procurement contracts to the Italian aeronautics industry are particu-

---

196 MAE, DGAE-Ufficio IV a CIR-Segreteria Generale, 'Aiuti americani all'Italia', 16 February 1952, in ACS, PCM, CIR, b. 60;

197 Pro-memoria per SE Alessandrini, 'collaborazione italo-franco-tedesca nel campo aeronautico', 6 November 1954, in ASMAE, Ambasciata d'Italia a Parigi, 1951-1958 (1954), b. 38, fold. R11/19-1, s.f. year 1954 (Collaborazione italo-franco-tedesca nel campo aeronautico);

198 C.Cavalli, Nota per il signor prof. V.Valletta, 'F-86K per la Germania', 12 July 1956; U.Morabito to C.Cavalli, 10 July 1956, both documents are in ASF, USA-Delibere, b. Contratto USAF-Governo italiano e licenza North American Aviation-Governo italiano-Fiat, year 1956;

199 MCE, Servizio Coordinamento Commesse e Affari Patto Atlantico, 'appunto', 26 February 1954, in ACS, MICA, Segreteria Campilli, b. 4; MSA-Mission to Italy to the Ambassador in Italy, 'Status of Offshore procurement contracts in Italy as of May 11, 1953', in NARA, RG469, Mission to Italy, Of-fice of the Director, Subject Files (Central Files), 1948-1957, b. 22, fold. 3 (Defense OSP Program Contracts- Production 1953);

200 ASF, Minutes of the board of directors, meeting of 1 August 1952;

larly representative in illustrating both the extent to which the Italians took advantage of the OSP to launch a process of industrial modernization and technological innovation, and the American position. The American authorities and NATO stubbornly insisted on allotting both contracts to repair and update weapons and military equipment to be transferred from the Pentagon to the European armies, and contracts for maintenance work on spare parts and machine tools of the American troops stationing in Europe, to the Fiat company. The insistence of the United States on distributing contracts of this type to the Italian economy can be explained by their intention to integrate the European manufacturing industries within the broader transatlantic market economy along a low-capital intensive model of industrial modernization[201]. On the other hand, however, the involvement of the Italian capital-intensive manufacturing sectors in the industrial mobilization demonstrates that they were seeking a balance between a low added value industrial reorganization and modernization, and the most technologically updated industries. In turn the redress of this balance was conducive to making the European defense industry self-sufficient in the American production models, an objective that the Americans had maintained from the inception of rearmament across the Atlantic community. In this respect it is indicative that the American military authorities applauded the technological leap Fiat accomplished in order to produce components and to assemble the F86K jet aircrafts. The production of the F86K OSP was made possible thanks to the concession of production licenses by the North American Aviation Company and this allowed Fiat to supply both the United States Air Force and the armies of other member states of NATO[202].

---

201 A.Morante (consigliere commerciale di ambasciata) to MCE-DG Accordi commerciali, 'Acquisti delle Forze Armate Aeronautiche americane in Europa', 13 February 1952, in ASC, CED, b. 49.1/2 (commesse alle forze armate degli Stati Uniti), fold. Circolari, appunti, sgravi fiscali sulle commesse 'off-shore'. Indagine sulla situazione delle commesse estere, s.f. Indagine sulla situazione delle commesse estere; Pro-memoria, n.a. (probably Targiani), Pro-memoria, 'presentazione al TCC della richiesta di commesse off-shore', 23 January 1952, in ASC, CED, b. 49.1/2 (commesse alle forze armate degli Stati Uniti);
202 C.H.Shuff (Deputy for Mutual Security Assistance Affairs) to E.Ortona, 15 May 1953, in ASF, USA-Delibere, b. Contratto USAF-Governo italiano e licenza North American Aviation-Governo italiano-Fiat, year 1953; in order to get a better understanding regarding the total amount of this program, which was implemented over the following years , see), MAE, DGAE, Uff. I, to Fiat, 'Critiche agli aiuti americani all'estero-Accenni alla Fiat', 7 October 1959, in ASBI, Carte Caffè, Pratt., n. 48, fold. 1; a trace of the orders placed with the Italian industry to supply the US armies directly can be found in M.Roli to E.Hallbeck, 'Fiat-Ordinazioni militari di aerei', 17 June 1953; on the reproduction license contracts conceded by North American Aviation to Fiat as prime contractor through the intermediary role of the Italian and US governments, see Governo USA, 'Memorandum', 13 May 1953; J.H.Kindelberger North American Aviation)-V.Valletta (Fiat)-U.Tolino (Ministero Difesa-Aeronautica)-A.Tarchiani (Ambasciata d'Italia Washington), 'Accordo per licenza ed assistenza', 16 May 1953; R.Pacciardi (Ministro Difesa-Aeronautica) to Fiat, 'Licenza di riproduzione velivolo F86 Ditta North American Aviation', 20 June 1953. All of these documents are in ASF, USA-Delibere, b. Contratto USAF-Governo italiano e licenza North American Aviation-Governo italiano-Fiat, a. 1953.

2.5 Conclusion

The first post-war rearmament program launched by the US, and strictly controlled by Congress, was the MDAP of 1949. This program aimed to transfer end items and spare parts from the US to the European national armies for their post-war reorganization without expanding European industrial capacity and output. This strategy was based on Washington's firm belief that any pressure on the European defense industry might impede and delay the overall process of economic reconstruction across Europe. However, the second rearmament program that followed a year later envisaged a significant contribution by the West European manufacturing industries. This step forward meant that both the US and their European partners would now have to tackle two impending problems: the impact of rearmament on the European balance of payments and the extremely unstable monetary equilibrium that NATO's most important partners were facing. The United States was obliged to carefully monitor and support the European reserve assets, while the European governments had to put aside ever greater sums for a defense effort that strained public finance. This led to a clash between the Truman Administration and the European governments. The latter exerted pressure on the Americans to split the dollar inflow from military assistance between the financing of internal investment and imports necessary to meet the defense effort, and the impact of rearmament on the Europeans' public debt. The United States had to struggle to maintain their objective of limiting the use of dollar aid by their European partners to the tackling of imbalances on the foreign exchange equilibrium arising from industrial mobilization. The Italian case study, and the dynamics of economic diplomacy between Italy and the United States from 1950 to 1952, is particularly illustrative in this respect. It sheds light on both the interplay between rearmament and the early steps in the process of European economic integration, and on the model of economic growth and development that the Americans attempted to introduce in Italy. It should be stressed that Washington's attempts to influence Italian domestic and foreign economic policy required by industrial mobilization were closely bound to the American goal of laying down the foundations for a mass consumer market across the country.

On this re production license, see also Tarchiani to MAE, DGAP, 11 May 1953, in ASMAE, DGAP, Ufficio I 1950/57, b. 216 (politica estera americana in funzione economica). With reference to the process of industrial modernization and technological update adopted by Fiat in its plants according to the American style industrial organization models and fordist production methods after the implementation of the European Recovery Program, see F.Fauri, *The Role of Fiat in the Development of Italy's Car Industry in the 1950's*, in "Business History Review", n. 2, 1996, pp. 167 ff.; id., *Angelo Costa e la ricostruzione dell'economia italiana*, pp. 77-78. For an alternative interpretation of the impact that the F86K military contracts had on the technological drift of the Turin-based aeronautical plants of Fiat, see T.Geiger, L.Sebesta, *A Self-defeating Policy*, p. 72;

Chapter 3

Rearmament and economic reconstruction. Military aid to Italy from the early phases of the Atlantic Alliance to the Korean War

3.1 From London to Washington. The Western powers and the resurrection of the Italian armed forces before the birth of the Atlantic Pact

In the first two chapters I have repeatedly stressed how, from the birth of the Atlantic Alliance to the outbreak of the Korean War, the Truman Administration made every effort to encourage European governments to shift public finances according to the needs of rearmament. Washington consistently strove to impose a trade-off between a firm European commitment to expand the ratio of defense spending to total public expenditure, and the allotment of military aid. Against this background, the early military assistance programs were to both transfer surplus American military equipment and weapons, and to finance much needed European imports of raw material, strategic sources and spare parts to resurrect national armies. In this context, the inception of rearmament stands out as a process with rather limited impact on the reorganization of the European defense industry[203]. In fact, a reorganization of national armies in each European country to the pre-war defense posture was likely to reactivate war-torn industrial capacity and manufacturing plans. Accordingly, the rearming of formerly belligerent European countries like Italy was to reorganize wrecked production lines and to remobilize industrial manpower. For the most part, the financial constraints geared to the first Mutual Assistance Act, which was passed into law by the US Congress in 1949, account for the low scale and scope of the early American plans to rearm the West European allies. This American stance modeled US government policy regarding the reorganization of the Italian army throughout the implementation of the first MDAP[204].

Chapter two followed the events that shed light on the reluctance of the Italian and European governments to shift public expenditure from the civil sectors to the defense effort. The low ratio of defense spending to total public expenditure that characterized the rearmament program presented by Italy to the Temporary Council Committee in fall 1951 was the source of

---

203 J.Sherman (Secretary of the War Council), Memorandum for the Secretary of the Army, the Secretary of the Navy, the Secretary of the Air Force, 'Significant Actions of the Meeting of the War Council on 23 February 1949', 24 February 1949, in DDRS;
204 Bell to Ohly, 'Report of Activity, December 26-29', 30 December 1950, in DDRS;

much criticism by the United States government[205]. This Italian unwillingness stemmed from the rather limited scale and scope of rearmament that characterized the first MTDP. However, from as early as the winter of 1950 there was a gradual shift in the De Gasperi government's approach to the problem. This change mirrors the leap forward in the scale and scope that came with the rearmament programs implemented by the United States government over the following years. As a matter of fact, during winter 1950 the De Gasperi Cabinet showed it was more willing to consider a possible expansion of its financial commitment to the defense effort. During bilateral meetings with the United States government and negotiations held within NATO, the Italian government proposed a trade-off between extra budgetary appropriations to the Ministry for Defense and a broader inflow of dollar aid to finance the import of much needed raw materials and machinery for rearmament[206]. In fact, the closer the process of rearmament came to turning from reorganization to expansion of the Italian manufacturing system, the more the Italians were willing to broaden their defense effort and the greater their calls for increased dollar aid.

It is worth following the sequence of events that led the UK government to hand over its control on Italian defense and security policies to the United States shortly after the end of World War II in order to better understand how the scale and scope of military aid and rearmament was broadened and thus stimulated a rise in industrial output.

From the closing months of the Second World War and through the immediate post war period, the British and American representatives within the Allied military commands in the Mediterranean shared a twofold view on the fate of the Italian military forces. On one hand, they stressed the importance of reorganizing a national army; on the other they aimed to maintain a firm allied military presence across the Italian Peninsula to oversee the yet uncertain transition from war[207]. At that time Her Majesty's Allied military commanders argued that Italy

---

205 MSA, Mission to Italy, 'Status of the Italian Military Production Program', 29 February 1952, in NARA, RG469, Mission to Italy, Office of the Director, Subject files (Central files), b. 22, fold. 2(Defense, OSP program: contracts, Production); MAE-DGAE, Ufficio IV to CIR-Segreteria Generale, 'Aiuti americani all'Italia', 16 February 1952, in ACS, PCM, CIR, b. 60;

206 ' "Aide-Memoire" Minutes of Meeting held March 5, 1951, by the Deputies' Joint Committee' [Memorandum of conversation Malvestiti-Magistrati-Malagodi-Ferrari Aggradi-Jacobs-Dayton-Barnett-Chenery], in NARA, RG469, Mission to Italy, Office of the Director, Subject Files (Central Files) 1948-1957, b. 39, fold. 4; Luciolli (ambasciata d'Italia in USA to MAE, 'Contatti Ministri Pella e La Malfa con autorità statunitensi', 29 August 1952, in ASMAE, Cassaforte, b. 16, Posizione Cassaforte 500/51. NATO Temporary Council Committee 1952; 'Conversations with Italian Prime Minister: Italian Economic Problems'[memorandum of conversation Acheson-De Gasperi-Harriman-Pella-Bissell], 1 October 1951, in DDRS;

207 L.Nuti, *L'esercito italiano nel secondo dopoguerra. La sua ricostruzione e l'assistenza militare alleata 1945-1950*, Ufficio Storico Stato Maggiore esercito, Roma, 1989, chapter 1; L.Nuti, *US Forces in Italy 1945-1963*, in W.Krieger (ed.), *US Forces in Europe: the Early Years*, Westview, Boulder (Col.), 1994, pp. 250-251; memorandum by Chief Commissioner Ellery Stone, 'Future Policy toward

should be granted a national army with rather limited power to address issues of internal security and insurgency and protect its borders from external threats[208]. The UK government pursued this view even as it was about to reorganize its own national army[209]. This reorganization aimed to swiftly reduce British military commitment abroad. Indeed, by 1947 the British military presence abroad had been significantly cut[210].

From as early as 1944 the British representatives on the Allied military commands had drafted a plan for this reorganization of the Italian army. It is important to underline that the British plan entailed the complete dismantlement of the Italian war industry and the transfer of British military surplus stocks to the newly established Italian armed forces[211]. The British government struggled to implement this punitive policy toward most of the former belligerent nations. The most obvious case was Germany: between the end of World War II and 1947 the UK tried to impose strict limits on the industrial output of strategic sectors in Germany, above all the steel industry[212].

These two cornerstones of the British project to reorganize the Italian army followed a different path. The transfer of surplus war material from the British and the Americans to the Italian government was a pillar of the early initiatives carried out to resurrect the Italian defense and security system immediately following the war. These transfers were complemented by the activities of an Italian state-owned agency, the *Azienda per il Rilievo e l'Alienazione dei Residuati Bellici*, widely-known as ARAR, which recovered the war material and equipment that the Allied military forces had left in Italian territory during the conflict[213]. On the other hand, however, the British plan to dismantle the Italian military industrial complex was eventually discarded. The firm American belief that Italy would play a strategic role in the struggle to secure Middle East oil sources for the Western bloc economies meant that after the conclusion of the war the United States became increasingly interested in stabilizing the internal

---

Italy', 23 June 1945, in *FRUS 1945, The Conference of Berlin (The Potsdam Conference) 1945*, vol. 1, Government Printing Office, Washington DC, 1960, pp. 688 ff.;

208 L.Nuti, *La sfida nucleare. La politica estera italiana e le armi atomiche 1945-1991*, Il Mulino, Bologna 2007, p. 24; on the harsh British position towards Italy, see P.Craveri, *De Gasperi*, pp. 178-183;

209 A.Gorst, *British Military Planning for Postwar Defense 1943-45*, in A.Deighton (ed.), *Britain and the First Cold War*, MacMillan-the Graduate School of European and International Studies University of Reading, London and Reading, 1990, pp. 91-108;

210 T.Judt, *Postwar. A History of Europe since 1945*, Penguin Press, New York, 2005, p. 111;

211 L.Nuti, *Gli alleati e le forze armate italiane 1945-1948*, in E.Di Nolfo, R.Rainero, B.Vigezzi (eds), *L'Italia e la politica di potenza in Europa (1945-1950)*, Marzorati, Milano, 1990, pp. 576-77; id., *L'esercito italiano nel secondo dopoguerra*, pp. 30-31;

212 M.Peter, *Britain, the Cold War and the Economics of German Rearmament, 1949-51*, in A.Deighton (ed.), *Britain and the First Cold War*, p. 275;

213 See S.Selva, *Integrazione internazionale e sviluppo interno. Stati Uniti e Italia nei programmi di riarmo del blocco atlantico 1945-1955*, Carocci, Roma, 2009;

economic and political situation in Italy and the recovery of the Italian manufacturing system was a gateway to this objective[214]. A thorough examination highlights the expansion of output and technological updating of the Italian aeronautical industry which started in the early 1950s thanks to its role in supplying semi-finished and finished goods to the air forces of Italy's NATO partners. The desire by the British and Americans to resurrect the war industry consistently shaped their policy toward their former German enemy after 1949[215]. The Allied Powers' firm commitment to the recovery of German industry had two objectives. Firstly, it firmly bound their former enemy to the Atlantic Alliance and sustained the onset of rearmament across NATO. Secondly, it was linked to the idea that the reconstruction and further development of German foreign trade was essential for the implementation of defense and security policies and the continuation of economic recovery for all the West European partners after the demise of the ERP. More specifically, the Truman Administration considered the recovery of German industrial capacity and export structure as fundamental for the targeted stabilization of America's West European allies as this recovery would enable the integration of the resource-rich European economies with the manufacturing countries[216]. In particular, in American eyes the German economy was to play a twin role. On the one hand, Germany was expected to supply steel, aluminum, and copper for work on the military production programs. On the other, the German processing industry was to produce and supply instrumental goods and consumer goods to meet demand in the West European consumer markets over the coming years[217]. In fact, throughout the first half of the 1950s, the requirements of

---

214 'Report on Military, Naval, and Air Clauses of the Treaty of Peace With Italy by an ad Hoc Committee of the State-War-Navy Coordinating Committee', 6 September 1945, in *FRUS, 1945*, Vol. 4, *Europe*, Government Printing Office, Washington DC, pp. 1036-1040; over the postwar era the key strategic position of Italy against the backdrop of the Mediterranean region pushed the United States to provide the Italian governments with assistance to re-build the national armies in the framework of the Atlantic Alliance defense and rearmament plans. The National Security Council policy paper NSC67 remains a key policy document even many years after its declassification. 'The Position of the United States with respect to Communism in Italy', 12 April 1950, in Digital National Security Archive (http://nsarchive.chadwyck.com/marketing/index.jsp);

215 In 1951 the United Kingdom, the United States and France significantly revised the 1949 agreement on concerning control of German industry. This revision entailed the possibility to raise output level of key German strategic sector such as steel industry, and removed vetoes on the production of civilian machine tools, and any prohibition to produce synthetic rubber and oil produced from coal. For a detailed report on the removal of these restrictions posed on the German industry in the past years see Memorandum by the Secretary of State for Foreign Affairs, 'Control of German Industry', 19 March 1951, in PRO, Cabinet Papers, CAB/129/45;

216 'Report of the Special ad hoc Committee of the State-War-Navy coordinated Committee', 21 April 1947, in *FRUS, 1947*, Vol. 3, *The British Commonwealth: Europe*, Government Printing Office, Washington DC, 1972, pp. 214-215;

217 FACC, 'Germany and MAP', paper prepared by the Foreign Assistance Correlation Committee, 21 June 1949, in *FRUS 1949*, Vol. 3, *Council of Foreign Ministers, Germany and Austria*, Govern-

steel and other raw materials of both Italy and France were imported from Germany[218], while the United States government worked hard to ensure that German manufacturing firms produced and exported durables to feed an ever-expanding civilian demand in the West European economies. At the same time the European countries were engaged in working on the off-shore procurement programs and in expanding industrial effort for the requirements of rearmament[219]. The United States strongly pursued this expansion in the intra-European import-export trade which they viewed as the best solution for a continued improvement in the balance of payments of each West European country.

In fact, the US government considered that a fully-fledged equilibrium in the European balance of payments was a necessary pre-condition for European self-sufficiency in manufacturing and industrial output they so desired. As the American authorities put it, the economy of a country such as Italy which was dominated by manufacturing «could be expected to command sufficient supply of raw materials through the export of the more highly processed products into which they are incorporated»[220].

To better understand both why and how the UK and the USA adopted such strikingly different defense and security policies toward Italy at the end of the 1940s, it is worth going back to the period of transition from wartime to peace. The plans drafted by the British representatives on the Allied Powers' military Commands envisaged a rather limited reorganization of Italy's armed forces and were the result of the British government's skeptical and suspicious stance toward its former enemy. Throughout the period of co-belligerence, the British Prime Minister, Churchill, and Foreign Minister, Eden, were scared by the rising role that the Italian

---

ment Printing Office, Washington DC, 1949, p. 477 ff.; The Secretary of State to Certain Diplomatic Offices, 27 March 1950, in *FRUS 1950*, Vol. 3, *Western Europe*, p. 34; The Ambassador in the United Kingdom (Douglas) to the Secretary of State, 14 April 1950, *idem*, pp. 50-52; M.Peter, *Britain, the Cold War and the Economics of German Rearmament 1949-51*, p. 278; Acheson to McCloy (US High Commissioner for Germany), 'German Contribution to Production for Defense', 18 October 1950, in NARA, RG59, Central Files 1950-54, 740.5/10-1850; see also R.Pollard, *Economic Security and the Origins of the Cold War 1945-50*, pp. 226 ff., and M.Hogan, *The Marshall Plan. American, Britain and the Reconstruction of Western Europe 1947-1952*, Cambridge University Press, Cambridge, 1987, pp. 336 ff.;

218 The Executive Director of the Coordinating Committee of the Mutual Defense Assistance Program (Bonesteel) to the Deputy Director of that Program (Ohly), top secret, 29 March 1950, in *FRUS 1950*, Vol. 3, *Western Europe*, p. 39; in Italy, for example, Fiat imported steel sheets from the German company Bochum. See ASF, Minutes of meetings of the board of directors, meetings held in January 1952;

219 In this respect see The Secretary of State to the Embassy in the United Kingdom, top secret, 23 March 1950, in *FRUS 1950*, Vol. 3, *Western Europe*, p. 32; The Ambassador in France (Bruce) to the Secretary of State, 28 July 1950, *idem*, pp. 157-158;

220 Proposed Fiscal Year 1952 Foreign Assistance Program, Title I, Chapter V, Part G, Italy, in NARA, RG59, Lot file 52-56 [Bell-Rowe file], b. 3, p. 7;

Communist and Socialist Parties rank and file played within the National Liberation Movement[221]. Furthermore, the government of London retained Italy deeply co-responsible for the outbreak of the Second World War as it had been the main European ally of Nazi Germany [222]. However, after the end of the conflict the UK continued to play a key role in political and military developments in Italy. Three main reasons account for the postwar British involvement in the reconstruction of the Italian armed forces. First and foremost, the British had contributed quite significantly to the building up of the armed forces of the Southern Kingdom government that was born after the downfall of Fascism during summer 1944. The government of London had supplied military equipment and had trained the Italian military personnel. Secondly, the Allied Powers' military mission to Italy had been led by the British military[223]. Thirdly, the British had substantially borne the financial burden of rebuilding the Italian armed forces throughout the last months of the conflict. In particular, the British had financed and sustained training costs, fuel supply, and equipment[224], while the provision of weapons, military components and spare parts was shared more equitably among the British and the Americans as this book's analysis of the aeronautical industry demonstrates[225].

By maintaining its military involvement in Italian affairs after spring 1945, the UK hoped to make Italy subservient to Her Majesty's armed forces and to influence future defense policies. The British were deeply concerned by the internal instability and the uprisings that swept across Italy in 1946, and pinpointed the strengthening of the Italian internal Police and security corps as a much needed step to stabilize the country and lock it into the Western sphere of influence on a more stable basis. In fact, the UK considered the Italian *Carabinieri* and *Polizia* badly equipped and too short of personnel to manage the internal uprisings and to curb

---

221 H.Macmillan, *Memoirs* vol 2, *the Blast of War*, London, Macmillan, 1967; P.Ginsborg, *A History of Contemporary Italy. Society and Politics 1943-1980*, Penguin, New York, 1990, pp. 48-49; P.Craveri, *De Gasperi*, pp. 159-160;

222 On the punitive British approach towards Italy in the period from 1943 through to 1945 see A.Varsori, *Le scelte internazionali*, in G.Sabbatucci, V.Vidotto (eds), *Storia d'Italia*, Vol. 5, *La Repubblica 1943-1963*, Laterza, Roma and Bari, 1997, pp. 260-267; F.Barbagallo, *La formazione dell'Italia democratica*, in AA.VV. *Storia dell'Italia repubblicana*, Vol. 1, *La costruzione della democrazia*, pp. 24 and 37; D.Ellwood, *Italy 1943-45*, Leicester University Press, Leicester 1985;

223 The Supreme Allied Commander, Mediterranean Theater (Morgan) to the combined Chiefs of Staff, 8 March 1947, in *FRUS 1947*, Vol. 3, *The British Commonwealth, Europe*, pp. 872-873; The Deputy US Political Adviser, Allied Force Headquarters (Byington) to the Secretary of State, 28 May 1946; The Commanding General, Mediterranean Theater of Operations (Lee) to the War Department, 17 August 1946, both in *FRUS 1946*, vol. 5, *The British Commonwealth, Western and Central Europe*, Washington DC, 1969, at pages 917-918 e 929-930 respectively;

224 E.Pedaliu, *Britain, Italy and the Origins of the Cold War*, Palgrave, London, 2003, p. 38;

225 L.Nuti, *Continuity and Change in Italian Defense Policy 1945-1995*, in M.Dumoulin (ed.) *La Communauté Européenne de Défense. Leçons pour demain?*, PeterLang P.I.E., Bruxelles 2000, p. 376; id., *La sfida nucleare*, p. 24 ;

84

the riots[226]. Over the following years, a consistent follow-up to this policy was the firm British opposition to the revision of the military clauses of the Peace Treaty signed with Italy soon after the end of the conflict: as late as 1951 the government of London was strongly reluctant to revise the Peace Treaty.

This British approach, combined with the Italian disappointment in the Peace Treaty, repeatedly termed as a diktat, was the source for much Italian resentment[227]. These frictions led to a stalemate in political and military relations between Rome and London from 1945 to 1947[228]. The deterioration of British-Italian relations was paralleled by the rising interest of the Truman Administration in the political and economic stabilization of the country. The origins of postwar American involvement in Italian affairs stretch back to the position that the US government assumed between 1944 and 1945 regarding the conditions and fate of Italy's industrial and communication systems. Within the Allied Powers' military commands, the US representatives proved receptive to the Badoglio government's call for military assistance shortly

226 The Chargé in Italy (Key) to the Secretary of State, 17 October 1946, in *FRUS 1946*, vol. 5, *The British of Commonwealth, Western and Central Europe*, Government Printing Office, Washington DC, 1946, pp. 940-941;

227 the Italian government viewed the Peace Treaty imposed on Italy as far removed from the expectations of the Italians as it had been drafted without any participation by the Rome Cabinet. At the Paris Peace Conference De Gasperi himself reiterated this view. See minutes of Cabinet Meeting 24 August 1946, in *Verbali del Consiglio dei Ministri*, luglio 1943-maggio 1948, Vol. 7, tome 1, *Governo De Gasperi* 13/7/1946-2/2/1947, Presidenza del Consiglio dei Ministri, Roma 1997; As regards the resentment of Italian public opinion against the Peace Treaty see E.Pedaliu, *Britain and the Reconstruction of the Post-Fascist Italian Armed Forces, 1943-48*, in "Cold War History", n. 1, 2001, p. 50; On the Italian Christian Democrats' firm opposition to the Peace Treaty, the internal divisions and the political realignment it produced, see for example , L.Sturzo to A.De Gasperi, 9 October 1946, in G.Antonazzi (ed.), *Carteggio Sturzo-De Gasperi 1920-1953*, Morcelliana, Brescia 1999, pp. 173-174; Sturzo to De Gasperi, 5 February1947, in M.R.De Gasperi (ed.), *De Gasperi scrive. Corrispondenza con capi di stato cardinali uomini politici giornalisti diplomatici*, Morcelliana, Brescia 1974, vol. 2, pp. 51-52; Sturzo to Sforza, 20 July 1947, in G.F.Marcucci (ed.), *Carteggio Sturzo-Scelba* (1923-1956), Istituto Luigi Sturzo, Roma 1994, pp. 296-298; on the definition of the Peace Treaty as a diktat see Sforza's speech given in Genoa in 1951. On that occasion the Italian Foreign Minister called for a revision of the military clauses of the Peace Treaty, in D.Folliot, *Documents on International Affairs*, 1951, p. 78, and The Ambassador in Italy (Dunn) to the Secretary of State, Rome, 23 May 1951, *FRUS 1951*, Vol. 4, Part 1, *Europe: Political and Economic Relations*, p. 613; for a different interpretation of De Gasperi' strategy and stance at the Paris Peace Conference see S.Lorenzini, *The roots of a 'statesman'. De Gasperi's Foreign Policy*, in "Modern Italy", Vol. 14, n. 4, November 2009, 473-484; 228 Memorandum of Conversation J.Greene (Office of Western European Affairs, State Department)-Boyd (British Embassy in Washington), 'Military Clauses of the Italian Peace Treaty', 1 March 1951, in *FRUS 1951*, Vol. 4, Part 1, p. 576;

after the Italian declaration of war on Nazi Germany[229]. Later, the US Administration pressed the Allied Powers' military commands to make sure the Italian Resistance Movement ignored a former allied directive to sabotage industrial plants and machinery across the Peninsula. In early 1945, the Americans ensured that Allied military forces instructed the Italian Partisans to defend industrial infrastructures and machinery from the sabotage of the withdrawing Germans[230]. The Department of State within the Roosevelt Administration had pursued this military policy firmly and consistently throughout the last year of the conflict, in order to both speed up a much needed transition from wartime production lines to civilian productions[231], and to rehabilitate output capacity in anticipation of rearmament[232]. Way before the end of World War II, the Americans engaged to defend both war production lines that could be converted to peacetime productions, and a strategic sector such as the electrical industry, which was considered essential to the restructuring of both civilian and military production chains[233].

The succession from the Roosevelt Administration to the Truman Administration set the ideal political conditions in Washington for the deepening of active American involvement in Italian political and military affairs. This transition marked a turning point from the previous presidency's view of a post war world clearly based on distinctive spheres of influence, to the growing involvement of the new democrat Administration in European political and security affairs as the outbreak of the Cold War loomed on the horizon[234]. Nevertheless, the Ameri-

---

229 The Chargé at Algier (Chapin) to the Secretary of State, 15 January 1944, in *FRUS 1944*, Vol. 3, *The British Commonwealth and Europe*, Government Printing Office, Washington DC, 1965, p. 1000;

230 P.Ferrari, *Un'arma versatile. I bombardamenti strategici anglo-americani e l'industria italiana*, in id. (ed.), *L'aeronautica italiana. Una storia del Novecento*, FrancoAngeli, Milano 2004, pp. 421ff.; see also M.Fini, *Oligarchia elettrica e resistenza di fronte al problema della difesa degli impianti . Prime considerazioni sul caso della società Edison*, in *Milano fra guerra e dopoguerra*, De Donato, Milano, 1979, p. 259; G.Rochat (ed.), *Atti del Comando generale del Corpo Volontari della libertà (gennaio 1944-aprile 1945)*, FrancoAngeli, Milano, 1972, pp. 181-183, 244-247;

231 Statement of the Secretary of State (Hull), 19 May 1944, in *Documents on American Foreign Relations*, Vol. 4, July 1943-June 1944, the World Peace Foundation and Princeton University Press, Princeton (NJ), 1976; *The Economic Basis for Lasting Peace. Address by the Secretary of State (Stettinius) before the Council on Foreign Relations*, Chicago, 4 April 1945, in *Documents on American Foreign Relations*, vol. 7, The World Peace Foundation and Princeton University Press, Princeton (NJ), 1976; *Post-War International Economic Problems. Statement of Assistant Secretary of State Acheson*, 30 November 1944, in *Documents on American Foreign Relations, idem*, pp. 464-479;

232 'Report on Military, Naval, and Air Clauses of the Treaty of Peace with Italy by an ad Hoc Committee of the State-War-Navy Coordinating Committee', in *FRUS 1945*, Vol. 4, *Europe*, Government Printing Office, Washington DC, 1945, p. 1039;

233 P.Ferrari, *Un'arma versatile*, pp. 402-430;

234 F.Barbagallo, *La formazione dell'Italia democratica*, pp. 49 and 72; G.Formigoni, *La democrazia cristiana e l'alleanza occidentale*, pp. 54 ff.; P.Craveri, *De Gasperi*, pp. 220 ff.; J.Harper, *America and the Reconstruction of Italy, 1945-48*, Cambridge University Press, Cambridge, 1986;

cans did not succeed the British in Italy until a few months after the end of the conflict. In fact, throughout the early months following Italy's liberation, the Truman Administration showed a rather limited interest in Italian military and political affairs[235]. By contrast it is widely known that throughout the period prior to the signing of the Atlantic Pact, United States foreign policy toward Italy focused on the reorganization of this country's economy and the stabilization of its social scenario[236]. This belated and slow American move to get involved in the rebuilding of the Italian defense and security forces explains why the Americans let the British take the lead in erecting and providing Italy with a national army in 1945, the so called *Esercito di transizione* (transition army), in the period before the Peace Treaty became effective. It was thus General Alexander, the British-born Supreme Allied Commander in the Mediterranean, who played a central role in drafting the structure and planning the functions of this transitory national army. According to the British project, the Anglo-American military forces were to let the Italians keep the land army under their full control, and to retain the navy and the air forces within the military structures of the Allied Powers. This platform for the transitory army in Italy, paired with the 1944 British plan, laid down the foundations of Allied military aid programs as they were implemented throughout the period that the reorganization of the Italian defense posture was under the British sphere of influence. In fact, the transition army was set up by transferring war material, equipment, military and training services from the British and American military forces, but it did not entail a reactivation of the formerly operative production lines that had been discontinued or damaged during the recent conflict. From late summer 1945 through the beginning of 1947, the Italian governments engaged in negotiations with the Americans and the British to bargain both cost-free transfers and the selling of war material previously used by the Allied military forces and war surplus. The War Department of the Truman Administration fully endorsed the project designed by General Alexander which coincided with the British tendency to curb domestic political uprisings and to protect Italy from external threats without supporting any reorganization or expansion of the Italian war industry's output. From the fall of 1945 to the end of 1946, the British led the Military Mission to the Italian Army and negotiated with Italy on the supply of war surplus to the Italian land and air forces[237]. A complement to these transfers was the Allied Powers' move to hand over the *Arma dei Carabinieri* and the land forces to the Italian government.

Even as the transition army was being set up Britain actively pursued the reorganization of the Italian armed forces, as a move to substantially revise and reduce British military involvement across the Mediterranean. The new Labor government in London wished to substantially cut the large amount of public spending devoted to the military after the end of World War II.

---

235 A.Brogi, *Confronting America. The Cold War between the United States and the Communists in France and Italy*, The University of North Carolina Press, Chapel Hill (NC), 2011, p. 66;
236 J.Harper, *America and the Reconstruction of Italy*;
237 L.Nuti, *La sfida nucleare*, p. 24;

The British decision to redress the balance between welfare spending and military expenditure induced London to remove its military forces from Greece and Italy due to budgetary constraints[238].

This turn in the UK's international military policy came at a time when there was growing concern in Washington over the exposure of the Italian territory to Soviet-inspired pressure and interest from Yugoslavia that the British withdrawal from the Peninsula might entail[239]. This combination between the British withdrawal and the State Department's rising fears over the future of Italy drew the government of the United States closer to Italy and increased US involvement in the reconstruction of the Italian army. This American move accelerated between late 1946 and 1947, and the reconstruction of the Italian air forces and the mechanical and metalworking Italian sectors can be regarded as a blueprint for that turn. In fact, American-born General William Morgan, Supreme Allied Military Commander in the Mediterranean, retained command of the Italian air forces even when the land forces returned under the aegis of the Italian government in November 1945[240]. In early 1946, Morgan formulated a plan to resurrect the Italian air forces by supplying them with high added value aircraft components and instruments such as radar, and very recent models of jet fighters produced in either the United States or the United Kingdom. The Supreme Allied Military Commander planned to equip Italy with sixteen British-processed spitfires and sixteen P-38 aircrafts produced by the US aeronautical industry[241]. At the Paris Peace Conference the Truman Administration re-appraised the Morgan plan and turned it into a military assistance program aimed to provide the Italian air forces with as many as two hundred new and technologically up-to-date fighters[242]. This new program was twofold in its aim as it would both bypass a number of quantitative constraints on production of recent fighters that the Peace Treaty imposed on Italy, and cool off rising Italian resentment and disappointment over the Peace Treaty. This American directive to smooth over and ease the impact of the Peace Treaty limitations on Italian rearmament was partly the result of the growing importance accorded by Washington to Italy in the Mediterranean in the post war years[243]. Thus, the Americans believed the punitive and restrictive approach of Britain to the reorganization of the Italian armed forces should be removed, whereas the resurrection of the Italian military was to be encouraged and sup-

---

238 D.Ellwood, *Italy 1943-45*; F.Barbagallo, *La formazione dell'Italia democratica*, p. 72;

239 As regards this American concern, Leopoldo Nuti stressed that over the following years it led the United States to get increasingly involved in the reorganisation of the Italian military. See L.Nuti, *US Forces in Italy*, pp. 254-255;

240 The Supreme Allied Commander, Mediterranean Theater (Morgan) to the Combined Chiefs of Staff, 30 May 1946, in *FRUS 1946*, Vol. 5, p. 846;

241 L.Nuti, *L'esercito italiano nel secondo dopoguerra 1945-1950*, pp. 77-79;

242 *Idem*, pp. 113-114;

243 Central Intelligence Agency, 'The Current Situation in Italy', 10 February 1948, in DDRS;

ported in order to secure the country to the Western bloc sphere of influence[244]. As soon as the American authorities drew closer to the Italian defense and security policies, the Truman Administration showed a growing interest in the economic, financial and budgetary burden that came with the reconstruction of the Italian air forces. The issue of raw material and its supply had actually been addressed by the United States as early as the second half of 1945. At that time the Foreign Economic Administration, an agency of the Federal government involved in the postwar economic assistance programs abroad, financed the import of carbon required for the reactivation of the Italian war industry[245]. However, this early American move to help the Italians in the reorganization of their military productions led the Washington elites to engage in large scale financing of import requirements and to support Italy in smoothing the impact of the rearmament effort on its foreign exchange balance. This occurred only a few months later, when the British started reducing their financial and military commitment in Italy. In the framework of trilateral negotiations among the British, the Italians and the Americans on the implementation of the military assistance program to Italy launched by the Truman Administration at the Paris Peace Conference, the London Cabinet proposed that only a rather limited amount of jet aircrafts and spare parts be transferred cost-free to Italy. The UK requested that some equipment and services discarded by Her Majesty's armies and planned for delivery to Italy be rewarded in hard currency. The United States formulated a proposal midway between Rome and London to accommodate both the Italian need to speed up rearmament and the British budgetary constraints. This offer envisaged that the Americans purchase a number of obsolete P-38 fighters held by the Italian air forces. In turn, these American purchases were to finance Italy's imports of British made P-51 fighters[246]. This American plan both proved Washington's increasing involvement in the reconstruction of the Italian armed forces, and anticipated the payments system revolving around the off-shore procurement programs which came into effect in the first half of the 1950s.

Therefore, as the Americans took over from the British in leading the rebuilding of the Italian armies, two distinctive features emerged that were to characterize the military assistance programs in Western Europe and Italy after 1948. From 1945 to 1948 the bulk of military assistance revolved around the transfer of a variety of war surplus to the Italian state. From weapons to instrumental goods and machine tools, most of this surplus war material came from the US War Assets Administration and was transferred cost-free or below market price to the war-torn European armies. These transfers took place in line with the principle of mutual de-

---

244 'Report on Military, Naval and Air Clauses of the Treaty of Peace with Italy by an ad Hoc Committee of the State-War-Navy Coordinating Committee', in *FRUS 1945*, Vol. 4, *Europe*, p. 1039;

245 J.Harper, *America and the Reconstruction of Italy*;

246 E.Pedaliu, *Britain and the Reconstruction of the Post-Fascist Italian Armed Forces*, pp. 52-53;

fense that underpinned the dawn of the Atlantic Alliance at that time[247]. In the case of Italy, these transfers met a pressing need to update and renovate military equipment and weaponry under use by the land and air forces. Accordingly, up to the very end of 1948[248] the Pentagon and the Department of State conducted further negotiations «to supplement obsolescent and insufficient material»[249] at the request of Italy. As I have outlined briefly, this pressing need to furnish and update the Italian military stemmed from the Anglo-American concerns for both the defense of the country from external threats, and a must-do commitment to stabilize its internal political and social context.

Shortly after the end of the Second World War the British project to dismantle the Italian war industry was discarded. Indeed, when the American authorities took over from the UK on the Italian political scenario, the reconstruction of the country's war industry was actively promoted. Washington's firm commitment to make the Italian military industrial complex once again fully operative stemmed from this sector's key role in stabilizing a wrecked Italian industrial system, and the monetary and financial implications of such a process[250]. Hence, from the late 1940s to the mid-1950s the United States government supported the reconstruction of the Italian and European war industry for reasons that changed strikingly over time. Prior to 1950, and the launch of the Atlantic Alliance's rearmament program, the widely shared reluctance among Americans to military spending and to American involvement in the defense effort of America's European allies underpinned the stance of the United States government[251]. Later, a pressing need to cope with the worsening of the US balance of payments,

---

247 Memorandum by E.Jacobs 'Reduction in Italian Funds for Italy's Defense', 23 November 1953, in NARA, RG 469, Mission to Italy, Office of the Director, Subject Files (Central Files) 1948-57, b. 37, fold. 4 (Internal Finance Defense Expenditures);

248 Basic Policies (Politico-Military matters), Basic Policies, 2. Military Assistance Policies', 1949, in DDRS.

249 Central Intelligence Agency, 'The Current Situation in Italy', 10 February 1948, p. 4, in DDRS;

250 on the role of the OSP contracts and the ERP-typed economic aid programs in this respect, against the backdrop of the American anti-communist biased stance, see Dayton to Secretary of State, 21 April 1952, in NARA, RG 469, Mission to Italy, Office of the Director, Subject Files (Central Files) 1948-57, b. 20, fold. 10 (Defense Contracts); F.Freeman (Deputy Special Assistant for MDAP Affairs) to LT Colonel W.B.Loomis (ordinance Procurement Center Rome), 21 May 1953, in NARA, RG 469, Mission to Italy, Office to the Director, Subject Files (Central Files) 1948-57, b. 41, fold. 1, and A.P.Battleman (Rome Embassy Controller) to A.Most (ECA Mission to Rome, Industrial Production Division), 29 August 1951; F.Moraglia (Ufficio Forniture Officine Reggiane) to ECA Special Mission to Italy, 25 August 1951, both in NARA, RG 469, Mission to Italy, Office of the Director, Subject Files (Central Files), 1948-57, b. 33, fold. 6 (Industry);

251 Among the huge amount of scholarly works so far produced on this point it is worth mentioning D.Yergin, *Shattered Peace*; J.L.Gaddis, *Strategies of Containment*; R.J.Donovan, *The Presidency of Harry S.Truman 1945-1948. Conflict and Crisis*, W.W. Norton, New York, 1977; for a different historical interpretation of the the economic policies implemented by the Truman Administration ,which

coupled with the Eisenhower's Administration shift towards orthodox fiscal policies, led Washington to cut foreign economic and military assistance programs substantially, and to support the establishment of self-sufficient production chains in most key European manufacturing sectors.

3.2 The first military assistance program: steps towards domestic growth, market integration and stability on the foreign exchange markets, 1949-1951

The first military assistance plan implemented under the aegis of the Mutual Defense Assistance Program in 1949, highlights the main features of rearmament prior to the launch of the coordinated production programs that were based on both full exploitation of strategic materials and manufacturing capacity, and transfer of instrumental goods and end items among the economies of the Atlantic Alliance's member states. The strain of this first program, widely-known as Additional Military Productions (AMP), on the federal budget of the United States was considerable as it came into force prior to the conclusion of the European Recovery Program[252].

Its first aim was to maximize the exploitation of strategic resources and to rehabilitate output capacity in the West-European countries to prevent internal political insurgencies or social upheaval, and to protect them from foreign threats on their borders. According to Title VI of the Foreign Assistance Act of 1948, from the outset the AMP program envisaged the building up of «a coordinated military assistance program in which the quotas of each recipient would be related to overall needs, production capabilities, political considerations and strategic concepts». In pursuing these targets, according to the US National Security Council, this program was to encourage the Europeans to cooperate with each other «in integrating their armaments industries with a view ultimately to maintaining and re-supplying their own equipment when economic conditions permit»[253]. By promoting cooperation in raw material supply and manufacturing, the AMP were to be the first step in making the rearmament of Western Europe conducive to the process of European trade and industrial integration[254].

---

intended «to reconcile the demands of the warfare state with the needs of the welfare state», see M.Hogan, *A Cross of Iron*;

252 'MSA, Proposed Fiscal Year 1952 Foreign Assistance Program, Title I, Europe', in NARA, RG59, Lot File 52-56 (Bell Rowe File), b.3, p. 74;

253 National Security Council, NSC14/1, 'The Position of the United States with Respect to Providing Military Assistance to Nations of the non-Soviet World', 1 July 1948, pp. 3 and 8, in DDRS;

254 S.Selva, *Recovery and Security. Early US Military Assistance to Italy and the Beginning of European Economic Integration*, in M.Rasmussen, A.C.Knudsen (eds), *The Road to a United Europe. Interpretations of the Pro cess fo European Integration*, PeterLang, Bruxelles 2009, pp. 137 ff.; for a

Secondly, despite its rather limited financial assets, the AMP was to provide continued military assistance rather than the discontinuous transfers of war surplus conducted over the previous three years. From its inception, the United States made it clear that a key note of the program was «that over the long term the production of arms and equipment be increasingly produced and financed by the recipients of our military assistance. »[255] The AMP aid was to reorganize and stimulate output capacity of the average capital intensive and labor intensive mechanical sectors. In so doing, the American authorities aimed to resurrect the industrial capability and market competitiveness of European industries through the standardization and rationalization of production lines and the introduction of American labor organization methods that were consistent with the technical assistance programs implemented at that time in the framework of the ERP[256]. The involvement of the Italian economy was a showcase for all of the features that characterized the AMP, thanks to both its underutilized industrial capability and manpower, and its position and role within postwar international relations following the signing of the Peace Treaty. The first Mutual Defense Assistance Program was implemented in Italy in early 1950, when the conditions imposed on Italy's armed forces and on the Italian war industry by the Peace Treaty were already effective[257]. This Peace Treaty had fixed limits on Italy's rearmament of land, naval and air forces as well as prohibiting Italian industries from raising physical output to supply the national armies of other European countries. In fact, these conditions were well suited to a military assistance program that had the precise target of reactivating the existing, war-wrecked production lines and protecting the

different interpretation inclined to see industrial cooperation for rearmament as a failure see P.Pitman, *The Economic consequences of Mr. Eden: The Paris Accords, Europe's Strategic Industries and the Atlantic Political Economy*, in *L'Europe et L'OTAN face aux défis des élargissements de 1952 et 1954. Organisation Internationale et Relations Internationales*, Actes du colloque organisé par le Centre d'études d'Histoire de la defense et l'Université de Paris I, Panthéon Sorbonne, Paris, 22-24 January 2004, Emile Bruylant, Bruxelles, 2005, pp. 155-172 ; a recent reinterpretation is in T.Geiger, *Western Defense, Economic Cooperation and the Atlantic Paradox: Multilateralism and Governmentality in the Cold War 1949-1960*, in R.Perron, G. Thiemeyer (eds), *Multilateralism and the Trente Glorieuses in Europe. New Perspectives in European Integration history*, Editions Alphil, Neuchâtel, 2011, particularly pp. 186 ff.;

255 J.Sherman (Secretary of the War Council), Memorandum for the Secretary of the Army, The Secretary of the Navy, the Secretary of the Air Force, 'Significant Actions of the Meeting of the War Council on 23 February1949', 24 February 1949, in DDRS;

256 'The Problem of Productivity in Italy', 23 March 1950, in NARA, RG469, Mission to Italy, Office of the Director, Subject Files (Central Files) 1948-1957 (1948-54), b. 45, fold. 1 (Productivity); 'IRI Programme for technical assistance in the companies of the Finmeccanica group', 28 May 1952, in NARA, RG469, Mission to Italy, Office of the Director, Subject Files (Central Files) 1948-1957 (1948-1954), b. 55, fold. 7 (Technical Assistance);

257 'Summary Statement on Status of Italian AMP Projects Nos. 1-141', 7 April 1952, in NARA, RG469, Mission to Italy, Office of the Director, Subject Files (Central Files) 1948-1957 (1948-54), b. 20, fold. 8 (Defense AMP Projects);

country from a meteoric rise of the Soviet-inspired red scare on its Eastern and South-Eastern borders[258]. Despite the considerable industrial and military constraints, with the implementation of the first MDAP the Italian government struggled to make the Italian economy into a manufacturing hub that could serve coordinated rearmament programs at continental level[259]. Analysis of the AMP is worthwhile as it summed up all of these features germane to the first MDAP[260]. In fact, this program revived the on-stream production capability of the Italian war industry without starting up new production lines. Furthermore, it triggered a first leap forward in the added value of the Italian mechanical sectors, and an early modernization of the Italian armed forces. Furthermore, the AMP stimulated a rise in physical output of the operative plants and production chains. To achieve these targets and increase the technological content of production[261], the program financed the import not only of raw materials, semi-manufactured goods and components[262], but also of spare parts for machinery from other economies of the Atlantic Alliance.

To tackle the twin objective to first strengthen the Italian armies and the national defense system, then to «transfer to other NATO countries on an equitable method of payments»[263], the Additional Military Productions drew on a low to average capital intensive reorganization of the Italian war industries and of the mechanical and metalworking firms that collaborated closely with them. The revamping of productions, machinery and machine tools engaged in

---

258 Foreign Military Assistance Coordinating Committee, 'The Current Situation in Italy', 17 April 1950, in DDRS;

259 Governo italiano, 'Italian Memorandum', 19 December 1950, in NARA, RG59, Lot File 52-56, Bell Rowe File 1949-1952, b. 2, pp. 25-30;

260 So far a widely-shared historical interpretation has viewed the AMP as rather limited in scale and discarded it as a failing initiative, whereas the US Mission to Italy christened it as an abortive program. With regard to both views see on the one side T.Geiger-L.Sebesta, *National Defense Policies*, p. 258; L.Segreto, *Arar*, p. 179; I.Megens, *Problems of Military Production Coordination*, in B.Heuser, R.O'Neill (eds), *Securing Peace in Europe, 1945-62. Thoughts for the Post Cold War Era*, MacMillan, London, 1992, p. 280; L.Sebesta, *L'Europa indifesa*, pp. 168-69; J.McGlade, *NATO Procurement and the Revival of European Defense 1950-1960*, in G.Schmidt (ed.), *A History of NATO: The First Fifty Years*, Vol. 3, Palgrave, New York 2001, pp. 14 and 376; on the other, the stance of the US Mission to Italy can be found in H.Chenery to V.Barnett, 'Use of Counterpart for Defense Production', 1 February1952, in NARA, RG 469, Mission to Italy, Office of the Director, Subject Files (Central Files) 1948-57, b. 22, fold. 2 (Defense OSP program: contracts, production), p. 2;

261 C.Parker (MSA Rome) to MSA Washington, 'US Materials Assistance to Italian AMP Projects', 13 February 1953, in NARA, RG469, Mission to Italy, Office of the Director, Subject Files (Central Files) 1948-1957, b. 20, fold. 8 (Defense AMP Project);

262 L.Sebesta, *I programmi di aiuto militare nella politica americana per l'Europa. L'esperienza italiana 1948-52*, in "Italia contemporanea", n. 173, 1988, pp. 43-63;

263 R.Whittet, Memorandum to the Files, 'Italian HPPP', in NARA, RG59, Lot File 52-56, Records of the Mutual Defense Assistance Program, Subject File Relating to Program Management ("Bell-Rowe F ile"), 1949-1952 , b. 3;

by the state shareholding of Finmeccanica to equip the Italian government's defense effort, is a case in point[264]. From 1949 to 1951, following the first rearmament program, the US authorities combined this limited, capital intensive recovery of the Italian mechanical sectors with strong pressure to encourage the Italian ruling class to expand physical output and improve price competitiveness by means of a comprehensive rationalization of labor based on an industrial policy that would slash labor costs. This combination of a low to average technological modernization and reduced labor costs assumed there would be a boost in market penetration abroad and no curb on labor purchasing power and domestic aggregate demand for durables in Italy[265]. The extension of the technical assistance programs, along the lines of the Marshall Plan to the defense industry, was essential to achieving this twin objective[266]. From 1949 onward the *Productivity and Technical Assistance Program* had been promoted in Italy by the Truman Administration to encourage improved competitiveness of Italian manufacturers on foreign markets and expansionary domestic demand for consumer goods[267]. In the wake of these initiatives, the Italian mechanical and metalworking industries that were working on military procurements were involved in technical assistance programs aimed at ensuring "greater per capita output".

Furthermore, a cost-cutting rationalization of the Italian production chains in line with American-style productivity trends aimed also to standardize the European war industry on the American models then in production or those just discarded by the United States' firms[268].

This labor-intensive rationalization of production costs aimed to improve competitiveness and raise the international demand for semi-manufactured and manufactured war material induced by the rearmament of Western Europe, while neither starting new productions lines nor curbing nominal wages and labor purchasing power[269]. In a country like Italy that was still in the

---

264 Finmeccanica, 'Per una graduale ripresa della produzione di interesse militare', 20 July 1948, in ACS, ASIRI, Numerazione rossa, Finmeccanica varie, S3-f.200.9.2;

265 Joint ECA Mission to Rome-American Embassy in Rome report, 'Speech of President of Confindustria on Productivity', 15 November 1951, in NARA, RG469, Mission to Italy, Office of the Director, Subject Files (Central Files) 1948-1957, b. 3, fold. 1(Industry Productivity);

266 For a different interpretation from mine on the American style productivity drive in Italy as revolving around a significant leap forward in technological advance and industrial efficiency see, for example , M.E.Guasconi *L'altra faccia della medaglia. Guerra psicologica e diplomazia sindacale nelle relazioni Italia-Stati Uniti durante la prima fase della guerra fredda 1947-1955*, Rubettino, Soveria Mannelli (CZ), 1999, p. 94;

267 J.McGlade, *Lo zio Sam ingegnere industriale. Il programma americano per la produttività e la ripresa economica dell'Europa occidentale (1948-1958)*, in "Studi Storici", n. 1, 1996, pp. 9-40;

268 'MSA, Proposed Fiscal Year 1952 Foreign Assistance Program, Title I, Europe', in NARA, RG59, Lot File 52-56, Bell Rowe File 1949-1952, b. 3, pp. 83-84;

269 ECA Special Mission to Italy, 'The Problem of Productivity in Italy', 23 March 1950, in NARA, RG469, Mission to Italy, Office of the Director, Subject Files (Central Files) 1948-1957 (1948-54), b. 45, fold. 1 (Productivity);

early stages of economic recovery in the aftermath of war a rearmament program based predominantly on the start-up of new productions and the reabsorption of unemployed and skilled labor in the short-term, was likely to induce a sharp and sudden economic downturn. On the contrary, a rapid rise in industrial productivity that could couple price competitiveness on foreign markets with inflation-linked wages, to ensure steady labor purchasing power, would make rearmament a viable method for achieving the internationalization of the Italian market and would sow the seeds for a domestic mass consumer market[270]. The United States pursued this highly ambitious, twofold objective not only through the introduction of the American-style labor organization and production methods geared to the technical assistance programs, but also by pressurizing the Italians to dismantle the monopolistic structure that characterized Italian capitalism. In the combined pursuit of laying the foundations of a domestic market oriented towards mass consumption, and of creating a competitive edge among exporters, the United States complemented the introduction of technical assistance to the war industry with a continued campaign to force the Italian government remove the so called «restrictive business practices»[271]. According to the experts working on industrial policy-related issues within the State Department, the Italian industrial cartels were a malaise that prevented the Italian economy from setting fair prices and competing fairly, on both Italian and foreign markets.

The third reason why the AMP is worthy of consideration is that it permits us to gain a comprehensive understanding of what military assistance was about and which aspects of the European economies it affected, thanks to the attention it addressed to the implications of the defense effort on the European balance of payments against the US dollar[272]. Most of the, rather limited, financial aid in US dollars allotted to the West European allies went to financing the import of the raw materials and investment goods required for military production. From the time of the first MDAP there had been an evident imbalance between the requirements for raw material and investment goods and their supply by the markets of the European currency and of the British Pound areas. This imbalance forced the European economies to

---

270 H.Cleveland (Assistant Director for Europe MSA), 'Notes on Italy', 1 December 1952, in NARA, RG469, Mission to Italy, Office of the Director, Subject Files (Central Files) 1948-1957, b. 36, fold. 6 (Italy Economic Problems); regarding the interplay between the US productivity drive towards Italy and the issue of unemployment see, S.Chillé, *Il 'Productivity and Technical Assistance Program' per l'economia italiana 1949-1954: accettazione e resistenze ai progetti statunitensi di rinnovamento del sistema produttivo nazionale*, in "Annali della Fondazione Giulio Pastore",vol. 22, 1993, pp. 80-81;
271 Italian Monopolies and Industrial Productivity, in NARA, RG469, Mission to Italy, Office of the Director, Subject Files (Central Files) 1948-1957, b. 3, fold. 1 (Industry Productivity).
272 NAC Meeting n. 160, 2 August 1950, in NARA, RG56, Nac Papers, Nac Minutes, b. 2 (9 February 1950-28 December 1950);

import from supplying economies other than the European and British ones[273]. As the markets that supplied raw materials and the economies producing investments goods that revolved around the US dollar trade area could easily satisfy these import requirements, the American idea was to channel currency aid to the Europeans through the AMP appropriations in order to ease the pressure of rearmament on the current account of each country's balance of payments against the US dollar. In this respect, from its inception in 1950 through to its conclusion in 1952, the first MDAP program rewarded the European economies belonging to the Atlantic bloc with roughly $40 million[274]. Under the same military assistance program, Washington managed to reduce the impact of rearmament on the European external monetary balance by transferring a significant amount of armaments and instrumental goods to its allies. This transfer aimed to prevent industrial mobilization caused by rising imports all across the European manufacturing economies[275]. From 1949 to 1950, import requirements were mostly met through either the free-of-charge distribution of American goods, or the ERP loans, as well as a by drawing on the counterpart funds accrued on the assets of the West European balance-sheets[276]. Indeed, the transfers channeled through the AMP were worth up to $100 million[277]. This twofold approach meant that the AMP program was able to finance both the purchase or the transfer of the equipment, spare parts for weapons, training and technical services needed to revive the European armies, as well as providing a large quantity of investment goods and instrumental goods for the recovery of the European defense industry[278]. The aids granted to Italy offer a neat sample of this twofold structure. In fact, the AMP program supplied the Italian armed forced with end items essential to their recovery, ranging from combat vehicles, jet fighters and munitions, to electronic equipment and average added value machinery to update both the national air forces and the Italian aircraft industry which was still under reorganiza-

---

273 Ragioneria generale dello Stato, Promemoria per il Ministro del Tesoro, 'Piani di aiuto militari-Problemi tecnici', 14 September 1950, in ACS, Ministero Bilancio e Programmazione economica, b. 106, fold. 648;

274 C.Parker (MSA Rome) to MSA Washington, 'Assistance to Italian Production of Military Equipment-Status of AMP Projects', 4 February 1953, in NARA, RG469, Mission to Italy, Office of the Director, Subject Files (Central Files) 1948-1957, b. 20, fold. 8 (Defense AMP Projects);

275 O.Bradley (chairman, Joint Chiefs of Staff), 'Memorandum to the Secretary of Defense', 27 October 1950, in HSTPL, President's Secretary's Files;

276 C.Spagnolo, La stabilizzazione incompiuta, pp. 217-229;

277 C.Parker (MSA Rome) a MSA Washington, 'Assistance to Italian Production of Military Equipment-Status of AMP Projects', 4 February 1953, in NARA, RG469, Mission to Italy, Office of the Director, Subject Files (Central Files) 1948-1957, b. 20, fold. 8 (Defense AMP Projects);

278 O.Bradley (chairman, Joint Chiefs of Staff), 'Memorandum to the Secretary of Defense', 27 October 1950, in HSTPL, President's Secretary's Files;

tion[279]. Therefore, the AMP anticipated the subsequent military assistance programs enacted within a multilateral rearmament framework, such as the off-shore procurement programs, in two ways. On the one hand, the AMP directed its financial appropriations to prevent industrial mobilization from straining the equilibrium in the European balance of payments. On the other hand, it helped the Rome Cabinet to reconstruct its national armies without putting pressure on its import-export trade.

The last distinctive feature of the AMP is that its implementation overlapped with the period of industrial mobilization resulting from the Korean War and its impact on the European economies as they moved from postwar economic recovery to the beginning of continued upward growth[280]. In the case of Italy, the outbreak and development of war in Far East Asia dramatically changed both the structure and dynamics of the domestic market, and its foreign trade and monetary balance[281]. Therefore, the following paragraphs of this chapter are specifically devoted to understanding this overlap and the changes it induced in the pattern of development both in Italy's domestic market and in the country's economic position on the international markets.

3.3 Industrial co-production and financial share out: the AMP as the antecedent of NATO cooperation on rearmament

The AMP military assistance program, launched in March 1949, was the first attempt by the Brussels Pact countries to expand and coordinate production of manufactured weapons, components and equipment; over the next two years it funded dozens of multilateral production programs among the NATO member countries for a total value of $600 million[282]. It absorbed the vast majority of the dollar aid provided for in the budget of the first Mutual Defense Assistance Program. Most of the AMP projects financed new orders for the West European aeronautical industry, which was strongly dominated by British aeronautics in the post war period. This British industry drew on its long-standing history and experience to lead the re-

---

279 'Material for House Appropriations Committee Group Visiting Italy October 14 through 21', 28 August 1953, in NARA, RG469, Mission to Italy, Office of the Director, Subject Files (Central Files) 1948-1957, b. 18, fold. 3 (Congress House Appropriations Committee Visit);

280 J.E.Jacobs (US Embassy Rome) to G.Perkins (Assistant Secretary of State), 7 July 1950, in NARA, RG59, Central files 1950-1954, b. 2838, 611.65/7-2750;

281 R.Gualtieri, *L'Italia dal 1943 al 1992*, pp.118-119;

282 A.H.Cornell, *International Collaboration in Weapons and Equipment Development and Production by the NATO allies*, Martinus Nijhoff Publishers, The Hague, 1981; the most part of this amount, between $400 million and $500 million, were to increase physical output of the existing production lines;

covery of the sector. Moreover, despite the fact that the rapid expansion of this industry did not take place until 1952, as early as 1946 the Labor government's Air Ministry had opted to maintain production levels through the allotment of both repair and maintenance contracts, as well as research and development[283]. This meant that the British government refrained from scheduling new military aircrafts and concentrated both its attention and financial assets on updating the most recent operative jet fighters. This choice was crucial in allowing the British firms to head the recovery and growth of the European aeronautical sector. The AMP programs favoured the revamping of the British industry and established a series of co-production programs that involved all the economies of the Atlantic Pact[284].

Against this background, the AMP prompted France to produce the British Vampire jet aircrafts and the Nene Jet Engines, whereas the Benelux countries cooperated to manufacture the British Gloster Meteors, with Belgium and the Netherlands processing the engines and the airframes respectively[285]. On the other hand, after the outbreak of war in Korea the United Kingdom gave orders that meant that France, Belgium and the Netherlands worked on the Vampire and the Meteor Jet Fighters[286]. From the beginning of the program, the Italian manufacturing firms headed by Fiat, were also involved in these productions. The Italian mechanical industries contributed by processing both end items, such as the Vampire airplanes, and components as the de Havilland Ghost gas turbine engines[287].

On the American side, an economic analysis unit was established within the ECA to study the interplay between military assistance and economic aid styled on the Marshall Plan, and the ECA itself managed US military assistance by channeling aid from these early co-production programs among its European partners and allies[288]. The US assistance program did not provide any aid to countries such as Austria and Sweden, but assigned most of its funds, the sum of $350 million, to the United Kingdom with the sole purpose of financing the import of the

---

283 T.Geiger, 'The next War is Bound to Come': Defence Production Policy, Supply Departments and Defense contractors in Britain, 1945-57, in A.Gorst, L.Johnman, W.Scott Lucas (eds), Contemporary British History 1931-61. Politics and the Limits of Policy, Pinter Publishers, London and New York, 1991, pp. 97 ff.;

284 The most recent historical works on the history of the European air industry argue that this sector was an outstanding case in point for the post war co-production activities that ensued from continent-wide cooperation in manufacturing. See the introduction by David Burigana and Pascal Deloge, Le coopération aéronautiques en Europe dans les années 1950-1980: un opportunité par relire l'histoire del la constructionne Européenne?, in "Histoire, Economie et Societè", n. 4 (2010), a collection of original works that examine the subject from this viewpoint ;

285 I.Megens, Problems of Military Production Coordination, pp. 279-280;

286 T.Geiger, Britain and the Economic Problem of the Cold War, pp. 153-154;

287 ASF, Minutes of the board of directors, January 1952;

288 Tarchiani to Sforza, 'Aiuti dopo il 1952', Washington, 16 June 1950, telespresso, in ASBI, Carte Caffè, pratt., n. 50, fold. 1;

raw materials and investment goods needed for the defense effort[289]. Apart from this unbalanced distribution of funds among the European partners, it should be noted that the program was both limited in scale and quite slow in its progress and fulfillment. The US Congress not only prohibited supplying the Europeans with funds to expand physical output, but also limited the financing of imports of raw material, components and instrumental goods to those available in the dollar currency areas[290]. Furthermore, a detailed and time-consuming screening process of the European applications for assistance, coupled with the 1953 reorganization of ECA into the Foreign Operations Administration (FOA), meant the implementation of US military aid through the AMP programs was both slow and uncertain[291]. These difficulties led the US Congress to speculate on the ongoing waste of funds by the European allies and sparked several Congressmen to oppose the last portion of the program, implemented in 1954, even more fiercely than in the past[292].

From early 1950 the launch of the second fiscal year's military assistance program, termed the Mid -Term Defense Assistance Program (MTDP), paved the way for a process of multilateral rearmament that was increasingly bound to the defense and security plans formulated within NATO. This in turn meant that the industrial mobilization took on a multilateral design[293]. Despite this trend, the US authorities worked hard to improve the AMP before and during the implementation of the new program, and to speed up the process for their West European allies. As regards the constraint on purchasing materials outside the dollar currency areas, the US Mission to Rome, with the full backing of the Washington-based agency of the Italian government for negotiations with the US Administration, the *Delegazione Tecnica*

289 NAC Meeting n. 160, 2 August 1950, in NARA, RG56, Nac Papers, Nac Minutes, b. 2 (February 9, 1950-December 28, 1950). At this time, the military assistance program to the United Kingdom combined this financial assistance with a larger end-item weapons aid package. See on this T.Geiger, *The British Warfare State and the Challenge of Americanisation of Western Defence*[courtesy of the author], p. 19;

290 T.Geiger, L.Sebesta, *National Defense Policies*, p. 258; Ragioneria generale dello Stato, Promemoria per il Ministro del Tesoro, 'Piani di aiuto militari-Problemi tecnici',14 September 1950, in ACS, Ministero Bilancio e Programmazione economica, b. 106, fold. 648;

291 as regards the transformation of the MSA into the FOA see for reference MAE to CIR-Segreteria Generale, 'Foreign Operation Administration (FOA). Nuovi dirigenti', 14 October 1953, sent by cable, in ASBI, Carte Caffè, pratt., n. 50, fold. 1; Magistrati a CIR-Segreteria Generale, 'Foreign Operations Administration (FOA). Programmazione aiuti all'Europa', 15 October 1953, sent by cable, *idem*;

292 J.H.Ohly (FOA) to William J.Sheppard, 'FOA Responsabilities for and Handling of the Additional Military Production (AMP) Program', 9 April 1954, in NARA, RG469, Deputy to the Director, Subject Files of Glen A.Lloyd, Deputy to the Director 1953-55, b. 4, fold. Military Assistance; with respect to FOA and its role see also E.Ortona to MCE, Direzione Generale Servizi Importazioni Esportazioni, 'Riorganizzazione della FOA', 15 September 1953, in ACS, PCM, CIR, b. 98;

293 I.Megens, *Problems of Military Production Coordination*;

Italiana, found a loophole[294]. The American diplomats and economists based in Rome struggled to exploit AMP funds to finance not only the import of the much needed raw materials for the defense orders, but also the imports of the strategic material required to meet the rising aggregate demand for civilian goods that was triggered by the expansionary effect of the defense effort. This ploy made it possible to increase the total of raw material imports that could be supported by the AMP program. The primary aim of the US economic experts working in Rome was to finance, first and foremost, the import of copper, nickel and cobalt[295]. In addition, however, in the 1951 fiscal year alone, up to 14 million dollars' worth of cotton and wool for civilian production were imported using MTDP funding and the Italians put pressure on the Americans to finance up to one fourth of the yearly requirements of Italy for steel[296]. This produced a steady rise in the assets of the Italian economy that could be used to finance imports and thus stimulated domestic civilian investments both in Italy, and across the West European economies involved in the AMP military assistance program[297]. This strategy was to improve the AMP and to bypass its bottlenecks and aimed to satisfy the requirements of the defense effort and to complete the process of economic reconstruction at the same time. In the following years, a follow-up to this approach to improvement of the AMP within the framework of the Mutual Security Program were the so-called *defense support* aids. This type of financial aid was specifically budgeted to meet a sharp slowdown in either the buying power of the European economies on foreign markets, or possible internal monetary instability arising out of war mobilisation[298].

---

294 DELTEC, 'Richieste di fabbisogni di materiali scarsi', 26 January 1951, in ASC, Comitati permanenti, b. 30.1/1 (Comitato permanente per gli Affari economici. Biennio 1951/1952), fold. 149 (II riunione dell'8/3/1951. Distribuzione internazionale delle materie prime critiche e relativa politica economica interna ed esterna. Problemi industriali del riarmo occidentale. Commesse e relativi finanziamenti);

295 Ragioneria generale dello Stato, Promemoria per il Ministro del Tesoro, 'Piani di aiuto militari-Problemi tecnici', 14 September 1950, in ACS, Ministero Bilancio e Programmazione economica, b. 106, fold. 648;

296 H.B.Chenery to J.Dunn, 'Status of Raw Materials Procurement for Military Production', 5 April 1951, in NARA, RG469, Mission to Italy, Office of the Director, Subject Files (Central Files) 1948-1957, b. 22, fold. 2 (Defense, OSP program: contracts, Production);

297 Summary of events Prepared in the Office of the Director of International Security Affairs (Cabot), 23 June 1951, in *FRUS 1951*, Vol. 1, *National Security Affairs, Foreign Economic Policy*, pp. 329-331;

298 F.Caffè, Segnalazione per il sig. Governatore 'L'attività degli istituti internazionali nel periodo giugno-luglio', 30 July 1953, in ASBI, Carte Caffè, pratt., n. 48, fold. 1 . When the new Eisenhower Administration devised to unify defense appropriations to the Pentagon and defense spending allocated to finance foreign military assistance within one single defense budget in order to cope with the US Congress' cuts on military spending, this was likely to prevent Washington from using a very useful way to hide the economic aid type of financial appropriation to its West European allies. See on this

As regards the American commitment to ease the screening of European requests for financial assistance to their imports, the US officers in Rome in charge of dealing with military assistance requested that the ECA and the Pentagon should no longer link the import of strategic material to the approval of specific production programs. This reflected the desire to satisfy requests for the import of the raw materials required for groups of projects while the final approval for each single project was still pending[299].

Though the US Secretary for Defense, Wilson, fiercely opposed this method of speeding up the implementation of the military production program[300], a «review of raw material requirements on a project by project basis» geared to the early steps of the AMP was scrapped[301]. Thereafter, the US Mission to Rome was skilful in getting the import requirements approved according to an «over-all program rather than a multiplicity of small unrelated projects»[302]. In his correspondence with the Secretary of State, Acheson, the US ambassador to Italy, James Dunn, maintained that improvement to the AMP would both streamline the bureaucracy governing the AMP programs, and stimulate a fully cooperative and active participation by the De Gasperi Cabinet. Furthermore, this device was likely to stimulate a rise in the production volumes of the Italian manufacturing firms to meet the defense efforts and to strengthen the three national armies[303].

All these initiatives for the improvement of the AMP programs were led by the Country Team in Rome, a technical organization established within each US Embassy to the West European allies that were involved in the military assistance programs. On the conclusion of the AMP program toward Italy the Country Team, which combined both a consultative advisory role and the right to express binding decisions, stressed that this ending of the program implied no

---

Ministero degli Affari Esteri to Governatore della Banca d'Italia, 'Aiuti americani per il 1953-54', 31 October 1953, classified, not sent by mail, in ASBI, Carte Caffè, pratt., n. 50, fold. 1;

299 with respect to this effort by the US officers in Rome see H.Chenery, Memorandum to J.Dunn (Ambassador to Italy) 'Status of Raw Materials Procurement for Military Production', 5 April 1951, in NARA, RG469, Mission to Italy, Office of the Director, Subject Files (Central Files) 1948-57, b. 22, fold. 2 (Defense OSP program: contracts, production);

300 'Appunto sulla riunione del DPB nella quale il coordinatore della produzione ed i membri delle varie delegazioni si sono incontrati con MR Wilson', 2 May 1951, in ASC, CED, b. 49.1/2 (Commesse alle forze armate degli Stati Uniti), fold. Commesse. Promemoria del dottor Mattei-Targiani-Campilli, s.f. Relazioni varie sui lavori del DPB-NATO;

301 H.Chenery to V.Barnett, 'Use of Counterpart for Defense Production', 1 February 1952, in NARA, RG469, Mission to Italy, Office of the Director, Subject Files (Central Files) 1948-1957, b. 20, fold. 12 (Defense-Correspondence);

302 The Ambassador in Italy (Dunn) to the Secretary of State, 1 February 1951, in FRUS 1951, Vol. 4, Europe: Political and Economic Relations , part 1, p. 565;

303 idem, p. 565;

withdrawal of America's commitment to Italy[304]. On the contrary, American military assistance would be continued, but in such a way as to rationalize and speed up the process of rearmament. In this respect, the US Embassy in Rome reported to the Italian Chief of Defense Staff, Efisio Marras, that in the future any kind of military aid and financial assistance required to meet the imports connected with industrial mobilisation «will be based in the first instance on an analysis of and general agreement on the overall Italian military production program rather than on individual production projects as formerly»[305]

After a round of negotiations between the De Gasperi government and the US authorities based in Rome where the total figures of the program were discussed, as well as the number and type of production programs it was supposed to back through grants and financial support, the two countries reached an agreement on a production program worth up to $250 million of industrial investments over the following three years[306]. In order to get a better sense of the scale of the AMP and its impact on the recovery of the Italian military and on the reactivation of the defense industry, it is worth mentioning that even as the AMP program was being implemented, the US transferred discarded military end items and weapons to the Italian government to a value of $101 million[307]. The United States financial contribution to cover the import requirements of the Italian manufacturers involved in the program was $37 million in aid. It was to co-fund up to 137 new military production programs and to finance

---

304 The ECA had already underlined this point in 1950, when its officials assured the Italians that a perspective of closing down of the AMP «would not mean a complete stoppage on projects». H.Cleveland (ECA Acting Assistant Administrator for Program) to Dayton (Chief ECA Mission to Italy), 20 October 1950, in NARA, RG469, Mission to Italy, Office of the Director, Subject Files (Central Files) 1948-1957, b. 23, fold. 5(Economic conditions);

305 J.E.Jacobs (Special Assistant for MDAP Affairs) to E.Marras (Capo di Stato Maggiore della Difesa), in NARA, RG469, Mission to Italy, Office of the Director, Subject Files (Central Files), 1948-57, b. 20, fold. 8 (Defense AMP Projects); as regards raw materials see, H.Chenery to V.Barnett, 'Use of Counterpart for Defense Production', 1 February 1952, in NARA, RG469, Mission to Italy, Office of the Director, Subject Files (Central Files) 1948-57, b. 22, fold. 2 (Defense OSP program: contracts, Production); This policy guideline had come to the forefront of American foreign aid policy over the preceding two years. The US-sponsored committee chaired by Gordon Gray was a front runner in this respect. See A.Tarchiani to C.Sforza, 13 November 1950, classified, 'Rapporto Gordon Gray', in ACS, Ministero delle Finanze, Gab., Ufficio Paesi esteri, b. 32; on the Gordon Gray Report see also F.Fauri, *Il Piano Marshall in Italia*, pp. 248-249;

306 US Embassy in Italy-Rome Country Team, 'Italian Defense Production. Preliminary Study Prepared by Rome Country Team for Fiscal Year 1954 Congressional Presentation', 26 March 1953, in NARA, RG469, Mission to Italy, Office of the Director, Subjects Files (Central Files) 1948-1957, b. 23, fold. 1 (Defense-Production);

307 MSA Rome to MSA Washington, 'US Material Assistance to Italian AMP Projects', 13 February 1953; MSA Rome (C.Parker) to MSA Washington, 4 February 1953, both in NARA, RG469, Mission to Italy, Office of the Director, Subject Files (Central Files) 1948-57, b. 20, fold. 8 (Defense AMP Projects);

the import of raw materials, commodities and semi-manufactured goods to be used in the Italian plants, mostly by the shipbuilding industry[308]. The import of naval components was financed with up to $19.2 million aid, out of a total of $37 million[309]. If we break this down in more detail, the American assistance enabled the Italian shipyards to import a series of materials for specific production programs that had already been agreed upon by the two governments: predominantly, copper for a value of up to $3.9 million, iron and steel worth up to $1.8 million, and nickel ($1.8 million). On the other hand, this military assistance program offered financial support to import raw materials not directly linked to any production programs. Thus, the AMP met the import requirements of unrefined cotton ($2.6 million), crude carbon and oil ($1.8 million)[310].

Irrespective of its support to the shipyards, over its three-year lifetime, the AMP program fuelled the production of three-fifths of the military or civilian consumer goods required by the three Italian armies[311]. Above all, it stimulated a rise in production of components and semi-manufactured goods for the Italian navy and air forces, above all training aircrafts, jet engines, anti-torpedo nets, engine gunboats and anti-aircraft cartridges[312]. In addition to enabling the Italian firms to achieve a dramatic growth in production volume for the strengthening of the Italian armies, the program permitted Italian manufacturers to increase the production that supplied the defense systems of other NATO member countries. The AMP expanded the physical output of every Italian industrial sector involved in military production programs apart from combat vehicles[313].

---

308 C.Parker (MSA Rome) a MSA Washington, 'US Materials Assistance to Italian AMP Projects', 13 February 1953, in NARA, RG469, Mission to Italy, Office of the Director, Subjects Files (Central Files) 1948-1957, b. 20, fold. 8(Defense AMP Project);

309 MSA Rome to MSA Washington, 'US Material Assistance to Italian AMP Projects', 13 February 1953; MSA Rome (C.Parker) to MSA Washington, 4 February 1953, both in NARA, RG469, Mission to Italy, Office of the Director, Subject Files (Central Files) 1948-57, b. 20, fold. 8 (Defense AMP Projects);

310 for all of these figures I drew on D.McClelland-H.Chenery, 'Summary Statement on Status of Italian AMP Projects', 7 April 1952, in NARA, RG469, Mission to Italy, Office of the Director, Subject Files (Central Files) 1948-57, b. 20, fold. 8 (Defense AMP Projects);

311 D.H.McClelland-H.Chenery, 'Summary Statement on Status of Italian AMP Projects', 7 April 1952, in NARA,RG469, Mission to Italy, Office of the Director, Subject Files (Central Files) 1948-57, b. 20, fold. 8 (Defense AMP Projects);

312 Finmeccanica was the Italian financial holding that grouped together most of the mechanical and metalworking firms owned by the State shareholding IRI. The firms held by Finmeccanica produced up to 27 per cent of the total production volumes of the sector nation-wide. See 'Per una graduale ripresa della produzione di interesse militare', 20 July 1948, in ACS, ASIRI, Numerazione rossa (pratiche societarie), Finmeccanica, Varie, s3-f.200.9.2;

313 'Italian Defense Production. Preliminary Study', Prepared by Rome Country Team for Fiscal Year 1954 Congressional Presentation, 25 March 1953, in NARA, RG469, Mission to Italy, Office of the Director, Subject Files (Central Files) 1948-1957, b. 23, fold. 1 (Defense-Production), p. 23;

Notwithstanding these remarkable achievements, most of the AMP programs limited their support to the on-stream mechanical and aeronautical production lines to maximize productivity and to favour the reactivation of under-utilized plants and manpower. In fact, upon the conclusion of the program in 1952, the year when it overlapped with the beginning of the offshore procurement programs, the Italian economy was still not manufacturing new models of combat vehicles, and the Italian car and truck industry was committed to rehabilitation and repair programs which were mostly undertaken at the Fiat and Finmeccanica plants[314]. Both the structure of the Italian foreign trade policy, and the Pentagon's guidelines on the way Rome was to make use of the AMP funds, account for this almost complete lack of new production lines and the absence of any scheduling for the manufacture of new models. The De Gasperi Cabinet in no way assisted Italian firms to be geared for price competition. In fact, due to the American authority's choice of financing only the European production of military goods that featured a selling price no higher than 10 per cent of that by the United States manufacturers, the Italian Finance Minister Ezio Vanoni was slow in passing a series of decrees to introduce tax rebates and exemptions on the Italian export industries[315]. On the other hand, the United States had a firm commitment to assign repair and rehabilitation orders to the Italian military industrial complex. The main target underpinning this stance was to recover and to update scores of military trucks and vehicles hitherto used by the US troops stationing across Western Europe, before casting them off and transferring them to the German and Austrian land forces[316]. Furthermore, the implementation of the AMP suffered from delays due to the Italian government's decision to modify some production programs financed through the AMP. The De Gasperi government engaged in a continued review which led to as

---

314 Most of these industries were located on Southern Italy, the hub of which was in Naples where two leading firms, Navalmeccanica and Industria Meccanica Napoletana were operative. They worked on sub marines to provide repair and maintenance activities on behalf of the Italian Navy. See for reference Silurificio Italiano, 'Coordinamento dell'industria meccanica IRI del Mezzogiorno' in ACS, ASIRI, Numerazione rossa (pratiche societarie), Silurificio Italiano (poi Industria Meccanica Napoletana), 'Relazione di revisione e diverse', s3-f.silurificio it.21.12;

315 Confindustria, Appunto per il Segretario Generale, 'Commesse PAM-restituzione oneri fiscali settore autoveicoli', 22 April 1952; Confindustria, Appunto per il Segretario Generale, 'Commesse PAM-Restituzione oneri fiscali', 16 April 1952, both in ASC, CED, b. 49.1/2 (Commesse alle Forze Armate degli Stati Uniti), fold. Circolari. Appunti. Sgravi fiscali sulle commesse off-shore. Indagine sulla situazione delle commesse estere, s.f. Commesse off-shore. Trattamento fiscale;

316 L. Targiani, Pro-memoria, 'Perché ritardano le commesse e come si potrebbero accelerare', 7 January 1952, in ASC, CED, b. 49.1/2, fold. Commesse Promemoria del dottor Mattei-Targiani-Campilli, s.f. 1952. Promemoria Targiani-Campilli-commesse; Ambasciata d'Italia in Germania. Ufficio del consigliere commerciale a MCE-DGAC, 'Acquisti delle Forze Armate Aeronautiche americane in Europa', 13 February 1952, in ASC, CED, b. 49.1/2 (commesse alle forze armate degli Stati Uniti), fold. Circolari. Appunti.Sgravi fiscali sulle commesse off-shore. Indagine sulla situazione delle commesse estere, s.f. Indagine sulla situazione delle commesse estere;

many as half of the AMP programs already endorsed by the American authorities being changed. This Italian stance was determined both by military and strategic considerations and, even more revealingly from my point of view, by the quarrel between Rome and Washington over the extent of the burden that the Italian public finances were to bear for the financing of the project[317]. The Italian government maintained that the extra-budgetary appropriations necessary to enable the Ministry for Defense to purchase material and weapons scheduled for production under the AMP projects ‹‹need not be budgeted for›[318]. In other words, the government led by the Christian Democrats in Rome assumed that the United States would both finance the AMP projects and pay for the materials and end-items scheduled for transfer to the Italian armies.

This Italian position anticipated another issue at the centre of the negotiations that took place between 1949 and 1951 between the European governments and Washington on the sharing out of American financial aid at nation-level. The Italian stance was all the more important as it was a blueprint for a common European insistence on getting the US taxpayer involved not only in coping with the impact of the defense effort on the European balances of payments, but also in dealing with the strains on the balance-sheet liabilities that came with the extraordinary defense appropriations necessary for the national armies that were to purchase that material. The persisting public debt that dogged the public finances of most of the European countries meant that this request for assistance, coming not only from Italy but also from France and the United Kingdom, was to become an instrument of net aid for financing the public deficit of the European countries. From the negotiations on the AMP through the beginning of the Eisenhower Administration the Italian government drove to channel the US financial aid allotted under the military assistance programs to both ease the pressure on the balance-sheet and to cope with the strain of industrial mobilization on the Italian balance of payments. The Rome Cabinet regarded these two issues as complementary to each other[319].

---

317 L.Segreto, *Arar*, p. 179;

318 MSA Rome to MSA Paris, 4 February 1953, in NARA, RG469, Mission to Italy, Office of the Director, Subject Files (Central Files) 1948-57, b. 20, fold. 8 (Defense AMP Projects);

319 A.Tarchiani to Ministero degli Esteri, 'Aiuti americani, Anno finanziario 1953-54', Washington 8 May 1953, classified cable, in ASBI, Carte Caffè, pratt., n. 50, fold. 1; 'Economic Memorandum for NATO', n.d. (probably 1953), in NARA, RG469, Mission to Italy, Office of the Director, Subject Files (Central Files) 1948-57, b.21, fold. 7 (Defense: NATO Annual Review); Memorandum of conversation Dayton-Chenery-Pella-Ferrari Aggradi-Magistrati, 10 March 1952, in NARA, RG469, Mission to Italy, Office of the Director, Subject Files (Central Files) 1948-57 (1948-54), b. 47 fold. 4 (Programs-Aid Negotiations); Memorandum of conversation Pella-La Malfa-Luciolli (incaricato d'affari , ambasciata italiana a Washington)-Magistrati (direttore Generale Cooperazione Europea Affari Esteri)-Ortona (consigliere, Ambasciata Italiana a Washington)-Bruce (Acting Secretary of State)-Linder (European Division State Department)-Knight (Western Europe Division State Dept.)-Tesoro (Western Europe Division State Dept.), 'Italy's Economic Problems', 29 August 1952, in NARA, RG469, Office of the Director, Subject Files (Central Files) 1948-57, b. 36, fold. 6 (Italy Eco-

Right from the beginning of the MDAP, the US government and its ECA Mission to Rome were well aware of this Italian effort to combine monetary stability and foreign exchange balance[320]. As this position by the Rome Cabinet was the hallmark for a stance widely shared by the European member states of the Atlantic Alliance, throughout 1950 the Truman Administration worked hard to devise a viable solution to this disagreement with the aim of reaching a compromise with its European partners. Washington's efforts at economic diplomacy in both London and Paris were typical of the American approach. In London the Americans proposed that the British government use the entire amount of $350 million aid appropriated to the UK by the AMP program to cope with the impact of the rearmament programs on both the country's public finances and balance of payments. Richard Bissell, a high-ranking ECA official, maintained for example «that if Britain adopted an adequate rearmament program the interference with her economy would put her again in a position where there would be a serious foreign exchange deficit». Although Bissell remarked that this would-be scenario «was dependent wholly on a large-scale war mobilization in the United Kingdom»[321], it was all the more probable as the Additional Military Productions allotted to the UK, worth up to $114 million in 1950, were likely to be expanded during 1951 to meet the war mobilization.

This American inclination to direct AMP funds in an attempt to both finance monetary stability and to ease pressure on the balance of payments was furthered through the end items grant programs. In fact, the transfer of discarded weapons and military components from the American military forces to the British armies, which formed the bulk of the military assistance program to London during 1950, was intended to reduce liabilities of the balance of payments[322]. At the urging of Bissell this same approach was adopted towards France. The ECA formulated a platform for military assistance which was to cover the import of military supplies ranging from components to end-items worth up to $300 million. In so doing, Bissell

---

nomic Problems); on the Italian Treasury Minister Pella insistance in pursuing this perspective by circa 1953 see M.Magistrati (direttore Generale Cooperazione internazionale Ministero Affari Esteri), 'Appunto-verbale di conversazione De Gasperi-Pella-Pacciardi-La Malfa-Dulles-Stassen (direttore MSA)', 4 February 1953, secret, in ACS, ULM, b. 18, fold. 2;

320 'Italy. Defense requirements and capabilities', n.d. (probably 1950), in NARA, RG469, Mission to Italy, Office of the Director, Subject Files (Central Files) 1948-1957, b. 20, fold. 12 (Defense-Correspondence); The US Mission to Rome was well aware of this Italian approach from as early as the inception of the MDAP;

321 Nac Meeting n. 160, 2 August 1950, in NARA, RG56, Nac Papers, Nac Minutes, b. 2 (February 9, 1950-December 28, 1950);

322 T.Geiger, *Britain and the Economic Problem of the Cold War*, pp. 73–75; H.Leigh-Phippard, *US Military Aid to Britain: Interdependence and Dependence, 1949–56*, Macmillan, Basingstoke, 1995, pp.49–52;

stressed that this move was intended to support the French balance of payments and to prevent France from risking an imbalance in foreign exchange[323].

Washington chose a two-step approach to prevent the process of rearmament from creating debts for the European public finances. In the short term, before the start of the rearmament programs introduced under the umbrella of NATO, the American policy was a combination between a firm opposition to European requests and a more open-door approach to bearing the burden of the extra-budgetary defense appropriations that weighed on the European public finances. On the one hand, the military procurements of end-items paid for in US dollars were indexed as cost-free transfers[324], while on the other, there was the American tendency to draw on the ERP-type counterpart funds to relieve the pressure of rearmament on the government debts of the Europeans[325]. In the long run, the United States government placed the redressing of the European public finances at the centre of bilateral political relations with the European countries for as long as the rearmament effort placed them under pressure. Once more, the case of Italy would be typical. In fact, from the inception of the MDAP, Washington engaged in lengthy bilateral discussions with its Italian counterpart on this point. This early bargaining process on the problem of internal monetary stability and the impact of the defense effort on the Italian balance-sheet can be considered as a blueprint for the subsequent attempts to draft a platform of burden sharing that would lead to the multi-lateralisation of rearmament.

The United States move to launch the OSP programs and to set up a NATO common fund consistently built on this early effort to tackle both the issue of monetary stability and the impairing of the European balance of payments arising out of the defense efforts[326]. In fact, the

---

323 Nac Meeting n. 160, 2 August 1950, in NARA, RG56, Nac Papers, Nac Minutes, b. 2 (February 9, 1950-December 28, 1950);

324 As we have already explained, this ploy was to make the American taxpayer bear the financial burden of both the Italian firms' investments and import requirements, and the extraordinary defense spending necessary to permit the Italian Defense Ministry to purchase end item weapons, military components and the like, produced under the umbrella of the AMP programs;

325 Ministero della Difesa Aeronautica, Ufficio Bilancio a Direzione Generale dei Servizi, 14 April 1958, in ACS, Ministero dell'Aeronautica, Segretariato Generale, a. 1958, b. 136; Nac Meeting n. 160, 2 August1950, in NARA, RG56, Nac Papers, Nac Minutes, b. 2 (February 9, 1950-December 28, 1950); C.Spagnolo, *La stabilizzazione incompiuta*, p. 225; see also Oral History Interview with John W. Snyder, Washington DC, 13 August 1969, in HSTPL, Oral History interviews, pp. 1806-1807. This American guidance was also to influence both the defense efforts currently underway across Western Europe and the list of raw and critical material imports required to meet industrial mobilization;

326 The Ambassador in France (Bruce) to the Secretary of State, 28 July 1950, in *FRUS 1950*,Vol. 3, pp. 154-159; 'Summary of Telegrams by the State Department to unspecified recipients', 31 July 1950, in G.Olcese, Appunto per il sig. Governatore, 'Notizie di stampa sul progetto Van Zeeland per il finanziamento del riarmo', 29 September 1951, in ASBI, Carte Caffè, pratt., n. 48, fold. 1; il delegato della Banca d'Italia rappresentante dell'Ufficio Italiano Cambi per il Benelux to Menichella (Governatore Banca d'Italia), 'Piano belga tendente ad accelerare le commesse per armamenti', 20 July 1951,

burden sharing that came into effect within NATO over the following years was firstly to prevent the current account in the European balances of payments from downturns, and secondly
to strengthen monetary stability and to keep reserve assets steady across the European allies[327]. We will focus on this issue in the following chapter by examining the case of Italy to
further demonstrate how the Atlantic bloc countries used ERP-generated counterpart funds
that had accrued to the European public finances to cope with the defense effort. In addition,
the Italian case sheds light on the interplay between the US military assistance programs and
the changing dynamics in the trade relations of the West European member states of NATO.
The focus on this interplay will demonstrate how the Italian governments exploited the balance of payments issue throughout the early 1950s as a negotiating tool for its commitment to
rearm against the level of American military assistance.

3.4 The European economies and Korean War mobilization, straddling raw material requirements and import-export trade

In order to get a clear-cut picture of the AMP programs, it is necessary to direct our attention
briefly to the ways in which they influenced the supply of raw materials to the economies of
NATO during the period of Korean War mobilization and shortly afterwards. While the focus
of this study remains the situation in Italy, it is well worth reflecting on the situation of the
UK as regards raw and strategic material. Unlike most West European countries, the Korean
War-induced raw material price hike did not impair the balance in the British foreign exchange market. A detailed breakdown of the British import-export trade balance that takes
into consideration both the current account and the indirect quotations in the British balance
of payments at the time, clearly brings to light this distinction[328]. During the early period of

---

idem, n. 50, fold. 1; The United Stat es Deputy Representative on the North Atlantic Council
(Spofford) to the Secretary of State, 4 January 1951, in *FRUS 1951*, Vol. 3, *European Security and the
German Question*, pp. 10-12; B.Harvey to V.Barnett (MSA Mission to Italy), Memorandum, 'Brief
Summary of the Green Book', 16 Septermber 1952, in NARA, RG469, Mission to Italy, Office of the
Director, Subject Files (Central Files) 1948-1957, b. 21, fold. 7 (Defense: NATO Annual Review);
327 MSA Rome, 'Italy's Capacity to Support its Present and Possible Expanded Defense Program in
Fiscal Year 1954', n.d. (but 1952), in NARA, RG56, OASIA, b. 20, fold. NATO/4/25 Economic Ca-
pabilities for Rearmament;
328 In striking contrast with my own interpretation , the economic analysis staff working at the US
Embassy in Rome took for granted that a rise in output capacity was likely to trigger a worsening
balance of payments. On this see Military Assistance Advisory Committee, Minutes of Meetings,
'MSA Projections of Country Defense Expenditures and Country Aid, for Use in the Fiscal Year 1953
Presentation', 16 February 1952, in DDRS;

the Korean War mobilization, the British balance of payments remained steady as the process of rearmament stimulated a rise in the export of raw and strategic materials from the British Pound market areas to the member countries of the European Payments Union[329]. However, this early stage of improvement in the assets of the balance of payments was later reversed during the course of the Korean War and after its conclusion. In fact, the full commitment of the British manufacturing system to economic mobilization and war productions triggered a rise in the import of consumer goods and durables to supply British civilian demand. The full employment and full scale industrial mobilization that had been engendered in Britain as a result of the defense effort meant that industrial reconversion from military to civilian production had not come about. Following the end of the conflict in Far-East Asia, this dynamic was exacerbated and in the 1950s led to British dependence on imports of consumer and civilian goods from foreign markets, especially from Germany[330]. This increasing dependence on foreign imports, combined with the rather limited impact of the war mobilization on the British balance of payments which had protected the internal British market from skyrocketing inflation rates, accounts for the strong demand for supplies for the British civilian industries. As the post war Anglo-American vetoes and punitive peace settlement had imposed severe restraints on German manufacture of armaments and led German industries to specialize in the production and supply of consumer goods, the Federal Republic of Germany was ideally placed to satisfy the increased demands of the British civilian market[331].

In Italy, according to the analysis of the US Country Team operating in the Embassy in Rome, the overall situation of the economy during the two years of the Korean War was that of a country which was suffering from a net rise in unemployment and featuring, on the whole, a substantial price stability paired with a slight downward trend in wholesale prices[332]. Given this economic outlook, the US Embassy in Italy and the US Treasury representatives in Rome argued that, though the import of raw and strategic material might impact on the terms of trade and domestic prices, the process of rearmament was unlikely either to trigger a rise in domestic retail prices or to rock the internal monetary stability. On the basis of this analysis, the American authorities in Rome fiercely criticised the dominant guidelines for Italian eco-

---

329 This came about notwithstanding tight controls on the export of raw material, first and foremost steel, deemed crucial to accomplish the process of post war economic reconstruction. See R.Ranieri, *Inside or Outside the magic cirle? The Italian and the British steel industries face to face with the Schuman Plan and the European Coal Iron and Steel Community*, in AA.VV, *The Frontier of National Sovereignty. History and Theory 1945-1992*, Routledge, London and New York, 1993, pp. 132-33;

330 H.Zimmermann, *Money and Security. Troops, Monetary Policy, and West Germany's Relations with the United States and Britain, 1950-1971*, Cambridge University Press, Cambridge, 2002, pp. 61-62;

331 see the insights by V.De Grazia, *Irresistible Empire*;

332 'US Position in OEEC/NATO economic review', in NARA, RG469, Mission to Italy, Office of the Director, Subject Files (Central Files) 1948-57, b. 21, fold. 7 (Defense: NATO Annual Review), p. 7;

nomic policy, widely known as the Linea Pella-Menichella. This policy, named after Italy's Treasury Minister, Pella, and the Governor of the Italian Central Bank, Menichella, had determined the Italian government's monetary and investment policies from as far back as the post war period of monetary stabilization. According to this policy the reconstitution of the country's reserves assets was the first priority, to be followed by the launch of nation-wide investments aimed at completing the process of industrial reconstruction and furthering economic growth. In American eyes, this tight monetarist economic policy attempted to balance the budget and to curb retail prices and inflation rates at the expense of internal economic recovery[333]. In striking contrast with such an economic policy platform, the Truman Administration representatives in Rome maintained that a firm Italian commitment to re-launch nation-wide civilian investments was a much needed measure to both meet the expansion in the internal demand for consumer goods triggered by the industrial mobilization, and to avoid price rises generated by excess demand[334]. According to the Americans the industrial mobilization determined by the Korean War had led to pressure on the stability of the Italian Lira and the national accounts, whereas a set of much-wanted investments would stabilize prices and secure a continued upward economic trend to the country[335].

As regards the rearmament-related impact on Italy's foreign trade balance, the US Mission to Italy argued that the Italian balance of payments had suffered from overall losses in line with those of the European allies that were determined by the initial mobilization for the Korean War but that thereafter, in the course of the conflict, the Italian balance of payments had showed signs of strengthening. A steady rise in Italian exports, and the credit balance accrued

---

333 Office of the United States Special Representative in Europe(SRE)-Rome Mission: Finance and Trade Division, 'Italy. Counterpart Policies and Financial Stability', 16 June 1950, in NARA, RG56, OASIA, b. 63, fold. Italy-MSA-FOA-Counterpart policies;

334 E.Bunker (US Embassy Rome) to G.Perkins (Assistant Secretary of State for European Affairs), 15 August 1952, in NARA, RG469, Mission to Italy, Office of the Director, Subject Files (Central Files) 1948-57, (1948-1954), b. 2, fold. 2 (Aid Negotiations-papers);. This economic policy guideline found in the US Embassy in Rome its most active advocates, and stemmed from a keynesian multiplier oriented approach to the economics of defense and its impact on peacetime economies;

335 'Italy's Capacity to Support its Present and Possible Expanded Defense Program in Fiscal Year 1954', n.d. (probably 1953), in NARA, RG56, OASIA, b. 20, fold. NATO/4/25 Economic Capabilities for Rearmament; these contrasting views revolved around a much discussed debate between the Americans on the one hand , and the Italians on the other, on the so-called Country Study on Italy. On this lengthy bilateral quarrel see C.Spagnolo, *La polemica sul «Country Study», il fondo lire e la dimensione internazionale del Piano Marshall*, in "Studi Storici", n. 1, 1996, pp. 93-144; id., *La stabilizzazione incompiuta*, chapter 5; C.Esposito, *America's Feeble Weapon: Funding the Marshall Plan in France and Italy 1948-1950*, Greenwood Press, Westport 1994. As regards the American pressures on the Italian government to make it undertake a set of wide-ranging investment policies long after 1949 see M.Magistrati to Ministero del Tesoro, Gab., 'Atteggiamento Americano verso l'Italia nei confronti della divisione degli aiuti ERP', settembre 1949,highly classified, in ASBI, Carte Caffè, pratt., n. 50, fold. 1; Tarchiani to Banca d'Italia, 'Piano Bissel', 24 January1950, secret, *idem*;

through the off shore procurement contracts, as well as the expenses of the American troops stationing across the Peninsula, all contributed to this trend [336].

With respect to the first point, the American view aroused much criticism from the Italian economic technocracies and policymakers. Indeed, the Italian reaction to the upward trend in wholesale prices, which occurred in summer 1950, is a clear case in point. At that time both Pella and Menichella, who were reluctant to consider any kind of expansionary measure, excluded a possible currency revaluation for two reasons. In their view, a revaluation of the Italian Lira risked damaging the performance of Italian exports on foreign markets, particularly that of Italy's farmers. On the other hand, this measure would clash strongly with the long-term and structural dependence of the Italian economy on international trade and on world markets [337]. Notwithstanding this firm Italian stance, the Treasury minister and the Governor of the Central Bank of Italy opted to alter the discount rate by 1 per cent to enable Italian manufacturers to import raw and strategic materials at reasonable prices [338]. Overall, from October 1951 to September 1952 these measures triggered a rise in currency in circulation by some 133 billion Italian Lira [339].

One year after this change in the discount rate, Menichella again emphasized the need to find a balance between the inflation rate and the broad money supply available to Italian manufacturers and import-industries for working on the military procurements ordered by the Atlantic Alliance. When addressing a broader audience through the 1951 year-end report to the plenary executive board of the Italian Central Bank, he supported his arguments by venturing a neat comparison of the changing trends and balances between wholesale prices and means of payment in a wide range of industrialized economies, looking back over the whole decade of

---

336 'US Position in OEEC/NATO economic review', in NARA, RG469, Mission to Italy, Office of the Director, Subject Files (Central Files) 1948-57, b. 21, fold. 7 (Defense: NATO Annual Review), p. 10;

337 D.Menichella, *Considerazioni finali all'assemblea della Banca d'Italia 1951*, 31 May 1952, in F.Cotula, C.O.Gelsomino, A.Gigliobianco (eds), Donato Menichella. *Stabilità e sviluppo dell'economia italiana 1946-60*. Vol. 2, *Considerazioni finali all'Assemblea della Banca d'Italia*, Laterza, Roma and Bari, 1997, p. 116;

338 In Italy the literature of economic history has already insisted on this point. See the insights by L.Conte, *L'azione della Banca d'Italia (1948-1993)*, p. 664, and B.Bottiglieri, *La politica economica dell'Italia centrista 1948-1958*, Edizioni di Comunità, Milano, 1984, p. 87;

339 'Riunione del 18 novembre 1952 in occasione della visita del Ministro Sawyer del Dipartimento del Commercio americano. Dichiarazioni del Governatore della Banca d'Italia', novembre 1952, in ASBI, Fondo Studi, pratt., n. 338, fold. 11. In his 1950 annual report to the General assembly of the Central Bank of Italy, Governor Menichella estimated that the overall money supply to the Italian economy, including agriculture, public services, manufacturing and the trade sector, was 77 times higher than the pre-war level. See D.Menichella, *Considerazioni finali all'assemblea della Banca d'Italia 1950*, 31 May 1951, in F.Cotula, C.O.Gelsomino, A.Gigliobianco (eds), *Donato Menichella*, p. 87;

the 1940s. In his comparison he included the United States, Japan, France, the UK, Switzerland, Belgium and the recently-born Federal Republic of Germany, and concluded that Italy stood out as the country that had fared best over this period thanks to its economic policies. In Italy the means of payment had risen by 30 per cent against a 15 per cent rise in wholesale prices[340]. This asymmetry highlighted the impact that a shift in the discount rate, made to supply an economy geared to war mobilization, had had on such a wide range of industrialized economies. Furthermore, this discussion is significant as it sheds light on a much-debated historical interpretation of the Italian economic policy at that time. The historical literature that examined the economic and political history of Italy throughout the first post war decade assumed Alan Milward's historical concept of neo-mercantilism to be eye-opening and germane to the Italian experience during that period[341]. In his scholarly historical and theoretical works Milward uses the term neo-mercantilism to define a model of economic and industrial policy that merged trade liberalisation with quantitative restrictions and custom duties on imports in order to establish a path of economic growth based on two pillars. In Milward's defi-

---

340 D.Menichella, *Considerazioni finali all'assemblea della Banca d'Italia 1951*, p. 115; on this stance by Menichella see also *Discorso all'Assemblea dell'Associazione Bancaria Italiana*, Roma, 28 novembre 1950, in "Bancaria", n. 12, 1950, pp. 1177-82, now published in F.Cotula, C.O.Gelsomino, A.Gigliobianco (eds), *Donato Menichella. Stabilità e sviluppo dell'economia italiana 1946-60*, Vol. 1, particularly pp. 326-327;

341 for a sample of this historical interpretation see R.Petri, *Dalla ricostruzione al miracolo economico*, in G.Sabbatucci, V.Vidotto, *Storia d'Italia*, pp. 314 ff.; more recently this author placed this thesis against the backdrop of the Italian economic policymaking from the early 1930s and thereafter. See id., *Storia economica d'Italia. Dalla grande guerra al miracolo economico 1918-1963*, Il Mulino, Bologna, 2002; id., *Von der Autarkie zum Wirtschaftswunder. Wirtschaftspolitik und industrieller Wandel in Italien 1935-1963*, Niemeyer, Tubingen, 2001;V.Zamagni, *Dalla periferia al centro. La seconda rinascita economica dell'Italia 1861-1981*, Il Mulino, Bologna, 1990; as regards the role of the banking system within the Italian model of neo-mercantilism see S.Battilossi, *L'Italia nel sistema economico internazionale*, particularly pp. 327-342, and conclusions; even the historical literature that interprets the Italian political-economic governance from reconstruction to the late 1950s economic take-off as an extraordinary compromise between statalism and liberism, stressing the role of the Italian state shareholding system in stimulating economic growth, generally agrees with the neomercantilist approach. An exemplary case of this perspective is in F.Barca, *Compromesso senza riforme nel capitalismo italiano*, in id., *Storia del capitalismo italiano dal dopoguerra ad oggi*, Donzelli, Roma 1997; for a critical reappraisal of the historical concept of neo-mercantilism see R.Gualtieri, *Piano Marshall, commercio estero e sviluppo in Italia: alle origini dell'europeismo centrista*, in "Studi Storici", n. 3 (1998), pp. 853-895, and C.Spagnolo, *La stabilizzazione incompiuta*, chapter 4; an attempt to extend and check to what extent the concept of neo-mercantilism was a leading economic policy guidance under the De Gasperi Cabinets appears in R.Gualtieri, *La politica economica del centrismo e il quadro internazionale*, pp. 91-117. On the long-standing historical and theoretical accomplishment of Alan Milward see now for reference F.Guirao, F.Lynch, S.Ramirez Perez (eds), *Alan S. Milward and a Century of European Change*, Routledge, New York, 2012;

nition, neo-mercantilism is a model of economic policy that is based on high rates of labor productivity and real wages on the one hand, and on capital intensive updating of industrial plants and technology on the other[342]. It is worth noting that in Italy the De Gasperi governments protected most of the manufacturing sectors that were working on military orders, and highly dependent on the import of raw material, from trade liberalizations and from the removal of custom duties and quantitative restrictions. In this respect the car and motor industry, dominated by the Fiat group that was headquartered in the city of Turin, was a case in point. While Italy adopted a full-scale set of trade liberalizations in the early 1950s, the car and motor manufacturing sector continued to be protected with custom duties and tariff protection on foreign products[343]. In fact, from the beginning of the 1950s the case of the Italian car industry, which was both strongly protected from foreign markets and structurally dependent on foreign supply of raw material, anticipated a decade-long debate on the most appropriate means of payment for the imports of raw materials, which were rising in proportion to the expansion in domestic aggregate demand and the development of a mass consumer market in Italy. This issue highlights the interplay between the Italian economy's requirement for raw materials and Italy's trade policy which had its origins in the Italian post war industrial policy. As early as 1945 the Italian economic and business elites had decided to set up a nationwide steel industry and stake Italy's future on reviving and expanding the petrochemical sector, and then investing further to establish the production of top-quality steel components and spare parts for military and civilian manufacturing industries, determining a growth in demand for raw materials and derivatives that could never be met internally[344]. This Italian trade and industrial policy, geared to neo-mercantilism, should be borne in mind when considering how the Italian elites conducted negotiations on the provision of financial assistance through military assistance, from the first MDAP to the beginning of the off-shore procurement programs. Italy's attempts to trade off its defense effort and commitment to rearm against the massive inflow of dollars engendered by OSP productions worked by the Italian firms, and the dollar aid for financing the defense industry's import of required raw materials, should be considered in this context. The same is true for De Gasperi Cabinet's move to convert the excess credit that the Italian money market held against its EPU partner currency areas into hard currency. From an Italian point of view, all these measures were to smooth and

---

342 A.Milward, *The European Rescue of the Nation State*, Routledge, London and New York, 1992, p. 130;

343 V.Zamagni, *Betting on the Future. The Reconstruction of Italian Industry 1946-1952*, in J.Becker, F.Knipping (eds), *Power in Europe? Great Britain, France, Italy and Germany in a Post-war World, 1945-50*, W.de Gruyter, Berlin and New York, 1986; F.Fauri, *L'Italia e l'integrazione economica europea 1947-2000*, Il Mulino, Bologna, 2001, p. 61;

344 R.Ranieri, *L'approvvigionamento di materie prime nella ricostruzione italiana*, in L.Tosi (ed.), *Politica ed economia nelle relazioni internazionali dell'Italia del secondo dopoguerra*, Edizioni Studium, Roma, 2002, pp 216-218;

ease the impact of rearmament on the Italian balance of payments and this determined the country's stance at the bilateral and multilateral negotiations on the military assistance programs. These monetary and foreign trade policies shaped Italian foreign economic policy along the lines of neo-mercantilism. This approach meant that the Italian manufacturing system would be tightly bound to the dollar markets and the import-export trade between the Italian Lira and the US dollar would remain of the utmost importance.

3.5 Redressing the balance of foreign exchange equilibrium and internal monetary stability: the Italian reactions to the economic impacts of war mobilization in a comparative perspective

In the previous paragraphs I argued my case for the uneven impact that the import of raw materials, triggered by the process of rearmament, had on each economy of the Atlantic Alliance involved in the defense effort. In particular, the inflow of raw materials put the equilibrium in the European nations' balance of payments under pressure. The dollar currency market itself suffered from this escalation and price hike in the international trade of raw and strategic materials: from the first semester of 1950 to the first quarter of 1951 the average yearly imports of the United States rose from $7.5 billion to $12 billion[345]. The acceleration in the international trade of raw and strategic material thus had a widespread and deep impact on the balance of trade and the balance of payments of the NATO's member countries that contributed to the industrial mobilization induced by the Korean War, and the leapfrogging in prices also had another truly remarkable effect. In fact, it caused a rapid deterioration in the monetary stability of the West European countries and brought them to the verge of meltdown. The situation of the British economy clearly illustrates this trend as the upward trend in the wholesale prices of raw materials, which from December 1949 to June 1951 pushed up the average price of imports by 60 per cent[346], hit both the balance of payments and the Consumer Price Index. This twofold impact of the war mobilization on the British currency area is all the more noteworthy as it took place in a country where the process of rearmament had to some extent improved the assets in the indirect quotations of the current account of the balance of payments, while the early conclusion of the Marshall Plan in the United Kingdom reduced the economy's net imports and its dependence on foreign suppliers[347]. In the United States the

345 A.Tarchiani to MAE-DGAE, 'Bilancia dei pagamenti degli Stati Uniti', 20 September 1951, in ACS, PCM, CIR, b. 60;

346 P.Burnham, *The Political Economy of Postwar Reconstruction*, MacMillan, London, 1990, p. 171;

347 T.Geiger, *Britain and the Economic Problem of the Cold War*, pp. 97 ff.; P.G.Boyle, *Britain, America and the Transition from Economic to Military Assistance, 1948–51*, in "Journal of Contemporary History", n.3 (1987), pp. 533–35;

economy was running at full production and utilisation of resources. In the context of this maximum rate of growth in physical output, several civilian production lines were reconverted to war productions to satisfy the rise in demand for military goods and services. From the beginning of summer 1950 up to March 1951 the combination of this industrial reconversion with the on-going upward trend in raw material prices on world markets, produced a rise of 17 per cent in wholesale prices[348]. The worldwide rise in demand for raw materials and the rise in output in Western Europe boosted the inflationary trend in the United States. However, this trend had started prior to 1950 in the wake of two overlapping economic dynamics. On the one hand, before the outbreak of the conflict in Far East Asia the American business community had chosen to stockpile raw and strategic material nationwide in anticipation of rearmament. On the other hand, prior to the conflict a widespread speculative demand for semi-manufactured goods had hit the Western economies and contributed to boosting the price of strategic materials on world markets[349]. In the light of this pressing need to curb prices and keep the international supply and trade of raw materials under the control of the Western bloc economies, the United States, France and the United Kingdom established the International Materials conference, an economic organisation gathering together some 28 countries with the aim of further coordinating the distribution and exchange of strategic materials among the economies of the Atlantic Alliance[350].

If we investigate the twofold impact of the rise in raw material prices on the foreign exchange equilibrium and the internal monetary stability of the Western bloc economies through a comparison among differing European economies, it is quite clear just how divergent this impact was from country to country. In fact, if following consideration of the British case we move on to that of Italy, the picture would appear very different and the comparison quite extreme. The rise in prices on the international markets made the Italian economy, a long standing purchaser of raw materials on world markets; suffer a much greater deterioration in its domestic monetary stability than in its balance of payments. From 1947 to 1950 the Italian balance of payments against the US dollar showed a continual recovery. In fact, over this

---

348 D.Menichella, *Considerazioni finali all'Assemblea della Banca d'Italia 1951*, Roma, 31/5/1952, in Donato Menichella. *Stabilità e sviluppo dell'economia italiana 1946-1960*, Vol. 2. *Considerazioni finali all'assemblea della Banca d'Italia*, p. 118; R.L.Reierson, *Le banche commerciali e la inflazione post-bellica negli Stati Uniti*, in "Bancaria", n. 6,(1952), p. 555; G.Tullio, *Monete ed economie*, p. 274;

349 J.C.R.Dow, *The Management of the British Economy 1945-1960*, Cambridge University Press, Cambridge, 1964, p. 55;

350 S.Nocentini, *Building the Network: Raw Materials Shortages and the Western Bloc at the Beginning of the Cold War (1948-1951)*, paper presented at the Business History Conference Annual Meeting, June 17-19, 2004, Le Creusot, France 2004 (www.thebhc.org/annmeet/abstracts04.html); G.Tullio, *Monete ed economie*, p. 274;

three year period, its deficit fell from $618 million to $212 million[351]. Both a steady decline in the Italian import of agricultural products, and the twin foreign trade policy that Italy implemented from 1947 onward through parallel domestic currency devaluation and a revaluation of the Italian Lira on the foreign exchange rate, permitted an improvement of the Italian equilibrium on the foreign exchange market. Italy pursued this foreign trade policy at a time when bilateral exchanges set the stage for the reorganisation of international trade among the Western economies[352]. Contrary to what was expected, and despite a rise in the import of raw materials and fuel, during the crucial months of the Korean War the Italian currency continued to reduce its imbalances on the foreign exchange market. Both the rise in Italian exports, which from 1949 through 1951 edged up from $110 million to $190 million a year[353], and the inflow from the United States of some $143.5 million as part of the first two MDAP, triggered this steady improvement in the Italian balance of payments[354]. This combined rise in the assets of the Italian balance of payments' current accounts and the redressing of the balance in the indirect quotations enabled by the US financial assistance from the military assistance programs brought the deficit in the Italian balance of payments down to $ 88.5 million[355]. The dynamics of the Italian monetary standing on the foreign exchange markets at the time of the mobilization for the Korean War and the consequent process of rearmament, offers a vantage point from which to get a neat understanding of the interlocking relationships between rearmament, the changing equilibrium in the Italian balance of payments and its divergence from the US dollar and the most important European currencies, namely the French Franc and the British Pound. In this respect it is worthwhile to note how even as the Italian external monetary equilibrium against the US dollar recovered, the assets of the Lira against the other European currencies deteriorated. This changing standing of Italy's currency on the foreign exchange mar-

---

351 'Riunioni del CIR dei giorni 28 e 29 luglio 1952', Meeting held on July, classified, in NARA, RG 469, Mission to Italy, Office of the Director, Subject Files (Central Files), 1948-1957 (1948-54), b. 2, fold. 1 (Aid Negotiations);

352 R.Gualtieri, *La politica economica del centrismo e il quadro internazionale*, p. 97; J.C.Martinez Oliva, M.L.Stefani, *Dal Piano Marshall all'Unione europea dei pagamenti. Alle origini dell'integrazione economica europea*, in F.Cotula (ed.), *Stabilità e sviluppo negli anni Cinquanta*, Vol. 1, *L'Italia nel contesto internazionale*, Laterza, Roma-Bari 2000, p. 186;

353 'US position in OEEC/NATO economic review', in NARA, RG469, Mission to Italy, Office of the Director, Subject Files (Central Files) 1948-1957, b. 21, fold. 7(NATO Annual Review);

354 Out of that total amount of $143.5 million, as many as $64 million were put to cover the import of raw materials' requirements for military productions. H.B.Chenery to J.Dunn, 'Status of Raw Materials Procurement for Military Production', 5 April 1951, in NARA, RG469, Mission to Italy, Office of the Director, Subject Files (Central Files) 1948-1957, b. 22, fold. 2 (Defense, OSP program: contracts, Production);

355 'Appunto: Situazione valutaria e dei pagamenti italiani al 30.6.1952', in NARA, RG469, Mission to Italy, Office of the Director, Subject Files (Central Files) 1948-1957 (1948-54), b. 2 fold. 1 (Aid Negotiations);

kets was in line with the Italian economic policymakers' aim to erect a dual foreign trade and monetary policy to cut off the import-export trade with the US dollar and expand that with the leading French and British currency areas.

The issue of domestic monetary stability and reserve assets is a distinctive feature of the Italian economic situation when a comparative analysis is made of the effects on the European economies determined by the mobilization for the Korean War. When compared with the rather limited impact that the rise in raw material prices had on the balance of payments in other European countries, notably the British economy, in Italy this rise hit both domestic prices and reserve assets much more significantly. To support this line of argument and to shed light on the close relationship between raw material prices and domestic inflation, it is worth following the trends in wholesale prices from the beginning of rearmament and throughout the period of war mobilization. Following a remarkable process of stabilization during the implementation of the ERP in Italy from 1948 through 1950, with the outbreak of war in Korea wholesale prices rose by 2 per cent and peaked in February 1951, and then dropped slightly and stabilized further soon thereafter. In late 1950 this tendency triggered a rise in the cost of living that was 11 per cent higher than its growth rate at the time of the outbreak of the conflict[356]. What ensued from this considerable impact of raw and strategic material prices on the Italian economy was a significant redress in the bilateral economic negotiations that Washington and Rome engaged upon to fix the level and scope of American financial assistance to Italy. In particular, the upward trends in the Consumer Price Index and the rise in the cost of living weakened the American stance that aimed to exploit the ERP and the MDAP financial allotments to stimulate internal industrial investments and to spark an expansionary economic policy. On the contrary, the Italian monetary authorities and Christian Democrat political circles took advantage of these economic trends to criticize the United States and to make their case for implementing belt-tightening monetary policies. The showcase for this quarrel was the debate on the way the so-called counterpart funds accrued to the Italian Treasury through American financial aids channelled as part of either the ERP or the MDAP.

On the one hand, the United States' authorities were tireless in repeating to the Rome Cabinet that even in summer 1951, and hence well after the outbreak of the conflict in Far East Asia, «financial stability had persisted in Italy and the inflationary pressures created by deficit

---

356 'Memorandum: Italy's Current Economic Position and Prospects', 17 November 1952, in NARA, RG469, Mission to Italy, Office of the Director, Subject Files (Central Files) 1948-1957, b. 36, fold. 6 (Italy Economic Problems); 'US Position in OEEC/NATO Economic Review', in NARA, RG469, Mission to Italy, Office of the Director, Subject Files (Central Files) 1948-1957, b. 21, fold. 7 (Defense: NATO Annual Review); MSA, Mission to Italy, 'Objectives of US Aid to Italy in 1952/53', in NARA, RG469, Mission to Italy, Office of the Director, Subject Files (Central Files) 1948-1957, (1948-1954), b. 2, fold. 1 (Aid Negotiations), Annex A;

spending due to defense are weak and incipient»[357]. After the Truman Administration's Treasury representative in Italy stepped down from his office in 1954, the new American Embassy in Rome perpetuated this stance. The economic envoys to Italy of the new Eisenhower Administration remarked on how «although the outbreak of war in Korea gave rise to fresh inflationary pressures, the situation was successfully contained»[358].

On the other hand, the Italian elites emphasized a different way of understanding the interplay between the dynamics of raw material prices on world markets and domestic inflation in Italy. Already in 1948 the State-owned steel holding Finsider was showing signs of concern about the scarcity of raw materials which hampered Italy's post war reconstruction as this dependence on foreign suppliers limited the competitiveness of the country's steel producers[359]. Furthermore, during the period of mobilization linked to the Korean War they expressed even greater concern and argued the case for putting an end to the Italian economy's dependence on international markets[360]. In 1950, during talks concerning Italy's membership of the European Coal and Steel Community, Finsider pleaded for cost free access to raw material on the international markets, and the removal of price discrimination on the supply side of the international trade chain[361].

This concern of Finsider was widely shared by the Italian mechanical and metalworking industries working on steel products[362] and, as they rightly argued, the high price of much needed raw materials such as fossil coal, coal and coal scraps, which were predominantly purchased on foreign markets, hit the Italian steel industry's market penetration abroad[363].

---

357 Brown to Watson, 'comments on Letter n. 38 from Rome Proposing Budgetary Counterpart Use in Italy', 8 June 1951, in NARA, RG56, OASIA, b. 63, fold. Italy-MSA-FOA-Counterpart policies;

358 American Embassy, Rome-US Operations Mission to Italy, 'Italy. Economic Summary', October 1954, in NARA, RG59, Central Files 1955-59, b. 4809, 865.00/8-2255, p. 9;

359 O.Sinigaglia, 'Finsider. Promemoria sulla siderurgia italiana', January 1948, in ACS, ASIRI, numerazione nera, Siderurgia, Siderurgia-Siac-Finsider, fold. II, s2.6-f.2.2-p34';

360 Rossi Longhi, Appunto per il delegato italiano al Defense Production Board, 'Materie prime per i programmi di riarmo', 4 May 1951, in ASC, CED, b. 49.1/2 (Commesse alle Forze armate degli Stati Uniti), fold. Commesse. Promemoria del dottor Mattei-Targiani-Campilli, s.f. Relazioni varie sui lavori del DPB-NATO;

361 R.Ranieri, L'approvvigionamento di materie prime nella ricostruzione italiana, p. 212;

362 'Relazione sulla produzione di materie prime (lamiere inossidabili, lamiere in acciaio magnetico, lamiere e nastri di alluminio, silicio metallico e ferro-leghe), prodotti dell'industria meccanica, prodotti dell'industria elettrotecnica', n.d. (but 1948), in ACS, ASIRI, numerazione rossa (pratiche societarie), Programmi post bellici delle aziende meccaniche e relazioni varie (1943-1945). Relazioni;

363 V.Barnett (Deputy Chief, MSA Mission to Italy)-S.L.Mellon (First Secretary of Embassy) to the Department of State, 25 August 1952, 'Benton Amendment Aspects of Defense Production', in NARA, RG469, Office of the Deputy Director for Operations (1953-1961), Office of European Operations (1953-1955), Italy Division, Decimal File 1948-1954, b. 7 fold. Italy 5.3 (Government Regulations and Participation in Business/Cartels), p. 6;

These early and widespread concerns about the repercussions of war material prices and Italy's dependence on foreign supply were widely mirrored in the way the Italians struggled to channel the financial assistance granted to the Rome government through the ERP from shortly after the launch of the Marshall Plan in 1947. The Italian elites, led by the Treasury Ministry, were firm in their aim to invest a large part of American funds to finance the import of raw and strategic material, and hence leaving only a modest amount of Marshall Plan funds to fund the import of machinery and machine tools[364]. The Italian policy of using ERP and MDAP funds in such a way emerges clearly from the figures and data that the Italian Treasury, Pella, brought before the new Republican US Secretary of State, John Foster Dulles, and Harold Stassen, the new head of the Foreign Operations Administration, the US government agency that took over the administration and distribution of economic and military assistance to the European partners from the MSA. Pella's statistical sources showed that from the very beginning of the Marshall Plan through 1953 his government used as much as 78 per cent of the entire amount of dollar inflow from the US and NATO to finance the import of raw materials and grains[365]. This Italian policy confirmed a widely-shared and longstanding interest in the issue of raw and strategic material in the framework of the country's economic recovery

---

364 P.P.D'Attorre, *Aspetti dell'attuazione del Piano Marshall in Italia*, in E.Aga Rossi (ed.), *Il Piano Marshall e l'Europa*, Istituto della Enciclopedia italiana, Roma, 1983, p. 167; see also L.Sturzo to several Members of Parliament, 18 November 1949, in *Carteggio Sturzo-Scelba 1923-1956*, Istituto Luigi Sturzo, Roma 1994, pp. 326-327. One can get a better grip on this widely-shared Italian guidelines through a full command over the functioning of counterpart funds accrued to the Italian Treasury under the Marshall Plan. The Counterpart funds were the earnings resulting from the distribution on the Italian market of machine tools, machinery and instrumental goods imported through the ERP. The largest amount of those earnings, deposited on a special bank account held by the Italian Ministry for Treasury, were to finance domestic investments and their respective import requirements. This mechanism required that the Italian government anticipated on another bank account those earnings to grant the investments that they were planned to fund. That imposed to import material and goods that were much required in the Italian economy to prevent that unsold goods forced the Italian central bank to carry on expansionary measures to finance the scheduled platform of domestic investments. As in the context of a post war industrial reconstruction and the further Korean War related industrial mobilization demand for raw materials exceeded that for machinery and machine tools, and the price issue for raw and strategic material was the far pressing problem, the Italian government showed no sign of hesitation in its pursuit to channel the dollar aids provide under the ERP financial assistance programs to sustain the import of raw and strategic materials. The Italian historiography has dealt with the issue of counterpart funds and their domestic budgetary implication extensively. See, for example, R.Gualtieri, *La politica economica del centrismo e il quadro internazionale*, pp. 113-114, footnote 19; id., *L'Italia dal 1943 al 1992*, pp. 102-103; C.Spagnolo, *La stabilizzazione incompiuta*, pp. 139-142; id., *La polemica sul «Country Study», il fondo lire e la dimensione internazionale del Piano Marshall*, pp. 115-121; M.Del Pero, *Containing Containment: Rethinking Italy's Experience during the Cold War*, in "Journal of Modern Italian Studies", Vol. 8, n. 4 (2003), pp. 532-555;
365 M.Magistrati, 'Appunto', 4 February 1953, secret, in ACS, ULM, b. 18, fold. 1;

from its war-wrecked condition. All of the high-ranking economic policymakers across the country, from the Treasury Minister to the Governor of the Central Bank, and including influential politicians such as De Gasperi's leading economic advisor on the implications of rearmament, Piero Malvestiti, and the former Industry Minister, Ivan Matteo Lombardo, shared this concern[366]. This Italian approach to the way the US and NATO financial assistance was to be invested and the pressing need to both reverse the deterioration of the balance of payments, and halt the rise in wholesale prices and the rises in the Consumer Price Index and inflation explain the way financial assistance was exploited in those years. The reason why most of the AMP and MDAP funds were used ‹‹to purchase essential materials and equipment for the maintenance and expansion of the Italian economy, primarily raw cotton, coal, petroleum, iron and steel products, nonferrous metals, and industrial production equipment››[367] between 1950 and 1951 would thus appear clear. This financial support to the import requirements of the Italian economy was shared out almost equally between the industrial military complex and the civilian productions, with the state-owned steel industries and the mechanical and metalworking sectors being the most important manufacturing recipients.

In order to wind up my reconstruction of the first two military assistance programs to the West European members of NATO viewed through the case study of Italy, I should make a final remark on the issue of internal monetary stability as it is necessary to get a clear understanding of why the West European allies were partly successful in making Washington accept their use of financial assistance to revive reserve assets and to balance their budget. The Americans considered that a widespread commitment by the Atlantic bloc countries to both keep European currencies stable and curb inflation, was an essential prerequisite to laying down the foundations of a truly continental consumer goods market and to further domestic military and civilian investments across its partner economies[368]. As long as this view was shared by the high-ranking political and business community in Washington, bilateral economic relations between the United States and Italy, and the negotiations on US and NATO financial allotments to the economy of the Mediterranean Peninsula, were bound to revolve around a continuous bargaining on the use of both the counterpart funds accrued to the Italian

---

366 letter to Sforza (Ministro Affari Esteri), 'Il Piano Marshall, l'ECA e la situazione italiana', 2 December 1948, in ASCE, IML, b. 4; 'Verbale dei colloqui del ministro Lombardo presso l'Economic Cooperation Administration', in ASCE, IML, b. 4; with respect to Malvestiti's stance on the issue of raw material see Governo italiano, 'Italian Memorandum', 19 December 1950, in NARA, RG59, Lot File 52-56, Bell Rowe File 1949-1952, b. 2;

367 'Materials for House Appropriations Committee Group Visiting Italy October 14 through 21', 28 August 1953, in NARA, RG469, Mission to Italy, Office of the Director, Subject Files (Central Files) 1948-1957, b. 18, fold. 3 (Congress House Appropriation Committee Visit);

368 A.Milward, *The European Rescue of the Nation State*, p. 121;

Treasury through the ERP and the financial assistance directed to Italy through the MDAP[369]. The American objectives of currency convertibility and the process of intra-European trade integration could not be achieved until the West European countries had recovered their monetary stability. Within this framework of international monetary and trade policy targets the United States made some concessions to allow their West European allies to divert the financial assistance they were granted to support their budget deficit. As I have highlighted in this work, this transatlantic bargaining on whether to use American financial assistance to finance domestic investments and imports, on the one hand, or to balance the European budget on the other, had been the main issue on the table at the bilateral negotiations on military assistance from as early as 1950. From London to Rome and in Paris, the West European governments played on the American view that internal monetary stability and budgetary equilibrium was a prerequisite that had to be nurtured in order to achieve the much-desired intra-European trade integration and monetary cooperation. Throughout the period of the Korean War the process of European recovery was close to completion and economic growth, the starting of market integration among the European economies, as well as the US objective of currency convertibility, became prospective American targets, and the US and NATO divided up the financial assistance to sustain the foreign exchange equilibrium and internal monetary and price stability. In fact, the creation of a multilateral financial facility among NATO member states, widely known as the NATO common fund, fixed a binding ratio of budgetary defense appropriation to pro capita GNP for each member state. This eased the financial pressure of rearmament on the European public finances and forced the United States to bear a large share of the burden, but did not change the way financial allotments were granted to the European economies. In this respect, Italy's stance is worthy of note. In fact, it could be said that the case of Italy was unique as the Italians manoeuvred to use as much financial aid for import requirements as possible, so as to pay for raw materials. Indeed, an analysis of the financial assistance that accrued to the Italian Ministry of Treasury from the time of the MDAP annual allotments at the outbreak of war in Far East Asia, up to the period of lengthy negotiations in the Atlantic community that eventually led to the creation of the NATO common fund after 1952, shows a coherent development. In the 1953 year-end data on military assistance reported to the US Congress by the new Eisenhower Administration, «in

---

369 ECA-MSA Rome to ECA Washington, 27 September 1951, secret, in NARA, RG469, Mission to Italy, Office of the Director, Subject Files (Central Files) 1948-1957, b. 31, fold. 4 (Funds, Counterpart Lire); De Gasperi to Tarchiani, 26 February1951, in De Gasperi scrive, pp. 138-139; De Gasperi to Tarchiani, 31 March 1951, idem, pp. 139-140; Malvestiti to De Gasperi, 7/2/1951, in P.Malvestiti, Lettere al presidente, pp. 142-144; 'Memorandum by the ECA Mission in Italy to the Italian Government', 5 February1951, in FRUS 1951, Vol. 4, Europe: Political and Economic Relations, pp. 566-568; E.T.Smith, The United States, Italy and NATO, chapter 6; L.Sebesta, L'Europa indifesa, pp. 186-205;

1951-52 Italy was allotted $143.3 million of MSA Aid, of which $22.6 million was loaned, and in 1952-53 defense support aid totalled $102 million»[370]
It should also be pointed out that against the background of the Korean War, the issue of the increasingly essential, and ever more costly, raw materials was interweaved with this trend of linking both the bargaining positions of the Europeans and the concessions of the United States respectively, to diverting military assistance for a redress in the balance of payments. The aim was also to prevent a chain reaction in rising prices and a worsening in foreign exchange equilibrium from leading to currency devaluation that would eventually bring trade exchanges and market integration among the Western bloc economies to a stalemate.

---

370 'Materials for House Appropriations Committee Group Visiting Italy October 14 through 21', 28 August 1953, in NARA, RG469, Mission to Italy, Office of the Director, Subject Files (Central Files) 1948-1957, b. 18, fold. 3 (Congress House Appropriation Committee Visit);

Chapter 4

From the MDAP to the off-shore procurement programs: the resurrection and development of the Italian aircraft industry amidst internal stability and foreign exchange equilibrium

4.1 The re-birth of the Italian aeronautics industry and the revision of the Peace Treaty with Italy: domestic industrial expansion, American style technological drift, and market competitiveness

The Additional Military Productions program showed several limitations and gaps in both its scale and the industrial sectors involved in the process of rearmament conducted under its aegis. These limitations originated from the way the European countries had tackled issues in the aftermath of the Second World War. This monograph has aimed to provide a detailed examination of a case study of a defeated nation, in this case Italy, in order to illustrate how the peace conditions imposed by the Allied Powers on their former enemies contributed to shaping the military assistance program launched to aid both Germany and Italy by the Truman Administration. Moreover, I have explored how the US Administration's bilateral diplomatic relations with its German and Italian counterparts were affected by these peace conditions. Furthermore, it is worthwhile pointing out that the United States did not ease the limits imposed on both countries during the immediate post war peace settlement until bilateral military assistance paved the way for a coordinated process of rearmament among the economies of the Atlantic Alliance. In turn, this permitted the MDAP, and the subsequent aid programs directed toward the continental economies, to increase both their contribution to the recovery of national European armies, and to boost the level of industrial mobilisation fostered by the rearmament programs. Although the reasons varied from country to country, the removal of limits and vetoes on both the industrial production of armaments or the holding of weapons and the size of the national military in both Italy and Germany could be explained by an increasingly widely-shared conviction among the Washington elites. The Americans argued that the implementation of rearmament through the construction and development of a self-sufficient industrial capacity across the West European economies was conducive to the accomplishment of economic reconstruction and a step forward on the move to lay down the foundations of sustained and mutually interdependent mass consumer markets across restored continental European societies[371].

This being the broader picture, the case of Italy elucidates quite clearly both these early limits imposed on the first military aid program which aimed to revive a war torn national army, and the following American moves to step up from material reconstruction to expansionary economic policies triggered by the economic and industrial mobilisation of NATO's military build-up and the defense policy[372]. In turn, this interplay between the post war peace settlements, the rather limited industrial scale and military objectives characteristic of the AMP implemented in Italy[373], and the subsequent American stance, offer a viable lead-up to the centrepiece of this study: the Italian aeronautical industry. In fact, in the following paragraphs I will closely examine a set of key historical features. First that aeronautical industry was excluded from the framework of the ERP assistance initiatives and the reorganization of this industrial sector only took effect with the Atlantic Alliance; secondly, the airplane industry is an excellent vantage point from which to follow the American struggle and the European responses regarding the plans of the Atlantic Alliance to replace bilateral military assistance programs with coordinated cooperation in armaments production[374]. This move took place in the framework of the American struggle to make the process of rearmament a successful plat-

---

371 To get a sense of the convergence between the Americans and the British on the mutual relation between rearmament and market expansion within each NATO member country see for example Memorandum by the Secretary of State for Foreign Affairs, 'The Report of the Temporary Council Committee of the North Atlantic Council', 19 February 1952, in PRO, Cabinet Papers, CAB/129/49;

372 In this respect, according to the US Economic Cooperation Administration the Mutual Defense Assistance Program was likely to induce a rise in physical output and an upward trend in domestic aggregate demand in both the German and the Italian economies. Up to this point see 'MSA, Proposed Fiscal Year 1952 Foreign Assistance Program, Title I, Europe', in NARA, RG59, Lot File 52-56 Bell Rowe File, b. 3, p. 62;

373 It is worth noting that the AMP program to Italy did not include any procurement contract to manufacture investment goods for combat vehicles in Italy. At this early stage the Italian economy was not involved in the coordinated production lines of combat vehicles that had been set in motion among some of the West European economies. See Ambasciata d'Italia presso la RFT, Ufficio del consigliere commerciale to Ministero del Commercio con l'Estero, DG Accordi commerciali, 'Acquisti delle Forze Armate Aeronautiche americane in Europa', 13 February 1952, in ASC, CED, b. 49.1/2 (commesse alle forze armate degli Stati Uniti), fold. Circolari, Appunti, Sgravi fiscali sulle commesse "off-shore"; indagine sulla situazione delle commesse estere, s.f. Indagine sulla situazione delle commesse estere;

374 For a wide-ranging and up-to-date historiographical overview on the interplay between industrial cooperation on aeronautical production, European economic integration and transatlantic relations throughout the postwar era see "Histoire, économie et Société", n. 4 (2010), and particularly the introduction to the issue by D.Burigana, P.Deloge, *Introduction. Le coopérations aéronautiques en Europe dans les années 1950-1980: une opportunité pour relire l'histoire de la construction Européenne?*, pp. 3-18;

form to erect a continent-wide trade market in durables and investment goods, as well as strategic materials. Thirdly, the resurrection of the aircraft industry illustrates the process of industrial modernization and technological drift, as well as the capital mobility required for its financing, witnessed throughout the 1950s in Western Europe and Italy. Moreover, it is worth pointing out that the development of the air industry helps to shed light on this process as it was the highest added value industrial sector among those involved in the defense policies of NATO. In fact, the European cooperation in armaments production that followed from the very end of the 1950s and into the last quarter of the twentieth century hinged on the technologically advanced and high added value aeronautical industry venturing into new manufacturing sectors such as the helicopter and aerospace industry and so on[375].

An overview on the AMP to Italy analyzed according to the manufacturing sector involved in the industrial mobilization, highlights how the industries linked to producing combat vehicles and allied to aeronautics were not involved in its rearmament schedule. The Peace Treaty that the newly born Italian Republic agreed to with the Allied Powers required that Italy produced a rather limited amount of weapons that would enable it to reorganize the national armies as necessary to prevent the country from falling under the Soviet sphere of influence. Article 53 of the Peace Treaty, at the center of long negotiations between Rome and Washington, required that Italy neither manufacture nor hold for export weapons in excess of what was necessary to equip the three national armies according to the defence targets outlined and set down in the Peace Treaty[376]. Regarding the air force, the 1947 Peace Treaty specifically imposed a limit on Italy's air fleet of 350, and prevented it both from holding bomber aircraft[377], and from producing missiles, rockets, and nuclear power rockets[378]. In addition, Italy was forbidden from exporting armaments[379].

The United States government reversed this strict agreement altogether through 1951, when an increasing number of government branches, especially within the State Department, agreed that strict limitations on the production levels of the Italian war industry and its allied indus-

---

375 C.Bouneau, D.Burigana, A.Varsori (eds), *Les trajectoires de l'innovation technologique et la construction européenne. Des voies de structuration durable?*, PeterLang, Bruxelles, 2010;

376 Tarchiani to Ministero degli Esteri, Forniture per la marina da guerra venezuelana, Telespresso, 20 October 1949, Tarchiani to A.Moro (sottosegretario agli Esteri), 'Forniture armi al Venezuela. Articolo 53 del Trattato di Pace', 5 January 1950, both documents are in ASMAE, Cassaforte, b. 6, Ufficio I, Posizione Cassaforte 27 (Interpretazione Articolo 53);

377 M.Ferrari, *Trasformazioni e ridimensionamento dell'industria aeronautica nel secondo dopoguerra*, in id. (ed.), *L'aeronautica italiana. Una storia del Novecento*, FrancoAngeli, Milano, 2004, p. 121;

378 M.Arpino, *La dottrina di impiego delle forze aeree e i criteri della difesa aerea*, in C.Jean (ed.), *Storia delle forze armate italiane dalla ricostruzione postbellica alla 'ristrutturazione' del 1975*, Giuffrè, Milano, 1989, p. 209;

379 'Summary of Studies Prepared in the Department of Defense', 17 September 1951, 'The Effects of Limitations imposed by the Italian Peace Treaty on Italian Obligations under NATO Plans', in *FRUS 1951*, Vol 4, *Europe: Political and Economic Relations*, part 1, pp. 671;

tries were a drag on the Italian industrial reconstruction and the country's overall economic recovery[380]. This change in the American view overlapped with the shift from the first MDAP to the co-production programs among the manufacturing systems of the Atlantic Alliance that led Washington to fuel multilateral military assistance programs under the aegis of NATO. This change in the American approach regarding the impact of the Peace Treaty's strict limitations on the Italian economy and the output of its firms heralded the clear move subsequently made by the Truman Administration to adapt the rearmament programs of NATO to the rising growth rates ensuing across the West European manufacturing systems. This process gained momentum, and by the mid-1950s was thought to influence the expansionary output capability that featured in European industries over the course of the decade. To American eyes, that view was germane to both the Italian and the German economies, regarded in Washington as increasingly interdependent on each other[381].

Hitherto, from the signing of the Peace Treaty in 1947 and for at least the first three years of reconstruction, the US State Department headed by Dean Acheson had assumed that the Peace Treaty's vetoes that prevented weapon production exceeding the output levels of Italy's pre-war defence posture, would not be a drag on Italian recovery. In this perspective, the United States worked to better the existing military units and equipment which was regarded as largely insufficient[382]. In fact, over the course of lengthy and time-consuming bilateral negotiations in 1950 between Rome and Washington on the level of the Italian extraordinary budgetary appropriations to meet the defense effort required to revive the Italian armies, the State Department did not retain the Peace Treaty limitations a binding constraint on the Italian method of encouraging a nationwide industrial mobilisation to revive its military: «we do not consider that Italy has exhausted opportunities for increasing its strengths within these limitations.»[383] Thus, according to the Americans the Peace Treaty did not prevent the Italian

---

380 for this kind of periodization see the recent reconstruction by L.Nuti, *La sfida nucleare*, pp. 52-53;

381 'MSA, Proposed Fiscal Year 1952 Foreign Assistance Program, Title I, Europe', in NARA, RG59, Lot File 52-56 Bell Rowe File, b.3, p. 62;

382 'Proposed Fiscal Year 1952 Foreign Assistance Program. Title I. Part G. Italy', in NARA, RG59, Lot file 52-26 (Bell Rowe File), b. 3, p. 1-2;

383 the Secretary of State to Certain Diplomatic Offices, 27 October 1950, in *FRUS 1950*, Vol. 3, *Western Europe*, p. 410; the State Department extended the same approach to the impact of the Peace Treaty on the three national armies of the country, which were nowhere near working at full: «Although the Peace Treaty established limitations upon the size of Italy's military forces and upon the quantity and types of military production, the Italian Armed Forces at present are by no means up to the full efficiency possible within the Treaty limits. There is still much room for improvement within these limits by supplying forces with modern weapons, by improving the quality and morale of the corps of non-commissioned officers, and by developing the Italian Armed Forces into a highly trained organization capable of serving as a nucleus of rapid expansion at some future date.» Memorandum by the Assistant Secretary of State for European Affairs (Perkins) to the Deputy Director of the Mutual Defense Assistant Program (Ohly), 8 August 1950, *idem*, p. 1511;

manufacturing system from supplying both the Italian Ministry for Defense and its European partners. At a Congressional Briefing, the Economic advisor of the US Embassy in Rome Vincent Barnett remarked that «Italy could produce for her own use a substantially larger volume of defense items without violation of the Treaty.» According to the US Embassy in Rome Italy had to tackle its very narrow domestic capital markets and a rocky national budget. These two issues were in fact regarded as the linchpins preventing the Italian economy and its manufacturers from working at full capacity and the Ministry for Defense from meeting its targets for the military build-up[384]. On the other hand, however, Washington did not consider the Peace Treaty's strict limitations on the output ceilings of the Italian war industry to be in any way at variance with its role of supplying economy for other NATO member states. A remarkable example of this position was the series of bilateral meetings that took place in 1950 between the United States and each West European ally to coordinate and share out both output capacity and available industrial plants and raw materials among the Atlantic bloc economies. The State Department complemented this firm stance, pursued with particular strength within the Military and Supply Board of the Atlantic Alliance, with a command to impose a series of binding limits on the transfer of military weapons and spare parts cast off by the US armies occurring among the Europeans in the framework of the first MDAP[385]. In the case of Italy, Acheson instructed the Embassy in Rome to force the De Gasperi Cabinet to maintain the Peace Treaty limitations as the reference ceiling. Indeed, before transferring their war material surplus, the United States required that the Italian Ministry for Defense, and particularly its air forces, dismissed some aircrafts in use at the time and reduced the military units to respect the 1947 Peace Treaty ceilings[386]. Therefore, through 1950 the State Department maintained that the «participation by Italy in the MDAP is not of itself at variance with the Peace Treaty. In any instance where variance appears, the Peace Treaty must govern.»[387]

This firm American stance was in striking contrast with the Italian economic outlook on the level of defense effort called for by the United States. Piero Malvestiti, economic advisor on rearmament related problems, assumed that in Italy the American call-up to contribute to the defense effort of the Atlantic community would raise physical output way above the strict

384 'Remarks by Mr. Barnett at the Congressional Briefing', 2 July 1951, in NARA, RG469, Mission to Italy, Office of the Director, Subject Files (Central Files) 1948-1957, b. 17, fold. Congress, pp. 2-3; V.Barnett to M.Looram, 'Comments at Briefing Session', 2 July 1951, *idem*;
385 The Secretary of State to the Embassy in the United Kingdom, 23 March 1950, top secret, in NARA, RG59, Central Files 1950-54, 740.5/3-2450; 'Communiqué of the Military Production and Supply Board', 24 March 1950, in *FRUS 1950*, Vol. 3, *Western Europe*, pp. 33-34;
386 The Secretary of State to the Embassy in Italy, 2 June 1950, in NARA, RG59, Central Files 1950-54, 765.5 MAP/3-650; The Ambassador in Italy (Dunn) to the Secretary of State, 26 June 1950, secret, in *FRUS 1950*, Vol. 3, *Western Europe*, p. 1508;
387 G.W.Perkins, Position Paper Prepared in the Department of State, 'The Effect of the Italian Peace Treaty upon the MDAP for Italy', undated (probably spring 1950), in *FRUS 1950*, Vol.3, *Western Europe*, pp. 1506-1507; in this perspective see also NARA, RG59, Central Files 1950-54, 665.001;

limitations agreed on in 1947[388]. Italy's hope of making its commitment to rearmament conducive to the removal of the Peace Treaty limitations on its industry output ceilings was to emerge as early as 1951 when the implementation of coordinated military co-production programs, which in turn triggered the drive towards the birth of the off shore procurement industrial contracts, assigned a very precise role to the country: «the Treaty will then stand as an obstacle to two vitally important tasks —first the full utilization of Italy's extensive productive capacity for NATO rearmament, and, second, an increase in Italian forces to the extent required to provide an adequate defense of Italy against aggression. At that stage, continuance of the military clauses would prevent the maintenance of the Italian forces required by NATO defense plans»[389].

This shift in the American policy on the revision of the economic clauses of the Peace Treaty that occurred in 1951 was firmly linked to the shift that occurred in the same year from bilateral military aid to the foundation of multilateral military assistance programs set up under the institutional umbrella of NATO. Given that this shift heralded a solid coordination between the military policies, as well as the manufacturing and financial policies of the Atlantic bloc member states, constraints on production and exports of a country like Italy that manufactured and supplied end items, were likely to hamper the engineering and implementation of co-production programs among the Atlantic bloc economies. In particular, the limits imposed in 1947 on both the military items that could be produced and the volumes of production jeopardized the full use of manpower and production capability across the country that was needed to fit out the national armies of Italy and its allies. Accordingly, in early 1951 the Director of the State Department's Office of Western European Affairs, H.M.Byington, addressed a group of Congressmen close to the Italian American communities and the US-based Italian business interests that the Truman Administration strove continually to remove from the Peace Treaty's agreements any clause dragging on industrial production and economic growth[390]. At the same time the US Ambassador in Rome, James Dunn, worked hard to prevent the bilateral meetings and negotiations on the revision of the Peace Treaty from turning

---

388 P.Malvestiti, *Colloquio col Presidente del Consiglio del 16 febbraio 1951*, 17 February 1951, in id., *Lettere al presidente*, pp. 148-150;

389 Proposed Fiscal Year 1952 Foreign Assistance Program, Title I, Chapter V, Part G, Italy, in NARA, RG59, Lot file 52-56 [Bell-Rowe file], b. 3, p. 2;

390 Memorandum of Conversation H.M. Byington-H.Smith-Senator Pastore (democrat from Rhode Island), 20 March 1951, 'Italian Peace Treaty', in FRUS, 1951, Vol. 4, Europe: Political and Economic Relations, Part 1, pp. 584-585; see also NARA, RG59, Central Files 1950-1954, 665.001/3-2051; on this stance by Byington see also Memorandum by the Director of the Office of Western European Affairs (Byington) to the Assistant Secretary of State for European Affairs (Perkins), 26 March 1951, 'Italian Peace Treaty', *idem*, pp. 589-590;

into a trade-off between the two countries on the level of Italy's defense effort[391]. In the space of a few months, the US State Department had significantly advanced its approach:

> From a military viewpoint, the restrictions imposed by certain of the military clauses of the Peace Treaty are incompatible with the objectives of NATO. It is apparent that the successful defense of Western Europe will require a greater contribution of military manpower by Italy than is permitted by the terms of the Peace Treaty. Italy, with the forces at present allowed under the Peace Treaty, could not defend its northern frontiers in the events of an attack. The Peace Treaty also places strict limitations upon the type and quality of weapons and material which the Italian armed forces need for full combat effectiveness. In addition, the Peace Treaty by preventing Italy from manufacturing or possessing more war material than is needed for its own forces under the Treaty precludes Italy's full participation in the rearmament production effort of the North Atlantic Community.[392]

Therefore, on the eve of multilateral cooperation in armaments production and the launch of the off-shore procurement programs, the United States considered the Peace Treaty an agreement that would hamper the twofold objective of enabling the Italian manufacturing system to supply both its own national armies as well as the military of other Atlantic bloc countries in accordance with the goals on military force that had been agreed on within NATO.

This shifting American perspective emerged as a result of lengthy political and diplomatic disputes and negotiations which led to the revision of the Peace Treaty with Italy. The clauses concerning the military and industrial production of the 1947 Treaty were a key issue that was much discussed during the seventh session of the North Atlantic Council meeting, held in September 1951[393]. This preceded the final revision of the Peace Treaty, which took effect later on that year following a joint declaration by the United States, the United Kingdom and France to move forward in this direction[394].

---

391 The Ambassador in Italy (Dunn) to the Secretary of State, 8 March 1951, Secret, in *FRUS 1951*, Vol. 4, *Europe: Political and Economic Relations*, Part 1, p. 582;

392 The Department of State to the British Embassy, 22 June 1951, Top secret, 'Aide-Mémoire', in *FRUS 1951*, Vol. 4, *Europe: Political and Economic Relations*, Part 1, p. 623;

393 See for example NARA, RG43, Records of International Conferences, Commissions and Expositions, Records of International Meetings on Postwar Policy 1945-1955, Records Relating to the North Atlantic Council (NAC), Records concerning the seventh session of NAC, Ottawa, September 1951; *FRUS 1950*, Vol. 3, *Western Europe*, pp. 616 ff.;

394 Mutual Security Agency, Office of the Assistant Director for Europe, 'Italy', 6 February 1953, in NARA, RG469, Mission to Italy, Office of the Director, Subject Files (Central Files) 1948-1957, b. 25, fold. 6 (Evaluation Team), p. 13; 'Declaration by the United States, France, and the United Kingdom on the Italian Peace Treaty', 26 September 1951, in *FRUS 1951*, Vol. 4, *Europe: Political and Economic Relations*, Part 1, pp. 717-718; Conversations with Italian Prime Minister, 'Minutes of the

Against this background it is worth pointing out that the Pentagon and the State Department strongly insisted on the impacts and consequences of the Peace Treaty on the Italian aeronautical industry and its allied firms. The two US government departments contended that if the Italian aeronautical industry were free from the binding constraints of the Peace Treaty it could work as many procurement contracts as necessary to meet both the rearmament goals of the Italian air forces and the other Atlantic Allies' job orders to manufacture a stock of jet engines[395]. As the Department of Defense put it, in Italy the «industrial potential and present source of trained workers in the aviation industry, which are now working in other fields due to the Treaty limitations, would make her a European aviation producer surpassed only by the United Kingdom.»[396] According to the Americans, the military assistance programs were to promote and to finance the resurrection of the Italian pre-war defense posture, and the restoration of industrial output to meet the goals for the forces of the national armies without «immediate expansion in the immediate future"»[397]. The State Department and the Pentagon made their case for a follow up to integrate the Italian industry into the European aeronautical sector, against the prospective multilateral cooperation in the production and trade of armaments.

Therefore, from 1947 until the early 1950s, the Truman Administration reappraised and changed its view on the compatibility between the Peace Treaty and the industrial effort required to revive the national armies of the European member states of NATO[398]. From our own viewpoint the most salient point is that, according to the United States, a much needed move to overcome the strict limitations of the Peace Treaty on production was clearly linked to the American contention that it was necessary to expand Italy's industrial base if its economy were to become fully equipped to meet the NATO targets and to supply the national armies of its member states. By the end of 1951, therefore, Washington had moved away from the objective of promoting merely the reorganisation, technological updating and rationalisa-

---

First Meeting Acheson-De Gasperi', 24 September 1951, in NARA, RG59, Central Files 1950-54, b. 2973, 810.002; Department of State, Press Release n. 869, 26 September 1951; Draft Information Memorandum, 'United States Policy toward Italy', 23 November 1951, in NARA, RG59, Central Files 1950-54, b. 2838, 611.65/11-2651;

395 Summary of Studies Prepared in the Department of Defense, 'The Effects of Limitations imposed by the Italian Peace Treaty on Italian Obligations under NATO Plans', 17 September 1951, in *FRUS 1951*, Vol. 4, *Europe: Political and Economic Relations*, part 1, pp. 670-671; The Department of State to the British Embassy, NARA, RG 59, Central Files 1950-54, 665.001/6-2251;

396 Summary of Studies Prepared in the Department of Defense, 17 September 1951, 'The Effects of Limitations imposed by the Italian Peace Treaty on Italian Obligations under NATO Plans', in *FRUS 1951*, Vol. 4, *Europe: Political and Economic Relations*, pp. 670-671;

397 'Proposed Fiscal Year 1952 Foreign Assistance Program. Title I. Part G. Italy', in NARA, RG59, Lot File 52-56 (Bell Rowe File), b. 3, p. 2;

398 in this perspective see also L.Nuti, *La sfida nucleare*, pp. 48-49;

tion of the Italian aeronautical industry's production lines that were at the head of the early post war military assistance programs[399].

The changing perspective of the Truman Administration regarding the implications of the Peace Treaty on the recovery of the Italian aeronautical industry provides a clear-cut snapshot of what was going on in the Italian economy. In fact, a comparison between the rebirth of the military and that of the civilian aeronautical firms and production lines clearly shows that the reorganisation of military productions proved to be slower, and much more limited both in scale and in speed, from the end of the 1940s up to the beginning of the new decade. For example, a look at the American military aid packages in terms of dollar aid investments from 1950 through 1951 shows that the non-combat vehicle civilian aeronautical firms invested as much as $37 million. However, over the same period the firms manufacturing combat-vehicles lagged behind considerably: the five combat-vehicle producers that had shared the manufacturing burden of the off shore procurement programs from 1951 onwards, namely Fiat, the State-owned concerns of Finmeccanica, and the three smaller and private aircraft industries of Piaggio, Aer Macchi and SIAI-Marchetti, limited their investments to roughly $5 million[400]. In accordance with this trend, this asymmetry in the way the jet fighter producers and the concerns manufacturing civilian planes used the American funds was a result of a broader industrial reconversion of the war industry to civilian productions that was underway in Italy throughout the period of post war industrial reconstruction. By the end of 1951 the combat vehicle producers had placed orders with the industries linked to civilian production for spare parts and components that would have been equivalent to the manufacturing of 455 training aircrafts. This industrial reconversion changed the context of the Italian military aircraft industry altogether. In fact, soon after the end of World War II, a war-torn Italian aeronautical sector suffering from technological backwardness and financial distress had led to, on the one hand, the folding up of factories and, on the other hand, structural industrial reconversions. Over the late 1940s, many historical military aircraft producing firms, such as Caproni, Isotta Fraschini and Reggiane were forced to shut down. At the same time a group of firms that had formerly supplied war material for the Italian Defense Ministry during the Second World War, such as Macchi, started producing civilian aircrafts and took on orders for repair

---

399 I have dealt with this periodization further in my own S.Selva, *Recovery and Security*, particularly pp. 140 ff.;

400 These five combat vehicle manufacturers included Fiat, Finmeccanica, that run three firms – Aerfer, IMM and Alfa Romeo Aeronautica- all based in and around Naples, plus the three private-owned concerns of Piaggio, Aer Macchi and Siai-Marchetti. On this point see V.Barnett (Deputy Chief, MSA Mission to Italy)-L.Mellon (First Secretary of Rome Embassy) to the Department of State, 'Benton Amendment Aspects of Defense Production', 25 August 1952, in NARA, RG469, Office of the Deputy Director for Operations (1953-1961), Office of European Operations (1953-1955), Italy Division, Decimal File 1948-1954, b. 7, fold. Italy 5.3 (Government Regulations and Participation in Business/Cartels);

and maintenance activities at the request of the Italian Defense Ministry. This twin reactivation of both military and civilian production lines paved the way for a technical update that was brought about through the reorganisation of production lines to work orders on behalf of the Italian armies and the Atlantic Alliance. This technical update of the production chain aided the recovery of the whole sector and was a precondition for the prosperous Italian export of jet aircrafts during the 1960s[401].

This development based on the coupling of industrial modernization and market competitiveness actually began around 1948. In fact, that was when the leading Northern Italian company, Macchi entered into production of a twin-engine fighter, called the "320". This was to lead to the export of jet fighters becoming the firm's core business. Despite this early tendency of Italy's mid-sized enterprises to look towards the foreign markets, by the late 1940s the huge Turin-based Fiat group had taken the lead in pushing the mechanical and aircraft sectors in this direction. By 1948 Vittorio Valletta, president and chief executive director of Fiat[402], had opted to stake the group's recovery on the aeronautical productions[403]. In fact, in 1948 he engaged in lengthy negotiations with his counterparts in the United States to adopt American methods of industrial planning and to enter into production of American models of jet aircraft[404]. During a series of conversations and meetings he attended at the Department of State, Valletta put forward his case for converting the Fiat plants to produce American jet fighters and for reviving and modernizing the Italian production lines through massive

---

401 By the second half of that decade, the Italian airplane industry exported both on the western world markets and to the economies of the developing countries. See in this respect E.H.Hamilton, Memorandum for A.A.Hartman (Department of State), 'Conte/Long and Jets for the Congo', 9 May 1968, in DDRS;

402 A recent and up-to-date historical outline of the biography of the head of the Italian car producing multinational over the post World War II era is in C.Casalino, *Italian Big business and the Italian Automotive Industry. Fiat Internationalization in the Vittorio Valletta Era and its ongoing Reorganisation (1946-1972)*, in "Jahrbuch für wirtschaftsgeschichte", Vol. 51, n. 1 (2010), particularly pp. 91 ff.;

403 Valletta was a much appreciated managing director in both the United States and Italy. On both shores he was deemed fit to carry on negotiations to clinch an agreement on production contracts and orders. Over the post war years and throughout the1950s both the Department of State and the Italian civilian and military authorities considered him a key figure in voicing the interests of the Italian business community and to setting in motion the industrial and trade policy of the whole Italian aeronautical industry. In this respect see J.W.Joyce (Acting Science Advisor, Department of State), to W.E.Knox (President, Westinghouse Electric International Company), 19 January 1954, in NARA, RG59, Central Files 1950-1954, b. 3961, 765.56/1-1154; C.G.Parker, Memorandum for the Files, 'F-86D Contracts', 30 April 1953, in NARA, RG469, Mission to Italy, Office of the Director, Subject Files (Central Files) 1948-1957 (1948-1954), b. 4, fold. 5 (Aircraft-Documents);

404 P.Bairati, *Valletta*, Utet, Torino, 1983, p. 226; V.Castronovo, *Fiat 1899-1999. Un secolo di storia italiana*, Rizzoli, Milano, 1999, p. 837;

American technological transfers[405]. This position brought with it important consequences for future trade exchanges between the Italian firms producing air weapons and the British suppliers of high added value instrumental goods and aircraft components. In fact, Valletta's shift towards the American supply market meant that the Italian aircraft companies discarded British technologies, despite the insistence by the firms operating at a national level on the need to continue producing for the British industries and air forces, as well as to import patents and licences from the United Kingdom[406].

4.2 The Vampire production program amidst British technology, ERP-Lire Counterpart funds, and the Sterling currency area. The early resurrection of the Italian aircraft industry in the wake of the Anglo-Italian economic relations

Despite earlier moves, it was only after 1949 that Fiat took a true lead in the reactivation of the Italian military aircraft industry, resulting in the launch of the off-shore procurement programs among the member economies of NATO in 1951. The economic and military technocracies which cooperated closely with the De Gasperi Cabinet, or were directed by it, chose the Fiat group to work the procurement contracts that NATO was ready to place in Italy. In January 1950, for example, the Chief of Staff of the Italian air forces and the country's Ministries for Industry and Foreign Trade conducted their negotiations with the US Embassy in Rome and the ECA Mission to Italy to ensure that Fiat would secure a substantial amount of military procurement contracts[407]. In addition to this effort to permit Fiat to benefit from the production programs launched under the aegis of the Atlantic Alliance, between the launch of NATO's rearmament programs and the first phase of the war in Far East Asia, the Italian

---

405 To set in motion this business strategy the giant Italian automobile group worked hard to finance and to strengthen Aeritalia and Lingotto, the two most important plants involved in the aircraft production chains. The former was to produce airplane airframes, whereas the latter specialized in manufacturing aircraft motors and motor components. At the same time, the Turin group made investments to boost the Research and Development departments and to potentiate the industrial test and planning units. In this respect see Mutual Security Agency, Industry Division, Projects, A.J.Grant (Industrial Project Officer) to R.Whittet (Projects Committee, 'MSA Project N.° 67 Italy. Equipment for Production of Turbo Jet Parts by Fiat', 26 May 1953, secret, in NARA, RG469, Mission to Italy, Office of the Director, Subject files (Central Files) 1948-1957, b. 4, fold. 5 (Aircraft Documents);
406 'Situazione attuale DPB-NATO', 16 April 1951, in ASC, CED, b. 49.1/2 (Commesse alle forze armate degli Stati Uniti), fold. Commesse. Promemoria dottor Mattei-Targiani-Campilli, s.f. Relazioni varie sui lavori del DPB-NATO), p. 4;
407 J.E.Jacobs (Special Assistant for MDAP Affairs, Rome), Memorandum for the Files, 'Aircraft Production in Italy', 13 April 1953, in NARA, RG59, Central Files 1950-54, 765.5622/4-1753;

government itself and the Ministry for Defense placed a set of orders with Fiat for the manufacture of airplane and aircraft components. By the end of 1951 the Turin multinational had worked on orders from the Italian state to manufacture Vampire aircraft models and Ghost turbojet engines. Furthermore, Fiat was about to receive more orders from the Italian Ministry for Defense to carry out a follow-up program to produce both a further series of Ghosts and a number of Venom type military jet fighters[408]. Moreover, in 1952 NATO placed a series of military procurement contracts in Italy which were intended to start up the production of a stock of G80 jet fighters[409]. From the beginning of 1951 the Fiat industrial plants had been working on military procurements amounting to nearly 9 billion Italian Lira placed by the Italian land forces and 15 billion Italian Lira to supply the Italian air forces.[410]

Therefore, from the start of Atlantic bloc rearmament, the giant Turin-based car industry had accumulated production lines working for NATO and a series of procurement contracts placed by the Italian armies, that is two buyer accounts that would assist in the resurrection of the aeronautical production lines. Furthermore, another distinctive aspect of this early wave of defense procurement contracts was the importance of the British aeronautical industry and its aircraft models and airplane components in the recovery of the Italian aircraft production lines. Italy bought and acquired British technologies and production methods and these licenses were to play an important role in the early recovery of the Italian aeronautics. Thus, by the end of 1951 the American authorities firmly contended that Italy's recent decision to acquire and import British licenses and components to produce Venom jet fighters and Ghost jet engines[411] meant it was ready to receive and work on the large orders of 80 jet fighters and 100 jet engines that were placed in Italy within the framework of the Atlantic Alliance's early rearmament programs[412]. In Italy itself, this British oriented production reorganization and manufacturing update permitted the Italian firms to produce British model Vampire jet fighters to meet the defense targets of the Italian air forces. The bulk of Italian aeronautical concerns were involved in this early effort to meet the two sets of orders: from Fiat to Alfa Ro-

---

408 ASF, Minutes of the board of directors, session of January 1952;

409 ASF, Minutes of the board of directors, session of August 1, 1952, p. 58;

410 Memorandum of Fiat, Torino, Italy, 'Referring to Defense Orders and the Means to Facilitate the Defense Production', n.d. (probably April 1951), in NARA, RG59, Lot File 52-26, Records of the Mutual Defense Assistance Program, Subject File relating to Program Management ("Bell-Rowe File") 1949-52, b. 21;

411 Memorandum of Conversation Gen.C.Unia (Chief of NATO Air Force Section, Air Ministry Rome)-Col. E.Albanese (Chief of Production, Air Force Ministry Rome)-Gen. E.Cigerza (Air attache, Italian Embassy Washington)-Ten. Col. W.Adrove (Italian Military Delegation to Standing Group Washington)-Col. W.Glidden (ECA)-H.Hilton (Western Europe Division, Department of State), 'Aircraft Production in Italy', in NARA, RG59, Central Files 1950-54, b. 3961, 765.5622/8-1451;

412 For all of these figures see 'Production Program by Categories' in NARA, RG469, Mission to Italy, Office of the Director, Subject Files (Central Files), 1948-1957, b. 22, fold. 2 (Defense OSP Program: contracts, production);

meo Aeronautica, the main Italian industries worked continuously on these orders placed with them by either the Atlantic Alliance or the Italian government to supply jet engines or fuse-lage[413].

This approach clashed with the Fiat group's decision, underlined earlier, to reorganize its pro-duction chains based on its preferred trade partnership with the American aircraft industry and its allied firms, which would lead the Italian acronautical sector to perform a technological update linked to on the American models. Indeed, the Atlantic Alliance based the implemen-tation of all the early rearmament programs on a British oriented modernization of the Italian industry and production lines. Moreover, the Italian De Gasperi Cabinet collaborated with the Italian military and economic policy makers to enhance cooperation with British industry thus leading to the acquisition of British licenses and industrial models. In this respect the Vampire program, usually portrayed in the literature as a fly-wheel for the recovery and modernization of the Italian aircraft industry[414], clearly illustrates how far the buying of British licenses led to a substantial expansion in Italian output capacity and marked a step forward on the Italian move toward the British license market. In fact, during the period of the first military assis-tance program aimed at helping the Rome government to rebuild its air force in the second half of 1948, the high rank and file of the Italian military establishment had made initial ap-proaches to the British authorities to enquire about producing the British Vampire aircraft model in Italy. In 1948 the Chief of Staff of the Italian air forces made every possible effort to obtain licenses to produce the Vampire jet engines and spare parts from the British firm De Havilland[415]. These negotiations led the Italian government and the Vampire-producing Brit-ish firm to sign a contract enabling the Italians to acquire the rights to reproduce the reaction engines. Shortly thereafter, in 1949, Fiat, Alfa Romeo and Aeronautica Macchi[416], the three main aircraft manufacturing Italian firms, founded a new concern, named Sicmar, that was to take a lead in turning the Italian aeronautical production lines from air screw type aircrafts to jet propulsion airplanes[417]. Against the background of this new production program the Vam-pire assistance package came into effect to equip the new jet propulsion aircraft with British

---

413 J.C.Hudson (American Consul General Milan) to the Department of State, 'Italian Jet Airplane Production', 30 October 1951, in NARA, RG59 Central Files 1950-54, b. 3961, 765.5622/10-3051;
414 V.Spina, *L'Aeronautica e la NATO*, in R.H.Rainero, P.Alberini (eds), *L'Italia del dopoguerra. Le scelte internazionali dell'Italia*, Stabilimento Grafico Militare, 1999, pp. 134-135; C.Jean, *Ricerca, sviluppo e approvvigionamenti in ambito difesa*, p. 266; M.Arpino, *La dottrina di impiego delle forze aeree e i criteri della difesa aerea 1945-1975*, both in C.Jean (ed.), *Storia delle forze armate italiane dalla ricostruzione postbellica alla 'ristrutturazione del 1975*, pp. 222-223; M.Ferrari, *Trasformazioni e ridimensionamento dell'industria aeronautica nel secondo dopoguerra*, p. 127;
415 L.Nuti, *L'esercito italiano nel secondo dopoguerra 1945-1950*, p. 179;
416 P.Macchione, *L'aeronautica Macchi*, FrancoAngeli, Milano, 1985, p. 305-306; G.Lombardo, *L'Istituto Mobiliare Italiano*, Vol. 2, *Centralità per la ricostruzione 1945-1954*, Il Mulino, Bologna, 2000, p. 395;
417 P.Macchione, *L'aeronautica Macchi*, p. 305;

jet engines. The program envisaged 80 jet engines, the production of which was shared between Fiat and Macchi that manufactured 53 and 27 items respectively[418]. Leaving aside these technical details and focusing on the financial implications of the Vampire programs, we should note that the Italian Ministry for Defense was to partly bear the financial burden up to a sum of $4 billion. However, this extraordinary defense appropriation was financed neither through the ordinary balance-sheet of the Ministry nor through an American financial assistance package. Rather, the Christian Democrat-led Italian government and the Rome-based American authorities clinched a deal to draw on the ERP-Lire counterpart funds that had accrued to the Italian Treasury from the sale of goods distributed across the country under the aegis of the Marshall Plan. These ERP-Lire counterpart funds, which were allotted after approval of the US ERP Mission and the American Embassy in Rome in accordance with Marshall Plan procedures, were to finance that extraordinary defense appropriation required to enable the Italian Ministry for Defense to purchase the Vampire jet engines and the new jet propulsion aircrafts[419]. Over the course of the 1951-52 fiscal years this ploy to finance the extraordinary expenses was extended way beyond the expenses linked to the Vampire program. In fact, if we break down the Italian extraordinary defense expenditures we can clearly see that the ERP-Lire counterpart funds financed up to $9 billion worth of purchases. In this way the Italian air forces bought 150 M416 aircraft items, most of which were produced and assembled by Macchi[420]. Strictly speaking, in terms of volume and total amount of funds allotted, the use of ERP-Lire counterpart funds to ease financial pressure on the balance sheet of the Ministry for Defense was rather limited. A quick and very simple comparison between this ploy and the scale of the defense effort that the Italian Ministry engaged with to meet the rearmament efforts agreed on within NATO illustrates this point. As a matter of fact,

---

418 Ministero della Difesa Aeronautica, Direzione Generale delle Costruzioni e degli Approvvigionamenti, 'prospetto riassuntivo forniture', in ACS, Ministero dell'Aeronautica, Segretariato Generale, Archivio Generale, anno 1958, b. 136; V.Barnett (Deputy Chief, MSA Mission-S.Mellon (First Secretary of Embassy), to Department of State, 25 August 1952, in NARA, RG469, Office of the Deputy Director for Operations (1953-1961), Office of European Operations (1953-1955), Italy Division, Decimal File 1948-1954, b.7, fold. Italy 5.3 Government Regulations and Participation in Business/Cartels, p. 2;

419 Ministero della Difesa Aeronautica, 'Spese finanziate col "Fondo Lire ERP"-Progetti militari esercizio finanziario 1951/1952', in ACS, Ministero dell'Aeronautica, Segretariato Generale, Archivio Generale, anno 1958, b. 136;

420 Ministero della Difesa Aeronautica, Direzione Generale Costruzioni e Approvvigionamenti, to Min. Dif. Aer., Ufficio Segretariato Generale Bilancio, 'Spese finanziate col Fondo Lire Erp. Progetti militari per 34 miliardi. Esercizio Finanziario 1951/1952', 28 April 1958, in ACS, Ministero dell'Aeronautica, Segretariato Generale, Archivio Generale, anno 1958, b. 136; 'Spese finanziate col Fondo Lire Erp. Progetti militari. Esercizio finanziario 1951/1952', idem; A.Hoolihan (Capo Ufficio controllo ICA Italia) a Ministero della Difesa, Ufficio Bilancio e Coordinamento amministrativo, 11 March 1958, *idem*;

throughout the fiscal years of 1950-51 and 1951-52 the Ministry for Defense in Rome cleared military appropriations and expenditures for weapons and military services worth up to 328 billion Italian Lire[421]. If we focus our attention on the off-shore procurement contracts we find that from the beginning of 1952 through to the end of 1953 the Italian aeronautical firms received orders for over $44 million[422]. Notwithstanding the rather limited share of total defense expenditures that the ERP counterpart loans financed, this way of providing the Ministry for Defense with financial assistance to support its rearmament effort is important as it is relevant to the long-lasting quarrel between the United States and the European governments over who was to bear the financial burden of rearmament. This debate, which I have dealt with in other chapters of this work, further proves the historical definition of transatlantic cooperation in aircrafts production to be a «coproduction of hegemony» among the participant countries and economies[423]. In the case of Italy, this ploy offered quite a significant amount of funding to offset the extraordinary defense expenditures of the Italian government over a number of years[424].

On the other hand, the Vampire production program was of considerable importance as it changed the way that Italian industries working on military productions could pay off their imports and had a significant impact on the Italian external trade and balance of payments. In turn, this method of financing the import of instrumental and investment goods, as well as much needed military services, allowed Italian manufacturers to carry out rearmament production programs using funds from outside the extra budgetary defense appropriations or coupled different sources of funding. Thus, the Italian government could exploit not only the

---

421 Ministero dell'Industria e del Commercio, Servizio Coordinamento Commesse e Affari Patto Atlantico, 'Commesse nazionali ed estere', 19 September 1952, in ACS, MICA, Segreteria Campilli, b. 7, fold. 8;

422 Ministero dell'Industria e del Commercio, Servizio Coordinamento Commesse e Affari Patto Atlantico, 'Appunto', 26 February1954, in ACS, MICA, Segreteria Campilli, b. 4, p. 6;

423 D.Burigana, P.Deloge, *Le coopérations aéronautique en Europe dans les années 1950-1980: une opportunité par relire l'histoire de la construction européenne?*, in "Histoire, Economie et Societé", n. 4 (2010), p.10;

424 See for example Dayton to the Department of State, 'Fiscal Year 1952 Counterpart Program', 29 February 1952, in NARA, RG469, Mission to Italy, Office of the Director, Subject Files (Central Files) 1948-1957, b. 21, fold. 4 (Defense: Funds-Counterpars); R.Bissel to the Rome Embassy, 'Fiscal Year 1952 counterpart policy', 22 December 1952, telegram, *idem*; W.J.Acon to D.K.Hopkinson, 'Counterpart Program for Fiscal Year 1952-Italy', 3 November 1951, in NARA, RG469, Office of the Deputy Director for Operations (1953-1961), Office of European Operations (1953-1955), Italy Division, Decimal File 1948-1954, b. 13, fold. 6.3 (Project-Counterparts 1947-50); It is worth noting that the American authorities bound the use of the ERP counterpart funds to finance domestic investments and growth programs to Italy's commitment to take an active part in the military build-up of NATO's member countries. See Nac Meeting No. 160, 2 August 1950, in NARA, RG56, Nac Papers, Nac Minutes, b. 2, February 9, 1950-December 28, 1950;

ERP-Lire counterpart funds, but also the financial assets available on the Italian money market. A detailed analysis of these different sources of funding that permitted Italian manufactures to support their imports also highlights the relevance and influence of the British aeronautical industry and its jet aircrafts and components model on the Vampire production program and the early recovery of the Italian air forces. In this respect the Vampire program is noteworthy as it triggered a significant expansion in the import requirements of the Italian aeronautical firms. As it was a British jet fighter model equipped with British components, spare parts and technology, it imposed a radical reorganization of the Italian terms of trade with the British trade area and the sterling money market. Firstly, it was necessary to purchase spare parts, components, and building material for the start-up of the Vampire production lines on the commercial area of the British Pound. Secondly, there was a huge expansion of invisible imports determined by the importing the licenses and rights needed for the Vampire production.

Against this background, Valletta applied pressure to finance Sicmar's imports through frozen credit worth up to £80 million that Italy was waiting to claim back from the United Kingdom[425]. As shortly after its foundation Sicmar had to take out a loan with the *Istituto Mobiliare Italiano*[426], a major Italian medium-term credit institution, the Chief Executive of Fiat argued long and loud that Sicmar should guarantee this loan with this £80 million credit. Valletta's stance was consistent with the Italian law passed in 1950 that made it possible to draw on the current balance of payments surplus, at the time on deposit at the Italian Institute for Foreign Exchange, either to pay for the import of instrumental goods from the British trade area, or to finance construction works which the ERP failed completely to support[427]. The 1950 Italian law set up a specific fund, widely known as FAS, to place this balance of payments surplus at the disposal of Italian manufacturers. What is noteworthy is that the first and most important aim was to finance the imports made by Italian aeronautical concerns and their allied firms. As the £80 million credit was on deposit on FAS, it is evident that Valletta's strategy was consistent with Italian law and thus it is clear why he repeatedly insisted that Sicmar should employ this strategy. The Italian conglomerate acted on Valletta's advice and drew widely on FAS to finance its firms' imports. This came about at a very challenging time for the Italian terms of trade against the British money market due to London's devaluation of

---

425 P.Bairati, *Valletta*, p. 226;

426 Hereafter referred to as IMI. In 1949 IMI issued a loan to Sicmar, which in turn opened up a bank guaranty.

427 As regards the beginning and further development of the FAS funds see, G.Lombardo, *L'apporto dello European Recovery Program (Piano Marshall) alla ri-progettazione dell'industria italiana nel secondo dopoguerra: modernizzazione, conflitti e produzioni off limits*, in A.Bonoldi, G.Leonardi (eds), *La rinascita economica dell'Europa. Il Piano Marshall e l'area alpina*, FrancoAngeli, Milano, 2006, pp. 72-76;

the sterling in September 1949[428]. As soon as the recently established Italian conglomerate of Sicmar was provided with a loan by the IMI it set up a bank surety drawn from funds on deposit in FAS[429]. From this it is clear both that the implementation of the Vampire program in Italy was greatly dependent on the British supply of instrumental goods and average capital intensive components and reproduction licenses, and that the impact of that program on the Italian balance of payments concerned the Italian terms of trade with the British currency area, whereas the external trade of Italy with the dollar trade area did not contribute to shifting the country's balance of payments from a surplus to a deficit balance.

Last but not least, the Vampire military assistance program to Italy should be mentioned because the Italian government and military authorities accepted to share the financial burden it engendered with NATO and placed its implementation within the framework of Italian industrial policy, which at the very beginning of the 1950s was progressively shifting from the accomplishment of economic reconstruction to the early phases of industrial expansion and economic take off. The stance of the Italian authorities during their negotiations with De Havilland for the purchase of reproduction licenses and rights to produce the Vampire jet fighter provide an interesting insight. Form early in the second half of 1948, both the Chief of Staff of the Italian air forces and the Minister for Defense, Randolfo Pacciardi, did their best to convince Her Majesty's government that the Vampire items manufactured in Italy could stimulate the on stream process of intra-European trade exchange in durables and accelerate the birth of a continent-wide European trade area. According to the Italian government, a close and fruitful Anglo-Italian cooperation would lead to the export of the Vampire to European markets that were highly dependent on foreign supplies of durables and consumer goods in general[430]. Furthermore, from 1950 the Italian top level military officials and the Minister for Defense himself believed that a significant leap in production of the Vampire jet model might be the linchpin of a new defense and security system which would prevent the West European member states of NATO from falling under the Soviet sphere of influence in the case of a war between the two superpowers[431].

428 P.F.Asso, A.Biagioli, C.Piccozza, *Ordinamento valutario, politica del cambio e gestione delle riserve 1945-1960*, in F.Cotula (ed.), *Stabilità e sviluppo negli anni cinquanta*. Vol. 3, *Politica bancaria e struttura del sistema finanziario*, Laterza, Roma and Bari, 1999, pp. 133-152;

429 G.Lombardo, *L'Istituto Mobiliare Italiano*, Vol. 2, *Centralità per la ricostruzione*, pp. 394-395;

430 L.Nuti, *L'esercito italiano nel secondo dopoguerra 1945-1950*, pp. 180-181;

431 Pacciardi to De Gasperi, 7 July 1950, in *De Gasperi scrive*, Vol. 2, p. 277;

4.3 Sharing production chains and financial burden, finding new ways to balance the foreign exchange equilibrium, pursuing social cohesion and political stability. The evolution of multilateral rearmament programs from the demise of Venoms through the implementation of OSP contracts

Although the Italians attached much importance to the Vampire program and placed a remarkable amount of orders with Fiat to supply the Italian air force[432], by the year 1952 the United States had discontinued it once and for all. By the time it was discarded, the scale of the program was quite significant and had helped to resurrect the Italian air forces substantially. In fact, at the beginning of 1953 this first military assistance program to Italy provided the country's armies with 136 daytime jet fighters, of which 80 items had been processed in Italy. In addition, the program supplied the Italian Ministry for Defense with 14 night fighters[433] and a further 20 Vampires that the Italian government purchased by using an extraordinary spending appropriation from the Defense balance-sheet worth up to $5 million[434]. Shortly after the termination of the Vampire program, the Atlantic Alliance started a new military assistance program to place orders with the European industry which is worthy of discussion as it was equally important to the Vampire, though for very different reasons. When this new assistance program was being set up during 1951 the idea of the American authorities was to place limited orders with European industries. In fact the Venom Program, which was named after the new jet aircraft being produced, involved a pledge by the Americans to limit the contribution of European manufacturers to the production and assembly of this new jet aircraft, to the supplying of spare parts and to working on those maintenance services and repairs that were necessary to resurrect the European air forces. It is easier to understand the American objective if we consider that throughout the late 1940s the American reconstruction policies for the relief of the war-wrecked European economies aimed to encourage low capital intensive reactivation and the modernization of European industry by introducing labor intensive production methods and launching low capital intensive production chains[435]. Notwith-

---

432 ASF, Minutes of the board of directors, session of 1 August 1952;

433 General Staff Air Force, Office of the Atlantic Pact, 'Memorandum for MAAG Italy. Enclosure 2', 18 February 1953, in NARA, RG59, Records of the Office of the Special Assistant for Mutual Security Coordination, Office of the Undersecretary 1952-59, b. 25, fold. MAP-Italy (Fiscal Years 1952-54);

434 Col. W.A.R.Robertson, (Chief MAAG), Memorandum for the Record, 'Italian Government Counterproposal Regarding Defense Support Aid and Aircraft Industry', 26 February 1953, in NARA, RG469, Records of the Office of the Special Assistant for Mutual Security Coordination, Office of the Undersecretary 1952-59, b. 25, fold. MAP-Italy (Fiscal Year 1952-54);

435 Ambasciata d'Italia presso la RFT, Ufficio del consigliere commerciale to Ministero del Commercio con l'Estero, DG Accordi commerciali, 'Acquisti delle Forze Armate Aeronautiche americane in Europa', 13 February 1952, in ASC, CED, b. 49.1/2 (commesse alle forze armate degli Stati Uniti), fold. Circolari, Appunti, Sgravi fiscali sulle commesse "off-shore"; indagine sulla situazione delle

standing the rather limited scope of the program, it effectively turned out to be a watershed both as regards the shaping of transatlantic cooperation on military productions, and the full scale involvement of the European aircraft and metalworking industry in the defense effort of the Atlantic Alliance. Furthermore, the Venom program prepared the way for the implementation of the concept of burden sharing among the member countries of NATO and started production in full of jet aircrafts across West European industry shortly after its introduction.

As regards the coordination of manufacturing among the European economies and the introduction of full aircraft production lines across the Old continent, from the very beginning of 1951 the European governments, led by the French and British chancelleries, requested to the Americans that the Atlantic Alliance should produce the complete production of Venom in Europe. As a result of this pressure, in June 1952 the US representative to the Defense Production Board of NATO «announced American willingness to support the production of complete aircraft in Europe»[436]. In line with this American move, the Ismay-Batt working group presented a proposal to the International Secretariat of NATO that a fully coordinated production of jet aircrafts for as many as 1.700 end items should be produced in Europe. This proposal involved the production of Venom to supply the Italian air forces, as well as British-type Supermarine Swift jet aircraft and the French Mystère IV. Cooperation in the production and manufacturing of these models was to involve the economies of Belgium, France, Italy, the Netherlands and the United Kingdom[437].

From the start of discussions, studies were produced within the Atlantic Alliance to set up the program, and improvements were made to fully coordinate supply and use of raw materials as well as the industrial and financial resources that were available across the economies of NATO. Within the International Secretariat of NATO the working group Ismay-Batt, which was the first committee charged with defining and preparing the program, worked hard to engineer a mechanism aimed at ensuring that the member countries shared both production and costs[438]. The linchpin for the launching and implementation of a fair distribution of both production costs and payments for the transfer of military materials and end item weapons among the economies and national armies of NATO's member countries was the establishment of a financial facility, widely known at the time as a *NATO common fund*. Every mem-

---

commesse estere, s.f. Indagine sulla situazione delle commesse estere. For a recent assessment of the impact that the European Recovery Program had on the European industry, its scales and peculiarities see F.Fauri, P.Tedeschi (eds), *Novel Outlooks on the Marshall Plan. American Aid and European Re-Industrialization*;

436 I.Megens, *Problems of Military Production Co-ordination*, p. 284;

437 'Summary of the Report of the Aircraft Working Group of the NATO Secretariat', 27 June 1952, in NARA, RG469, Mission Files, Military Production Files (MP), b. 1;

438 L.Sebesta, *L'Europa indifesa*, p. 219; with regards to the International Secretariat of the Atlantic Alliance see R.S.Jordan, *The NATO International Staff-Secretariat 1952-1957. A Study in International Administration*, Oxford University Press, Oxford, 1967;

ber country contributed to this liquidity fund through a national contribution drawn on their national balance-sheets. This national contribution was directly proportional to the pro capita GNP of each member state of NATO[439]. A further source of funding to enhance burden sharing within NATO was the exploitation of the hard currency financial assets at the disposal of each member country which were used to finance the civilian investments that the process of rearmament nurtured[440]. In this case, the aim was to ease the pressure of rearmament on the balance of payments of the economies involved in the defense effort. Eventually a further ploy to mitigate the impact of the defense effort on the national public finances would be the setting up of *special defense financing funds*. These liquidity funds, diverted by NATO from its own budget to that of the member countries, were intended to deal with the growing impact on the national balance sheets of budgetary appropriations for defense spending[441]. Finally, each European member state involved in the rearmament program and in the new Venom production program was to divert some assets from its own national balance sheet to finance a rapidly expanding defense spending program[442]. The combination of these four sources of funding was a truly distinctive feature of the new Venom military assistance program. In this case there was no attempt to finance the production and payments of jet fighters among the member countries of NATO by either drawing on the counterpart funds or applying for loans from international financial institutions, such as the Export-Import Bank, as had happened previously with both the Vampire program and the financing of French rearmament respectively[443].

---

439 T.Geiger, *Sistemi di analisi o modelli di crescita? L'influenza americana nell'elaborazione delle statistiche europee sulla crescita economica dopo la seconda guerra mondiale*, in "Nuova civiltà delle macchine", n. 3 (1999), pp. 34-35;

440 International Cooperation Administration, 'Status Report to the National Security Council for the Period January 1-June 30, 1955. Part I, Mutual Security Programs in Support of Military Forces', n.d. (but, autumn 1955), in NARA, RG56, NAC Papers, Nac Documents and Supplements 1945-1968, b. 29; Mutual Security Agency, 'Fiscal Year 1954 Title I (Europe) Defense Support Program. Italy, Developmental Aid for fiscal Year 1954', 30 October 1952, in NARA, RG59, Records of the Office of the Special Assistant for Mutual Security Coordination, Office of the Undersecretary of State 1952-1959, Lot File 59D449, b. 25

441 Ambasciata italiana a Washington, 'Aiuti americani 1953-1954. Situazione al 25 giugno 1953', in ACS, Ministero del Tesoro, Direzione Generale del Tesoro, IRFE, b. 10, pp. 2-3;

442 'Summary of the Report of the Aircraft Working Group of the NATO Secretariat', 27 June 1952, in NARA, RG469, Mission Files, Military Production Files (MP), b. 1;

443 In the case of France, its commitment on the war in Indochina led Washington to provide Paris with a multiple set of military aid that coupled mutual assistance and the Atlantic Alliance rewards with a set of Export-Import Bank loans. The most path-breaking work on this point is W.H.Becker, W.M.McClenahan, *The Market, the State, and the Export-Import Bank of the United States 1934-2000*, Cambridge University Press, Cambridge, 2003, p. 81;

If we shift our attention from the Atlantic community as a whole, and focus particularly on Italy's involvement in the Venom program, we will note that the Atlantic Alliance planned to produce 400 vehicles and their spare parts in Italy for a value of up to $80 million. This plan envisaged that the Atlantic Alliance would pay the Italian manufacturers in US dollars predominantly to supply the Pentagon, but also to supply the national forces of Italy itself as well as of those of Belgium, the Netherlands, Denmark and Norway[444]. However, over the course of 1952 the US government and NATO did not actually implement this plan at all. The subsequent elaboration and rather limited implementation of the Venom program came about as a result of the Italian government's firm insistence on getting the country involved in this new production program. In fact, from 1951 the De Gasperi Cabinet managed to exert considerable pressure on the American authorities by drawing on the dual argument that Fiat had already acquired the machine tools and machinery needed to produce the Venom and Ghost jet engines, and that any upset in the recovery of the Italian aircraft industry and its allied firms might trigger painful repercussions on the employment rate, thus obtaining a series of military procurement contracts worth up to $200 million[445]. Though from the International Security Affairs of the State Department to the Department of Defense the US Administration showed signs of deep and widely shared skepticism on the scale of the Italian request, the Italians made their case for the launch and further implementation of the program in Italy. In the eyes of the Italian government that program would ensure some 70 million working hours per year equal to 35.000 employees for the country, while also securing the allotment of $26 million by the United States and NATO to the Italian economy to finance the import of much needed instrumental goods for Italy's production lines[446]. This latter consideration was especially important as by the end of winter 1953, the trade balance and the balance of payments of Italy against the currency areas of the European Payments Union had worsened substantially[447].

Over the course of 1952, even as the five member countries of NATO involved in the Venom program engaged in negotiations to set up military procurements, the Italian government moved in two directions to enable the national aircraft industry to manufacture the new jet

---

444 M.P.Arth to J.H.Ohly, 'Italian Aircraft Arrangement', 28 April 1953, secret, in NARA, RG469, Mission to Italy, Office fo the Director, Subject Files (Central Files) 1948-1957 (1948-1954), b. 4, fold. 5 (Aircraft-Documents);

445 State Department, Memorandum 'OSP Aviation Contract in Italy', 10 April 1953, in NARA, RG59, Records of the Office of the Special Assistant for Mutual Security Coordination, Office of the Undersecretary of State, 1952-1959, Lot File 59D449, b. 25;

446 Department of State, 'Osp Aviation Contract in Italy', n.d. (but 1953), in NARA, RG59, Central Files 1950-54, b. 3961; M.Levy-Hawes to Moore, 'Proposed Osp Contract for Aircraft in Italy', 13 April 1953, *idem*, 765.5622/4-1353;

447 'The Italian Balance of Payments. Position and Prospects', 1953, in ACS, Ministero delle Finanze, Gab., Ufficio Paesi Esteri, b. 13; E.Ortona to Ministero del Commercio con l'Estero, Direz. Gen. Importazioni e Esportazioni, 'Assegnazione fondi FOA', 20 February 1953, in ACS, PCM, CIR, b. 98;

aircraft and to ensure a sustained and continued level of production. Throughout the second half of 1952 the De Gasperi government approved a range of military procurement contracts designed to expand production and to raise the average working hours in the sector, as well as to supply the national air forces with the number of aircrafts it required. The implementation of this set of procurement contracts took effect irrespective of American approval and financial support. Hence, this production program bypassed the American prerogative to retain a final and binding right to approve or veto the implementation of those military production programs coordinated and worked thanks to full cooperation among the economies of the Atlantic Alliance[448]. The Italian initiative ran the risk of upsetting both the balance of payments and the country's public finances for neither the US Congress nor the financial facility set up within the Atlantic Alliance were at the time planning to provide financial support to this range of military procurement contracts. In late 1952 the Italian government's move to launch these procurement contracts to produce a set of Venom jet aircrafts regardless of the American stance was the result of the widespread Italian fear that the Americans were about to discard the program altogether. Such a decision on the part of the American authorities risked not only hampering the reorganization of the Italian aircraft industry but also cutting off essential mobilization of both resources and investments. At a meeting with the Officer in Charge for the Italian-Austrian Affairs of the State Department, a leading Italian diplomatic representative to Washington, Egidio Ortona, maintained that «the Italian Fiat factory which anticipates the OSP contract has spent 14 million dollars in the past, with US government encouragement for the purpose of tooling its factory to build the Venom and Vampire jet plane.»[449] This widely shared Italian concern was to influence the Americans: at the end of 1952 the US air force downgraded the Venom jet fighter which became an unacceptable model of jet aircraft. This led to the loss of procurement contracts to Norway and Denmark for as many as 20 and 26 airplanes respectively, whereas the program's downsizing hampered the manufacturing system of Belgium to an even greater extent as it was denied the opportunity to produce 74 Venom that had been previously scheduled by the Atlantic Alliance[450].

---

448 J.E.Jacobs (Special Assistant for MDAP Affairs), Memorandum for the Files, 'Aircraft Production in Italy', 13 April 1953, in NARA, RG59, Central Files 1950-54, b. 3961, 765.5622/4-1753;
449 Memorandum of conversation Ortona-V.Lansing Collins (Esquire, Officer in Charge, Italian-Austrian Affairs, Department of State)-E.Adams (Western European Division, State Department), OSP Aviation Contracts', 18 March 1953 , in NARA, RG84, Rome Embassy, Secret General Records 1953-55, b. 1, fold. 320.1 (off-shore procurements classified 1953-55); Ortona quoted in E.Jacobs, Memorandum for the Files, 'Aircraft Production in Italy', 13 April 1953, in NARA, RG59, Central Files 1950-54, b. 3961, 765.5622/4-1753;
450 State Department, Memorandum 'OSP Aviation Contract in Italy', 10 April 1953, in NARA, RG59, Records of the Office of the Special Assistant for Mutual Security Coordination, Office of the Undersecretary of State, 1952-1959, Lot File 59D449, b. 25;

In the light of the unsuccessful implementation of the Venom production program the Italians undertook a second series of initiatives to offset its cancellation and to ensure continuity in production and export to the Italian aircraft industry. From the end of 1952 through March of the following year, Italy's high-rank military officials and diplomatic representatives to Washington and NATO voiced the country's firm intention to pin down the United States to an agreement on an alternative production program to that of Venom[451]. After lengthy discussions and negotiations among a wide range of Italian economic Ministries and inter-Ministerial committees, ranging from those of Foreign Trade and Industry to the Ministry of the Treasury and the Foreign Office, the Inter ministerial Committee for Reconstruction and Fiat, the Italian authorities drafted a Memorandum on the Italian rearmament program and brought it to the attention of their American counterpart. This memorandum outlined the Italian plan to replace the Venom and to prevent the national manufacturers from experiencing a fall-off in production and export[452]. Moreover, it highlighted the concern and struggle in Italy to save the American financial aid that had been scheduled in the framework of the Venom program. In particular, as Ortona himself underlined on the occasion of his meetings and conversations in Washington, the annulment of Venom contracts meant that some $14 million, that had been allotted to modernize Italian industrial plants with new and updated machine tools and machinery, risked being blocked[453]. In this document the Italian government also maintained that the Italian economy was at imminent risk of experiencing a steady drop in its employment and growth rates, and that to face up to the pressing need to prevent such an economic downturn the government had appropriated extra budgetary military spending worth up to $5 million:

> The problem to be resolved immediately is that of the survival of the industry in
> the next few months, inasmuch as it is obvious that if this problem is not taken

---

451 Bunker (US Ambassador to Italy) to W.H.Draper (US Special Representative in Europe), 12 March 1953, 'Aircraft Production Program in Italy', in NARA, RG59, Records of the Office of the Special Assistant for Mutual Security Coordination, Office of the Undersecretary of State 1952-59, b. 25, fold. MAP-Italy (fiscal Years 1952-54);

452 Memorandum of conversation Col. Robertson (Chief MAAG)-Harvey (MSA)-Col.Albanesi (Italian Air Force)-Col. Bellini (Italian Air Force), 'Italian Government Counterproposal Regarding Defense Support Aid and Aircraft Industry', 26 February 1953, in NARA, RG59, Records of the Office of the Special Assistant for Mutual Security Coordination, Office of the Undersecretary 1952-59, b. 25, fold. MAP-Italy (Fiscal Year 1952-54);

453 Memorandum of conversation Ortona-V.Lansing Collins (Esquire, Officer in Charge, Italian-Austrian Affairs, Department of State)-E.Adams (Western European Division, State Department), OSP Aviation Contracts', 18 March 1953, in NARA, RG84, Rome Embassy, Secret General Records 1953-55, b. 1, fold. 320.1 (off-shore procurements classified 1953-55); Ortona quoted in E.Jacobs, Memorandum for the Files, 'Aircraft Production in Italy', 13 April 1953, in NARA, RG59, Central Files 1950-54, b. 3961, 765.5622/4-1753;

care of, there will be no purpose to formulating future programs. [...] The Italian government, in order to contribute to working out this difficulty, has recently placed orders with industry for a total of five million dollars[454].

According to the Italian Memorandum, this extraordinary financial effort had proved insufficient despite its size and it would be necessary to formulate and to set up an alternative production program to Venom that would be much greater in scale and scope. Thus, the document drew up a plan to produce and assemble a further set of Vampire jet fighters in Italy, intended to be a further program that would come into effect in addition to the five million dollar orders that had been recently placed with the Italian aircraft and metalworking firms:

These orders, although constituting a maximum extra financial effort on the part of Italy are a considerable distance from the tying-in of the production now under way (the Vampire) with that of the new type planes. The American contribution to be added to the maximum financial endeavor which the Italian Air Force will attempt in every way to meet in the near future and which is estimated at six to eight millions of dollars, is evaluated at least sixty more Vampires. The amount needed for the sixty Vampires and which is asked as US aid is ten million dollars and should be considered over and above the twenty six million destined exclusively for the production of the new aircraft.[455]

The Italian initiative to plead with the US government and NATO to permit Italy to manufacture and assemble a further sixty Vampires was conducted against the background of the impending Italian general elections, scheduled for early June 1953. The Rome Cabinet exploited US concerns over the election results, and their pressing desire to reduce the risk of growing political consensus to the left-wing parties, when it drew up its new plan to replace the Venom production program and brought it to the attention of the American authorities in Rome. The American concern for the Italian political outlook on the eve of the Italian polls meant the Cabinet had an important bargaining tool to influence the decisions of the US government. In

---

454 Governo italiano, 'Memorandum for MAAG Italy', December 1952, in NARA, RG59, Records of the Office of the Special Assistant for Mutual Security Coordination, Office of the Undersecretary 1952-59, b. 25, fold MAP-Italy (fiscal Year 1952-54); on the Italian Memorandum see also E.Bunker to W.H.Draper, Aircraft production Program in Italy', 12 March 1953, *idem*; A.Urbani (General Staff Air Force, Office of the Atlantic Pact, Chief of Staff) to US Force Section, American Embassy Rome, 'Aid Plan Amounting to 26 Million Dollars (MSA) for Defense Support of Aircraft Production', 18 February 1953, idem;
455 Governo italiano, 'Memorandum for MAAG Italy', December1952, in NARA, RG59, Records of the Office of the Special Assistant for Mutual Security Coordination, Office of the Undersecretary 1952-59, b. 25, fold MAP-Italy (fiscal Year 1952-54);

fact, in early 1953 the American foreign policy makers engaged in lengthy discussions over the most effective way to replace the Venom production program with other military assistance programs in Italy. The US Ambassador, Draper, suggested that the Atlantic Alliance place a set of procurements to produce in full and assemble an all-weather fighter model of choice with Italian industry. For its part, the Department of State firmly endorsed this idea, termed «worthy of the most sympathetic consideration»[456]. This widely-shared American concern for providing the Italian ally with continued military procurement contracts stemmed from a deep-rooted concern for the upcoming general elections. A drop off in the number of off-shore procurement contracts placed with the Italian manufacturing firms risked eroding the vote for the Christian Democrats and triggering an electoral leap forward for both the Italian Communist Party and for those on the far-right of Italian politics. A reduction in the number of defense procurements contracts placed with the Italian industry was indeed likely to make Italian public opinion and the electorate assume «a reduced US interest in supporting the Italian Defense effort»[457]. Furthermore, discontinuing military assistance increased the risk that the Italian Parliament would not pass a vote of confidence on the General Treaty drafted at European level to establish the European Defense Community. This interplay between the shaping, scale, scope and timing of military assistance programs on the one hand, and the American concern for influencing the Italian political outlook and its development on the other, was undoubtedly fundamental in influencing the setting up and implementation of the off-shore procurement contracts for Italy as part of the Atlantic Alliance's military assistance programs[458]. Moreover, Italy's call to schedule production in full for sixty more Vam-

---

456 Department of State, 'OSP Aviation Contract in Italy', 1953, in NARA, RG59, Records of the Office of the Special Assistant for Mutual Security Coordination, Office of the Undersecretary of State 1952-59, Lot File 59D449, p. 1;

457 Department of State, 'Fiscal Year Title I (Europe) Defense Support Program. Supplemental Note. Italy', in NARA, RG59, Lot File 58D357, b. 15, fold. 435.01 Direct Aid 1953-1954;

458 See for example Draper to the Secretary of State, 17 April 1952, telegram, in NARA, RG469, Mission to Italy, Office of the Director, Subject Files (Central Files) 1948-1957, b. 21, fold. 4 (Defense: Funds-Counterparts); H.Cleveland (Assistant Director for Europe), Memorandum for Members of MAAC, 'Allocation and Administration of Defense Support Funds for Fiscal Year 1953', 14 July 1952, in NARA, RG469, Mission to Italy, Office of the Director, Subject Files (Central Files) 1948-1957, b. 17, fold. 3 (Conferences- Chief of Missions); H.M.Byington to L.E.Thompson (American Embassy Rome), 2 July 1952, idem. In order to get a neat sense of understanding regarding to what extent the Italian political outlook and its polls influenced the American stance and decisions on the OSP to place with Italian industry, it is worth noting that in trying to tie in the launch and carry on of OSP contracts planned for allotment to Italy during 1953 with general election, the US Embassy argued loud and long that these contracts be compulsorily placed with the Italian aircraft industry several months in advance of that year's political polls. See in this respect The Ambassador in Italy (Bunker) to the General Director for Mutual Security (Harriman), in *FRUS 1952-54*, Vol. 6, *Western Europe and Canada*, Part 2, Government Printing Office, Washington DC, 1986, p. 1596.

pires stemmed from the Italian discontent with the effective successfulness and positive economic impact of producing spare parts for either the national armies or the military of other NATO member states, and the firm Italian belief that the American commitment to provide financial assistance and to speed up the implementation of off-shore procurement contracts among the member countries of NATO could be warranted only through the launch of production programs to manufacture and to supply end item weapons. This conviction was fuelled by the example of the Italian involvement in the Ghost production program to supply the national armies of other countries. From the end of 1951 the Defense Production Board of NATO had scheduled to place a substantial amount of OSP contracts with Italian industry to produce several Ghost jet engines, but these were long delayed[459].

The Italian Memorandum thus proposed to drive for Vampire production to resolve the problems posed by the abortion of the Venom procurement contracts. However, it also dealt with the American initiatives and proposals to involve Italian industry in off-shore procurement programs considered by Washington as alternatives to Venom and sufficient to ensure the continued recovery of the Italian aircraft manufacturing sector. From the fall of 1952 through summer 1953 and way beyond, the American authorities tried to plan a set of military procurement contracts to be placed with Italian industry which would permit it to work on both spare parts and production in full of jet fighters, namely the so called all-weather fighters. Through summer 1953 the US Mutual Security Agency's Special Representative in Europe showed a considerable and consistent commitment to save and reprogram financial allotments appropriated to finance the Venom production program in Italy. Furthermore, it made a case for initially placing contracts for spare part productions with Italian industry to be later followed by the production in full of an all-weather fighter to meet a series of force requirements agreed on for NATO[460]. Notwithstanding this firm commitment by the US Special Representative in Europe, the Military Assistance Advisory Group to Italy and the Country Team based at the US Embassy in Rome were at the forefront in bringing the American proposals formulated in Washington before the Italian government and in conducting the ensuing contacts and negotiations in Rome[461]. In late 1952 the US Department of Defense made its case

459 L.Targiani, 'Pro-memoria. Impressioni riportate da Londra in merito alle commesse-15-17 gennaio 1952', p. 1, 23 January 1952, in ASC, CED, b. 49.1/2, fold. Commesse. Promemoria del dottor Mattei-Targiani-Campilli, s.f. 1952. Promemoria Targiani-Campilli-commesse;

460 The Deputy US Special Representative in Europe (Anderson) to the Ambassador in Italy (Bunker), in FRUS 1952-54, Vol. 6, Western Europe and Canada, pp. 1599-1600; Department of State, Memorandum, 'OSP aviation Contract in Italy', n.d. (but, 1953), in NARA, RG59, Records of the Office of the Special Assistant for Mutual Security Coordination, Office of the Undersecretary of State 1952-59, Lot File 59D449, b. 25 ; M.Levy-Hawes to T.Shelling, 10 April 1953, idem;

461 Bunker (US Ambassador to Italy) to W.H.Draper (US Special Representative in Europe), 12 March 1953, 'Aircraft Production Program in Italy', in NARA, RG59, Records of the Office of the Special Assistant for Mutual Security Coordination, Office of the Undersecretary of State 1952-59, b. 25, fold. MAP-Italy (fiscal Years 1952-54);

for getting the Atlantic community to assign a series of off-shore procurement contracts to work on spare parts intended for the assembly lines of the F84G and J-65 jet fighters to Fiat and Finmeccanica, the only two Italian nation-level mechanical industries[462]. On the other hand, however, the US was intending to introduce assembly lines to produce in full a series of jet fighters to Italy: among a wide ranging array of hypotheses, in early 1953 Washington chose the technologically advanced Gloster Javeline, fully equipped with two Sapphire jet engines[463]. With a view to financing the launch of productions in full of jet fighters to compensate for the annulment of contracts for the assembly of Venoms, during the winter of 1953 the United States made the Italian government an offer for financial assistance of close to $26 million. This allotment was part of a broad global financial appropriation plan for the 1952-53 fiscal year to place a set of OSP contracts totaling up to $240 million with varying Italian manufacturing sectors[464], and aimed at triggering «a little new employment by date of elections directly resulting from placement of OSP contracts.»[465] Therefore, this chunk worth up to $26 million materialized in the framework of the on-going bilateral negotiations between Rome and Washington on the overall production planning of OSP contracts to place with Italian economy during the coming year[466]. This allotment of as many as $26 million was intended to tackle two issues arising out of the introduction of new production lines for the manufacture in full of new models of jet fighters. In fact, according to the Americans this sum was to meet both the costs of the import requirements of the Italian manufacturers involved in the OSP contracts, and to ease the impact of the rearmament effort on the national balance sheet. As regards the latter, the American authorities in Rome believed that the strain of the defense effort on the public finances was likely to trigger a drop in civilian productions and a sharp cut in consumer demand. A path-breaking new financial ploy underpinned the American offer and made it possible to tackle both the import requirements and the drag of the defense effort on the national budget at the same time.

In fact, the United States aimed to provide this $26 million to fuel import requirements required by Italian industry to produce aircrafts and aeronautical spare parts. The American plan envisaged that in the early stages the Italian companies themselves would be responsible for the issue of bonds or other sources of funding to cover start-up investments and production costs. Following this early financial effort, the United States would then draw on the $26 million sum to reimburse them. Thereafter, the Italian government was to set up a counterpart

462 Mutual Assistance Advisory Committee, 'Minutes', 29 October 1952, in DDRS;

463 ASF, Minutes of the board of directors, session of 12 January 1953;

464 CIR-Segreteria Generale, 'Aspetti della cooperazione economica con gli USA (Aiuti americani e prestiti esteri)', 22 January 1954, in ACS, PCM, GAB., 1951-1954, fold. 15-5;

465 Joint Cable Defense Department-State Department-MSA to AmEmbassy Rome, n.d. (but, January 1953), in NARA, RG59, Records of the Office of the Special Assistant for Mutual Security Coordination, Office of the Undersecretary 1952-59, b. 25, fold. MAP-Italy (Fiscal Year 1952-54);

466 E.Ortona, *Anni d'America. La diplomazia 1953-1961*, Il Mulino, Bologna, 1986, p. 27 ff.;

fund accruing from the distribution and selling of jet fighters and spare parts to other European partners. According to the American plan, this counterpart fund was intended to go towards national public expenditure on defense.

This American financial assistance program aimed at backing the investment efforts of the Italian concerns involved in working of the OSP contracts placed with Italy and the impact of rearmament on Rome's public finances was a remarkably new and original way of dealing with at twofold problem. However, it had a number of limitations as the Italian enterprises had to overcome a number of hurdles to achieve it. It was indeed a truly innovative way of financing the rearmament effort and clearly showed Washington's intention to make a shift from earlier methods used for the financing of the extra-budgetary defense appropriations that continued to increase the liability of the European budgets. The Atlantic community neither resorted to the US taxpayer nor considered diverting to the Defense Budget funds from the ERP-Lire counterpart funds, a ploy the United States drew on repeatedly in the framework of the early military assistance programs launched in Italy over the course of fiscal year 1951-52, when the Americans took a lead by putting up half the counterpart fund to feed government spending on defense[467].

This thoroughly new way of redressing the impact of the industrial effort that the OSP contracts were to stimulate, on both the balance of payments and public spending, was nonetheless the source of some trouble for the Italian firms because the industrial reconversion that was required to set up the new production lines for the all-weather fighters ran the risk of being very expensive and time consuming. In fact, in the framework of the Italian government's policy to enable the national metal-working and mechanical industry take advantage of the off-shore procurement programs, which led Rome to request that the 20 T-33 model aircrafts cast-off by the Pentagon be replaced by OSP contracts, the national industry was blocked by several industrial reconversion issues. Most of the Italian firms involved in the OSP contracts were not in any way capable of meeting the pre-production costs required before the allocation of reimbursements that would come later from the $26 million American financial aid package. Furthermore, the most important prime contractors ran the risk of seeing a sharp

---

467 ECA Mission to Italy, Finance Division to V.Barnett, 'Status of the Lira fund Program as of 30 June 1952', 17 July 1952, in NARA, RG469, Mission to Italy, Office of the Director, Subject Files (Central Files), 1948-1957, b. 31, fold. 4 (Funds, Counterparts Lire); Watson to Brown, 'comments on Letter No. 38 from Rome Proposing Budgetary Counterpart Use in Italy', 8 June 1951, in NARA, RG56, OASIA, b. 63, fold. Italy-MSA-FOA-Counterpart Policies; Ministero della Difesa Aeronautica, Ufficio Bilancio a Direzione Generale dei Servizi, 'Spese finanziate col "Fondo lire ERP" Progetti militari per £ 34 miliardi-Esercizio finanziario 1951/1952', 14 April 1958, in ACS, Ministero dell'Aeronautica, Segretariato Generale, a. 1958, b. 136. As regards the increasing tendency to resort to the counterpart funds to redress monetary stability and the balance sheet to prevent a dramatic deterioration, see IMF, Western Hemisphere Department, North American Division, Review of the United States Foreign Aid Program, 15 May 1953, in ASBI, Carte Caffè, pratt., n. 50, fold. 1, p. 6;

drop in production levels and employment rate during the transition period that would be necessary to set up the production chains for the all-weather fighters. The fact that the Fiat plants would have to tackle this problem was argued long and loud by Egidio Ortona during his discussions with the European Division of the State Department: «the Fiat aircraft factory may be idle, and it may be forced to reduce its employment force by hundreds or even thousands of workers»[468]. This Italian concern arose specifically from the industrial reconversion of Aeritalia plants required for the production of the new Javeline jet fighters and the jet engines with which they were fitted.

During the fall of 1952 the Atlantic Alliance devised a broad set of measures to pre-fund industrial reconversion and war production costs to start up and further jet aircraft off-shore procurements in Italy prior to the appropriation of American financial assistance in order to resolve this issue. The United States and NATO devised the so-called prefunding scheme to eliminate this hurdle to the launch and production of the OSP. This mechanism varied according to the diverse industrial and financial circumstances of each European country involved in the OSP contracts. It entailed a variety of ways of coping with the transition period. Two noteworthy measures were: on the one hand, compelling the European public finances to share the burden of pre-production costs of national industries such as start-up investments, industrial modernization and the reconversion or replacement of instrumental goods; on the other hand, the engineering of a pre-payment system aimed at spreading out the required start-up industrial investments for procurements over a longer period of time. This latter solution involved the national Ministry of Defense or the foreign buyers paying for each military procurement lot by lot as they were worked and thus ahead of the completion of each procurement and the final hand-over to the purchasers. This reorganization of the payment system was intended to ease the pressure of rearmament costs on the national budgets and the industry of the European manufacturing countries through the implementation of scaled down and short term industrial investments[469].

---

468 Memorandum of Conversation Ortona-V.Lansing Collins-E.Adams, 'OSP Aviation Contracts', 18 March 1953, in NARA, RG84, Rome Embassy, Secret General Records 1953-55, b. 1, fold. 320.1 (off-shore procurements classified 1953-55);

469 M.Magistrati to CIR-Segreteria Generale, 'Aiuti americani. Problemi del pre-finanziamento delle commesse', 20 May 1952, in ASBI, Carte Caffè, pratt., n. 50, fold. 1; F.Caffè, Appunto per il sig. Governatore 'Problemi del pre-finanziamento delle commesse', 17 June 1952, in ASBI, Carte Caffè, pratt., n. 48, fold. 1; G.Olcese, Appunto per il sig. Governatore 'Notizie di stampa sul progetto Van Zeeland per il finanziamento del riarmo', 29 September 1951, idem; Confindustria, n.a. (but, Targiani), 'Promemoria', 2 January 1952, in ASC, CED, b. 49.1/2, fold. Commesse. Promemoria del dottor Mattei-Targiani-Campilli, s.f. 1952. Promemoria Targiani-Campilli-commesse;

4.4 The government of the United States and the implementation of the OSP contracts across Western Europe: multilateral rearmament and its discontents

The US federal departments, the military and the inter-ministerial committees involved in either shaping or implementing the OSP, had contrasting views on the very significance of the off-shore procurement programs in the framework of American foreign economic policy toward the West European allies, as well as on the best way to conduct aid negotiations with the Italian counterpart. In this respect, the position adopted by the Pentagon is worthy of note. On the one hand, the Department of Defense fully endorsed the implementation of multilateral production programs aimed at coordinating the European economies and at making their resources and goods complimentary to each other. On the other hand, the American military proved to be, at the least, skeptical regarding the running of NATO's financial facility for the payment and transfer of raw materials, military spare parts and assembled weapons between the resource-rich and the manufacturing economies of NATO. In turn, the role of the Atlantic Alliance in placing orders with European industry was the source for much criticism at the Pentagon. In this paragraph I will try to elucidate this twofold stance of the American military and examine how it came to be at variance with other federal departments.

From as early as 1951, the Department of Defense showed less concern than the Secretary of State, Dean Acheson, and the ECA for the financial implications of the defense effort on the European balance of payments and the national balance-sheets, and strove to postpone any discussion on it[470]. In 1952, before the start of bilateral negotiations with each European country involved in the aircraft procurement contracts, the United States Air Force repeatedly exerted pressure to cut down the US budgetary contribution to NATO's common fund for the payment and transfer of raw and strategic materials, semi-manufactured goods and military end items among NATO's recipients[471]. Furthermore, the Pentagon insisted with the other member states of NATO that military assistance and negotiations on this issue should continue at bilateral level.

On the other hand, the US authorities consistently pursued the establishment of integrated production chains among the industrial systems of the European economies. Especially worthy of note is the fact that multilateral military productions involved both member states of NATO and some allied countries, which until then had been outside the Atlantic Alliance, in the architecture of the off-shore procurement programs. Thus, for example, the Federal Republic of Germany itself was partly involved in working on military orders placed by the Pentagon and NATO prior to joining NATO. In the fall of 1952 the US Department of Defense

---

470 Memorandum of Conversation by the Director of the Office of European Regional Affairs (Martin) Acheson-Marshall-Bradley-Foley-Bissell, 'Meeting the MTDP Gap-ISAC D-4/7a', 21 June 1951, in *FRUS 1951*, Vol. 3, *European Security and the German Question*, Part 1, pp. 197-204;
471 I. Megens, *Problems of Military Production Coordination*, pp. 284-285;

would both desire to have «components of finished goods produced in Germany but would keep the principle that we do not want the Germans in total armament production»[472].

The position that the Pentagon took toward Italy offers a vantage point from which to reconstruct the American stance regarding the reorganization of rearmament from 1951 onwards. It is useful to trace the continuation of military assistance to the Rome Cabinet in the framework of the off-shore procurement programs, as well as to consider the internal divisions that shook the US federal agencies and the American Embassy in Rome on the issue of multilateral rearmament and the American military assistance needed to nurture it. Hence, I will attempt to cast light on two off-shore procurement contracts that involved the Italian aeronautical industry from spring 1952 until around 1954. Firstly, we should consider that as early as 1950 the US military advanced the idea of placing a set of military productions for equipping the military of other European allies with Fiat and the other prime Italian contractors. In the same year, both the Under Secretary of Air Steward and the American-born General Stone, put forward their case during discussions with Valletta for placing maintenance orders for a series of American model F84 jet propellers with the Turin plants[473].

Two years later, in June 1952, the US Air Force acquired its manufacturing license from General Motors to produce the Allison jet engine's components and spare parts[474]. Soon thereafter, as part of a broader American aim to make the European industry completely independent of American suppliers[475] in the production of spare parts for military aircrafts, the US Department of Defense handed these manufacturing licenses over to Fiat. Later, in spring 1953 it appropriated a sum worth up to $2.2 million to finance pre-production expenditures by Fiat. The Americans set up a production program to enable the Turin based group to manufacture spare parts and components worth up to $6.5 million that were required to assemble a J-35 turbojet engine. This jet engine model was to equip the F84G jet fighter, an aircraft that NATO gave a pivotal role in its defense and security policies. Indeed, the Atlantic Alliance proposed that in the future each European member state of NATO was to equip its national air force with this model of jet fighter. The envisaged production program meant that Fiat would share the financial burden for the costs of industrial plants and capital assets for producing these materials by having recourse to the $2.2 million military assistance aid. The US Air Force took a lead by placing orders to produce spare parts and components with Fiat as part of

---

472 Mutual Assistance Advisory Committee, 'Minutes', 29 October 1952, in DDRS;

473 A.Most to Dayton, 'Conference with Professor Valletta', 4 June 1951, in NARA, RG469, Mission to Italy, Office of the Director, Subject Files (Central files) 1948-1957, b. 33, fold. 6 (Industry);

474 ASF, Minutes of the board of directors, session of 1 August 1952;

475 A.J.Grant (Industrial Projects Office-MSA) to R.Whittet (Chairman, Projects Committee-MSA), Memorandum, 'MSA Project 67 Italy. Equipment for Production of Turbo Jet Parts by Fiat', 26 May 1953, in NARA, RG469, Mission to Italy, Office of the Director, subject Files (Central Files) 1948-1957, (1948-54), b. 4, fold. 5 (Aircraft-Documents); A.Grant to T.E.Drumm, Fait Turbojet Application', 8 May 1953, idem;

the maintenance and replacement works of obsolete components for the F84G that had previously been carried out by KLM and AIA at their facility plants in the Netherlands and in Casablanca during the seven-year period that the jet fighter was in operation[476]. Soon thereafter the new US ambassador to Italy, Clare Boothe Luce, contended that the Italian economy gained no substantial industrial advantage in terms of GDP from these procurement orders, although they would put pressure on the Italian foreign exchange equilibrium against the other currency areas of the European Payments Union[477]. Despite the new Ambassador's fierce opposition, the shaping and implementation of this package of OSP contracts is noteworthy as it sheds light on the twofold intention of the US military to nurture the implementation of offshore procurement programs to produce and transfer weapons among the member states of the Atlantic Alliance, as well as bypassing the role of NATO by both placing orders with the national industries and appropriating payments on behalf of each European national army. In fact, when in spring 1953 the US Department of Defense allocated a lump sum of financial assistance of close to $2.2 million to Italy, the primary American objective was to finance Fiat's expenses on the dollar market to import industrial machinery and equipment for its plants «without requirement for dollar credit»[478]. As regards my reconstruction, the most remarkable feature of this OSP production program is that Italian industry was above all required to manufacture components and spare parts for other member countries of NATO. On the other hand, however, it is eye opening to note that the US Department of Defense strongly wished to eliminate any role being played by NATO. In fact, the Pentagon intended to finance the Italian imports for a total amount that was eventually close to $3.7 million, without resorting to the financial facility set up within NATO to address this target[479]. Rather, the American military planned to draw upon the military assistance funds held at the US Mutual Security Agency to ease the liabilities in the current account of the Italian balance of payments arising

---

476 T.E.Drumm to R.Whittet, Memorandum, 'Fiat Turbojet Application', 8 May 1953, in NARA, RG469, Mission to Italy, Office of the Director, Subject Files (Central Files), 1948-1957, (1948-1954), b. 4, fold. 5 (Aicraft-Documents);

477 Luce to Dulles, 'J-33 and J-35 overhaul facilities', 11 June 1953, in NARA, RG59, Records of the Office of the Special Assistant for Mutual Security Coordination, Office of the Undersecretary of State 1952-59, Lot File 59D449;

478 A.J.Grant (Industrial Projects Office-MSA) to R.Whittet (Chairman, Projects Committee-MSA), Memorandum, 'MSA Project 67 Italy. Equipment for Production of Turbo Jet Parts by Fiat', 26 May 1953, in NARA, RG469, Mission to Italy, Office of the Director, subject Files (Central Files) 1948-1957, (1948-54), b. 4, fold. 5 (Aircraft-Documents); A.Grant to T.E.Drumm, Fiat Turbojet Application', 8 May 1953, idem;

479 C.J.Baker (MSA) to A.J.Grant (MSA), 'Proposed Fiat Turbojet Project –Machine Tool Requirements', in NARA, RG469, Mission to Italy, Office of the Director, Subject Files (Central Files) 1948-1957, (1948-54), b. 4, fold. 5 (Aircraft-Documents);

from this new military production program[480]. Furthermore, the US Air Force was the prime buyer, and rewarded the Italian manufacturing concerns directly without envisaging that NATO would have any intermediary role.

The second series of off-shore procurement contracts that shed light on the stance and policy that the US Department of Defense maintained regarding the reorganization of rearmament in a multilateral framework was the order placed with Italian industry for production in full of 50 F86 all-weather fighters[481]. The agreement signed in late spring 1953 by the US-based North American Aviation that owned the license to produce and to assemble that all-weather fighter model with the Italian Air Force and Fiat meant that the Turin based multinational was to serve as the prime contractor[482]. Once again the United States Air Force bypassed the Atlantic Alliance both in placing the off-shore procurement contracts with the Italian metalworking and mechanical industry, and in financing the industrial effort of the Italian firms to work these manufacturing orders, as well as in making payments to the Italian companies. In fact, though these contracts were specifically intended to supply the Italian Air Force, it is worth remarking that the Pentagon placed this package of contracts with Italian industry in order to set up a production source in Italy that could supply the national air forces of all the other member countries of NATO[483]. In particular, the US Air Force aimed to set up the production in full of a turbojet engine model called *General Electric J-47* in Italy that was to equip the new F86 all-weather fighter model. On the other hand, this 1953 agreement also envisaged that the US Air Force would finance the imports of the Italian aircraft industry. In this respect it is worth pointing out that the Pentagon provided the Italian firms with financial aid both to acquire the licenses to reproduce the all-weather fighter model and the technical assistance services necessary to carry out maintenance work, and to import a wide array of spare parts such as jet engine cells, and machine tools ranging from assembly mask and tools

---

480 H.Tasca to FOA Washington, 'F-86-K Assembly', 23 November 1953, telegram, in NARA, RG469, Mission to Italy, Office of the Director, Subject Files (Central Files) 1948-1957, b. 22, fold. 4 (Defense : OSP programs Contracts production 1954); Ministero Commercio Estero, Direz. Gen. Importazioni e Esportazioni a CIR, 'Progetto Fiat Aeronautica', 9 March 1953, in ACS, PCM, CIR, b. 98;

481 A.Tarchiani to MAE, 10 May 1953, in ASMAE, DGAP, Ufficio I 1950/1957, b. 216 (politica estera americana in funzione economica);

482 V.Roli to E.Hallbeck (Vice President Bank of America), 'Fiat-Ordinazioni military di aerei', 17 June 1953, in ASF, USA-Delibere, b. Contratto USAF-Governo italiano e licenza North American Aviation-Governo italiano-Fiat, year 1953;

483 C.H.Shuff (Deputy for Mutual Security Assistance Affairs) to E.Ortona, 15 May 1953, in ASF, USA-Delibere, b. Contratto USAF-Governo italiano e licenza North American Aviation-Governo italiano-Fiat, year 1953;

to electronic devices from North American Aviation, all of which were essential to manufacture the J-47 turbo jet engine[484].

The Pentagon exhibited a long-lasting disappointment with the structure of multilateral rearmament as the Atlantic Alliance had shaped it prior to its launch and through the mid-1950s. In fact, the Department of Defense and other federal agencies of the US government conducted negotiations directly for the defining of the off-shore procurement contracts and the appropriations of funds to European industries that would enable them to manufacture and assemble the scores of F86 all-weather fighter models that went into production through the first half of the decade. In this period the US military and the Department of State repeatedly clashed with the International Staff of NATO, an Atlantic Alliance branch working on the definition and implementation of military assistance programs : the International Staff was the source of so much fierce criticism from the United States that the US Embassy in Rome blamed it for «prodding all European nations about aircraft production to fill large European deficiencies»[485]. On several occasions over the course of negotiations on the OSP programs, the US government strove to bypass NATO and to skip its role in placing orders and providing the Europeans with financial support. This occurred even when the OSP programs placed contracts with a US-based aeronautical industry and assigned subcontracting orders to the Italian firms. The case of the assembly of the most modern F86K all-weather fighter model clearly illustrates this, as we shall see in the following paragraphs. Following an earlier project, the F86 program highlights the unwillingness of the US to let Fiat assemble this all-weather fighter in full, which was ferociously opposed in Washington by a wide range of government agencies and bureaucratic branches. Indeed, the US government chose to place orders to carry out maintenance works on spare parts and to produce all-weather components with the Italian metal working and aircraft industry[486]. In fact, in the case of the F86K aircraft the United States government decided to place the contract for its assembly with North American Aviation, which in turn was to allocate subcontract orders to Italian industry to manufac-

---

484 Ambasciata italiana a Washington, 'Memorandum', 13 May 1953; R.Pacciardi to Fiat, 'Licenza di riproduzione di velivolo F86 ditta North American Aviation', 20 June 1953; see also for reference 'Accordo per licenza e assistenza', 16 May 1953, all of these documents are in ASF, USA-Delibere, b. Contratto USAF-Governo italiano e licenza North American Aviation-Governo italiano-Fiat, year 1953;

485 Memorandum of Conversation dated 18 March 1953, on the subject of OSP Aviation contracts, participated in by Mr. Ortona, Counselor of the Italian Embassy, Mr. V.Lansing Collins and Mr. Edwin Adams, 'Aircraft Production in Italy', 13 April 1953, in NARA, RG84, Rome Embassy, Secret General Records 1953-1955, b. 1, fold. 320.1 (off-shore procurement classified 1953-1955); H.M.Byington (Director, Office of Western European Affairs) to E.Dunbrow (Esquire, Counselor of AmEmbassy to Italy), 31 December 1952, in NARA, RG84, Rome Embassy, Secret General Records 1953-55, b. 1, fold. 320.1 Off-Shore Procurement Classified 1953-55;

486 'Draft Paper for Mission Chiefs' Meeting, 'F-86 Aircraft Program', 15 August 1953, in NARA, RG469, Mission to Italy, Office of the Director, Subject Files (Central Files) 1948-1957, b. 41, fold. 3;

ture and supply several spare parts. Here also the Pentagon retained the right to approve or withdraw the wide range of subcontract orders, and decide their allocation and funding[487]. By the mid-1950s the Pentagon had taken the lead in instructing the military assistance programs and in shaping the OSP contracts and their distribution across the Atlantic bloc economies. In fact, starting in spring 1954 the Secretary of Defense and the Assistant Secretary of Defense for the International Security Affairs assumed the power to shape and implement the military assistance programs from the three US armies and the intra-departmental committees, such as the US Munitions Allocation Council, the Mutual Defense Assistance Management Council, or the Joint Chiefs of Staff that had hitherto been responsible for these tasks. As a direct result of this reorganization and centralization of power on military assistance decision-making, thereafter the various Military Assistance Advisory Groups in operation at each US Embassy in Europe took instruction directly from the Secretary of Defense[488].

Although the decision-making process within the American government and among the US military branches had changed substantially over the first half of the 1950s, the dual stance of the US military on multilateral rearmament was advanced consistently over the course of those years. This widely shared view on how multilateral rearmament should be shaped from the early off-shore procurement programs through the middle of the decade, which was based on skipping the financial facility set up within NATO, on placing production orders directly with European industry through the implementation of bilateral military assistance, and at the same time on stimulating the industrial cooperation and trade exchange among the European economies through the launching of integrated production chains and a full exploitation of different natural or manufacturing resources available in each Atlantic bloc economy, was pursued coherently.

It is indeed difficult to account for the twin American stance on multilateral military production programs that have emerged from my study. Neither US military concern for the implications of US financial contributions to the financial facility of NATO on the ordinary budget of the Pentagon, nor American industry's firm opposition to handing over influence on the shaping of multilateral rearmament that any NATO-centered reorganization of military assistance might imply offer a convincing explanation. Contrary to the opinion of the European chancelleries and the claims of the American industries producing war materials, this Ameri-

---

487 Dunbrow (Rome Embassy) to the Secretary of State, 2 July 1955, telegram, in NARA, RG469, Office of the Deputy Director for Operations (1953-1961), Office of African and European Operations (1955-1961), Western Europe Division, Italy Subject File 1950-56, b. 1;

488 J.Ohly to H.Stassen, 'Department of Defense Directive', 30 April 1954, in NARA, RG469, Deputy to the Director, Subject Files of Glen A.Lloyd, Deputy to the Director 1953-55, b. 4, fold. Military Assistance; Department of Defense, Directive 5132.3, 'Policy, Organisation and Function Relating to the Mutual Defense Assistance Program', 26 April 1954, idem;

can position was based on a variety of reasons[489]. The Pentagon's concern with the impact of its financial contribution to the common fund established within NATO to finance the war material manufacturing European economies can only explain the American stance to a rather limited extent[490]. On the other hand, the pressure that the US industrial military complex exerted consistently to maintain influence on the shaping of the off-shore procurement contracts to European industry, contrasted with the Pentagon stance.

There is, in fact, a wealth of archival documentary evidence that demonstrates how American industry aimed to overshadow and eliminate any operative role being played by NATO in order to pursue its own industrial and profit-making interests. For instance, in early 1952 the authoritative periodical *Fortune* speaking for the US business community expressed their heartfelt criticism toward a prolonged lack of attention ‹‹on the part of either the military or the planners in Washington of the urgency of machine tools until about six or eight months after Korea›› [491]. Contrary to the claim of US manufacturers, the idea that underpinned the choice by the US Air Force and the Pentagon to set up a series of assembly lines to produce in full both all-weather fighters and their spare parts, and at the same time to overshadow any operative role of NATO in shaping the OSP programs, was that of establishing a structured production base in Western Europe. The aim was to enable the European allies to be fully independent of American aid and of the US war industry. This US military stance was directly connected to the American objective of rebuilding the European defense industry and consistently equipping the national armies using American production methods and military goods. This objective of introducing American-style production rationalization and standardization of goods was part of the long-term US aim to transfer most of the materials that the US armies discarded over time to the West European allies, as well as to extend and to introduce scores of technical services and machine tools in Europe that previously had been used by the United States military forces alone[492].

---

489 Confindustria, n.a. (authored by Targiani), 'Promemoria', 2 January 1952, in ASC, CED, b. 49.1/2, fold. Commesse. Promemoria del dottor Mattei-Targiani-Campilli, s.f. 1952. Promemoria Targiani-Campilli-commesse;

490 Tarchiani to MAE, DGAE, 'Aiuti americani. Off-Shore Procurement', 25 November 1952, both in ASC, CED, b. 49.1/2 (Commesse alle Forze armate degli Stati Uniti), fold. Commesse. Promemoria del Dottor Mattei-Targiani-Campilli, s.f. Commesse per le Forze Armate americane. Circolari. Appunti);

491 *The Machine-Tool fumble*, in "Fortune", January 1952, p. 56;

492 Mutual Assistance Advisory Committee, 'Minutes', 29 October 1952, in DDRS; L.Targiani, Promemoria, 'Considerazioni pratiche sulle commesse', 1 February 1952, in ASC, CED, b. 49.1/2, fold. Commesse. Promemoria del dottor Mattei-Targiani-Campilli, s.f. 1952. Promemoria Targiani-Campilli-commesse; Office of Secretary of Defense, 'Department of Defense Report to the National Security Council on Status of Military Assistance Programs as of 30 June 1955. Section II-Topical Report', 1 October 1955, in NARA, RG273, Records of the National Security Council, Policy Papers, b. 38, p. 33;

In both these off-shore procurement contracts, it is clear that the American military convincingly promoted the launch and implementation of multilateral and coordinated production programs to attain rearmament; on the other hand, the US armies maneuvered to contract out the off-shore procurements to European industry and to pay for them in such a way as to avoid any intermediary role by NATO. By the mid-1950s, with the implementation of the all-weather fighter OSP contracts, this US tendency to combine the implementation of coordinated industrial production chains among the European economies with tight bilateral economic relations that had been designed to enable the US Department of Defense and the Department of State to engage directly with the European counterparts in military procurement contracts and financial aid negotiations, was relentlessly furthered by all the military and the civilian government agencies in Washington.

4.5 The US military assistance programs to the Italian aeronautical industry amidst dumping and industrial modernization

The interplay between American military aid to help resurrect the Italian defense industry from its war-torn conditions and the process of technological update and production rationalization that involved the Italian mechanical and metalworking industry during the period of post war reconstruction has long engendered scholarly debate between economists and historians. With reference to the early 1950s, scholars from these two disciplines basically present two contrasting arguments. A first cohort of studies maintains that the military assistance programs promoted by the Atlantic Alliance triggered a dumping impact on the Italian war industry on the whole and specifically on aeronautics. According to these studies the US guideline to transfers military end items and spare parts cast off by the US troops would account for this dumping effect, whereas a significant slowdown in terms of technological modernization and capital upgrade ensued. In this respect, most of these studies contend that this delay in upgrading the Italian production lines prevented firms that produced items such as tanks and all-weather fighters from advancing in productivity, price competitiveness and output capacity[493]. On the other hand, a second strand of scholarly works that focused on reconstructing the impact of ERP on the reorganization of the Italian mechanical industry suggests a rather differ-

---

493 S.Parazzini, *Le trasformazioni dell'industria militare europea. Le politiche industriali per la ristrutturazione*, Giuffrè, Milano, 1996, p. 199; L.Sebesta, *L'Europa indifesa*, p. 238; M.Nones, *L'industria militare dalla ricostruzione all'espansione*, in C.Jean (ed.), *Storia delle forze armate italiane dalla ricostruzione postbellica alla 'ristrutturazione del 1975*; V.Ilari, *Storia militare della prima repubblica 1943-1993*, Nuove Ricerche, Ancona, 1994, p. 267; M.Ferrari, *Trasformazioni e ridimensionamento dell'industria aeronautica nel secondo dopoguerra*, p. 127;

ent interpretation. In fact, these reconstructions maintain that the ECA economic aid programs promoted under the umbrella of the European Recovery Program boosted a technological leap all across the majority of the large Italian manufacturing firms by introducing both American type labor organization methods and a significant turn over in terms of machine tools and instrumental goods to Italy[494]. We should note that though the US-promoted OSP programs played an essential role in the process of recovery and further development of the Italian aeronautical firms, it is all the more important to remark that it is still disputable whether ‹‹this development was a spin-off from American technology (transferred as part of the OSP contracts) or due mainly to indigenous engineering and managerial skills››[495]. However, the Fiat group, on which my own reconstruction is based, offers a clear example in favor of the latter interpretation.

To further analyze this point we should consider the impact of the MDAP on the technological update and production rationalization of the Turin-based production chains of the Italian multinational involved in the rearmament programs. This may shed light on the argument by offering a balanced view on a rather contested point such as the interplay between rearmament and productivity in the framework of the US governments' policies toward the West European allies.

When the MDAP began appropriating the OSP contracts across European industry, the car-producing giant headed by Vittorio Valletta was already on its way to achieving a capital intensive modernization. Although the Fiat group was traditionally very careful in adopting

---

494 M.Doria, *Note sull'industria meccanica nella ricostruzione*, in "Rivista di storia economica", n. 4 (1987), p. 54; A.Milward, *The Reconstruction of Western Europe 1945-1952*, Meuthen, London , 1984, p. 112; P.P. D'Attorre, *Aspetti dell'attuazione del Piano Marshall in Italia*, in E.Aga Rossi (a cura di), *Il Piano Marshall e l'Europa*, Istituto della Enciclopedia italiana, Roma, 1983, pp. 167-170; G.Gualerni, *Ricostruzione e industria. Per una interpretazione della politica industriale nel secondo dopoguerra 1943-1951*, Vita e Pensiero, Milano, 1980, pp. 88-89; L.Segreto, *Americanizzare o modernizzare l'economia? Progetti americani e risposte italiane negli anni cinquanta e sessanta*, in "Passato e Presente", n. 37 (1996), p. 79; M.E.Guasconi, *L'altra faccia della medaglia*, pp. 108-113; F.Romero, *Gli Stati Uniti in Italia. Il Piano Marshall e il Patto atlantico*, in *Storia dell'Italia repubblicana*, Vol. 1, *La costruzione della democrazia*, pp. 263-265; L.Sebesta, T.Geiger, *A Self-Defeating Policy. American Offshore Procurement and Integration of Western European Defense Production 1952-1956*, in "Journal of European Integration History", n. 1 (1998), p. 68; V.Castronovo, *Fiat. Una storia del capitalismo italiano*, Rizzoli, Milano, 2005, p. 420;
495 T.Geiger, L.Sebesta, *National Defense Policies and the Failure of Military Integration in NATO. American Military Assistance and Western European Rearmament 1949-1954*, in F.H.Heller, J.Gilllingham (eds), *The United States and the Integration of Europe. Legacies of the Postwar Era*, St. Martin Press, New York 1996, p. 265; See also L.Sebesta, *American Military Aid and European Rearmament: the Italian Case*, in F.H.Heller, J.R.Gillingham (eds), *NATO: the Founding of the Atlantic Alliance and the Integration of Europe*, p. 296;

American-style production lines and labor organization methods[496], from the early post World War II period American aid programs for a substantial technological upgrade deeply influenced the reorganization of the Italian multinational's production chains. Prior to the launch of the Marshall Plan, in 1947 a sum worth up to $10 million was allotted within an Export-Import Bank loan to Italy. This sum was used to import machinery and machine tools which would modernize the Turin-based manufacturing plants. From 1948 onwards, the ERP funds to Fiat financed the swift and important capital-intensive advances that characterized the industrial history of Fiat in the late 1940s. In particular, the European Recovery Program nurtured a technological advance in the steel producing sectors, as well as in the car and track assembling production chains[497]. For instance, from 1948 to 1950 the ERP funds permitted Fiat to renovate one fourth of the machinery operative at its Mirafiori plans, leading to an improvement in product quality, industrial productivity and market competitiveness both in the area of mass production and on demand production[498].

Over the course of the Mutual Security Program's first two years of operation, Fiat predominantly used most of the Mutual Security Programs funds intended to foster industrial modernization to upgrade the basic means of production, whereas both the manufacturing and the assembly lines were not involved in this process of technological turn over. In this respect, for example, from 1950 to 1952 this Washington financed capital intensive modernization enable the steel producing lines to raise their volumes of production of crude steel from some 120,000 to 240,000 tons per year. Moreover, the American funds were used to raise power capacity meaning that Fiat could produce a wider range of steel products and byproducts[499].

From 1952 onwards, with the allocation of off-shore procurement contracts to Fiat as part of multilateral cooperation on rearmament among the Atlantic bloc economies, the Turin-based group supplied both the Italian armies and other partners' Ministries for Defense. Against this multilateral rearmament framework, the military assistance channeled to this manufacturing group provided continued capital intensive upgrade and offered assistance programs to help train the Italian workers in order to improve their working skills. In 1955, within bilateral negotiations between Rome and Washington on the allocation to Italy of OSP contracts to assemble a set of F86K fighters «for day and night all weather fighter defense needs of Italy

---

496 D.Bigazzi, *La grande fabbrica. Organizzazione industriale e modello americano alla Fiat dal Lingotto a Mirafiori*, Feltrinelli, Milano, 1999, p. 131;

497 P.Bairati, *Valletta*, p. 218; G.Lombardo, *L'apporto dello European Recovery Program (Piano Marshall) alla ri-progettazione dell'industria italiana nel secondo dopoguerra: modernizzazione, conflitti e produzioni offlimits*, p. 72;

498 D.Bigazzi, *La grande fabbrica*, pp. 136-142;

499 A.J.Grant (Industrial Projects Officer) to R.Whittet (Chairman, Projects Committee), 'MSA Project 67 Italy. Equipment for Production of Turbo Jet Parts by Fiat', 26 May 1953, in NARA, RG469, Mission to Italy, Office of the Director, Subject Files (Central Files) 1948-1957 (1948-54), b. 4, fold. 5 (Aircraft-Documents);

and other NATO nations», a program to train Italian technicians and skilled workers was approved and launched to improve maintenance and revision work on J-47 jet propulsion models that was then underway at the Turin plants. The program was to provide Fiat with «necessary technical assistance and facilities and provide repair and overhaul training Italian technicians»[500]. Furthermore, technical assistance Missions were approved in Washington to send a number of technicians from the US Forces to Turin to improve the technical skills of the workers employed in the F86 assembly lines[501]. Fiat welcomed this military assistance policy guideline and strove to use the financial aid from the Mutual Security Program to enhance capital intensive modernization and to further improve the skills of its workers. This policy took effect while the Italian elites' pursued a tendency to devote an ever increasing amount of ERP counterpart funds to finance the import of instrumental goods for the Italian manufacturing industry to advance industrial modernization[502].

It should be noted that for the Americans the desire to use the military assistance programs and the OSP contracts to boost technological upgrading and technical assistance across the Italian defense industry's production lines and its allied metalworking concerns did not contrast with the transfers of American military end items and machine tools, which had been at the basis of the early rearmament programs and were still underway during the early 1950s. In fact, the transfer of American end items was undoubtedly central to military assistance throughout this period[503]. Prior to 1949 it had been much debated during bilateral negotiations on the US military aid program to Rome, whereas from 1950 to 1953 direct transfers of US end items and military products transferred to Italy as part of the OSP program amounted to a value of $900 million and helped re-equip all three of the Italian armed forces, providing them with munitions, electronic devices, spare parts for jet fighter or combat trucks[504]. Indeed these

---

500 The Secretary of State (J.F.Dulles) to the American Embassy in Rome, 11 April 1955, telegram, in NARA, RG56, OASIA, b. 63, fold. Italy/9/52 MSA-FOA Off shore Procurement vol. 2;

501 'Programma F86K. Missioni e visitatori stranieri'; 'Revisione velivolo F86D. Notizie e dati sul lavoro svolto nel trimestre ottobre-dicembre 1955'; both documents are in in ASF, USA-Delibere, b. Contratto USAF-Governo italiano e licenza North American Aviation-Governo italiano-Fiat, year 1955;

502 H.Tasca (US Operation Mission Rome) to Foreign Oparation Administration Washington, 23 November 1953, telegram, in NARA, RG469, Mission to Italy, Office of the Director, Subject Files (Central Files) 1948-1957, b. 22, fold. 4 (Defense: Osp programs Contracts Production 1954);

503 Military Assistance Advisory Committee, 'Minutes', 25 February 1952, in DDRS;

504 American Embassy Rome-US Operation Mission to Italy, 'Italy. Economic Summary, October 1954, in NARA, RG59, Central Files 1955-59, b. 4809, 865.00/8-2255, p. 14; in order to get a neat sense of understanding of the ratio of end-items to total military assistance over fiscal year 1953, as well as the US spending outlook for the following years see US Department of Commerce, "Survey of Current Business", April 1953; 'aiuti americani 1953-1954. Situazione al 25 giugno 1953', n.d. (but, 1953), in ACS, Ministero del Tesoro, Direzione Generale del Tesoro, IRFE, b. 10; IMF, Western

transfers, that by early 1955 had reached a value of nearly $1 billion, were never intended by Washington as an alternative to the creation of a production base in Europe[505]. Rather, the American military and the US federal agencies promoted this huge transfer of military goods with the twin aim of providing war material that the Italian manufacturers could not produce, and helping the Italian industry to set up self-sufficient output capacity[506]. In this respect the transfer of military goods was intended not only to offer immediate political support to the De Gasperi Cabinets in their effort to curb the internal communist anomaly but also to drive this principle of self-sufficiency that in turn could only be implemented with wide-ranging capital intensive modernization and technological update[507].

This American decision to both strongly promote a self-sufficient production base in Italy and Europe and to transfer instrumental goods, spare parts and end items that the US military and the American industry had cast off revolved also around two elements that the Americans had chosen to bet on in the mid-1950s. On one hand, by the early 1950s Washington had identified the Italian manufacturing system as an ideal defense production source for the Atlantic Alliance, as Italy had a widely unutilized industrial capability and a high rate of unemployed average-skilled and highly skilled workers. Italy's full involvement would therefore serve the defense needs of other NATO nations while at the same time tackling the unemployment issue; this latter move being essential to subdue social unrest and avoid any potential political uprisings which the Italian far-left was suspected of fomenting[508]. Furthermore, the introduction of American military goods and the US desire to introduce both American type production methods and US technology, which included offering technical assistance to train Italian workers, is clearly related to the American move to distribute OSP contracts to produce American technology based all-weather aircrafts and jet fighter components. This is highlighted by the launch and implementation in Italy of production lines to manufacture the F86 all-weather fighter models following the fold-up of the Venom program. In fact, transferring

Hemisphere Department, North American Division, 'Review of the United States Foreign Aid Program', 15 May 1953, in ASBI, Carte Caffè, Pratt., n. 50, fold. 1;

505 L.Sebesta, *American Military Aid and European Rearmament: the Italian Case*, p. 296; F.Fauri, *L'Italia e l'integrazione economica europea*, p. 51;

506 'Objectives of US Aid to Italy in 1952/53', 21 July 1952, Secret, in NARA, RG469, Mission to Italy, Office of the Director, Subject Files (Central Files) 1948-1957 (1948-54), b. 2, fold. 1 (Aid Negotiations), p. 8; H.B.Chenery (Chief, Program Division), to V.Barnett, 'Objectives of US Aid to Italy in 1952/53', 21 July 1952, *idem*;

507 In this respect the US Embassy in Rome shared the American government's view in full. See on this Dayton to Acheson, 27 June 1951, telegram, in NARA, RG469, Mission to Italy, Office of the Director, Subject Files (Central Files) 1948-1957, b. 22, fold. 2 (Defense, OSP Program: contracts, Production);

508 State Department, Memorandum 'OSP Aviation Contract in Italy', 10 April 1953, in NARA, RG59, Records of the Office of the Special Assistant for Mutual Security Coordination, Office of the Undersecretary of State, 1952-1959, Lot File 59D449, b. 25;

163

spare parts and instrumental goods to the Italian industry to produce this American style jet fighter would speed up the work and supply from European productions sources compared to the production through the early 1950s of military aircrafts based on British technology[509]. This modernization of the Italian aircraft industry based on American technology dominated the reorganization and industrial update of Fiat and its allied firms. In 1954, even as Rome and Washington engaged in lengthy negotiations on the OSP contracts to Italy designed to supply other NATO nations in the short term, Washington allotted very generous transfers of machine tools and industrial equipment to Italy. This massive transfer of instrumental goods from the US-based Allison concern[510], allowed Fiat to start producing spare parts for the J-35 jet engines that were to equip the F84G jet fighters. This American-led technological spin off continued thereafter with the production in Europe of the F86K all-weather fighter model. Against the background of the OSP programs the United States transferred technical equipment, services and instrumental goods to Turin to permit work on orders to produce J-47 jet engines spare parts and the assembly of J-47 jet engines[511].

---

509 M.P.Arth to Kohn Ohly, 28 April 1953, secret, in NARA, RG469, Mission to Italy, Office of the Director, Subject Files (Central Files) 1948-1957, (1948-1954), b. 4, fold. 5 (Aircraft-Documents);
510 V.Bowlby (Reimbursable Aid Branch), Memorandum for the Record, 'Conference Relative to Transfer of Machine Tools to Italy for the Fiat Corporation', 21 January 1954, in NARA, RG330, Country Files (CAIN) 1950-1955; G.C.Steward (Major General, US Army, Director, Office of Military Assistance, Memorandum for the Assistant Secretary of Defense International Security Affairs, 'Transfer of Machine Tools', 3 February 1954, idem;
511 Fiat, 'Notizie e dati al 30 giugno 1956', in ASF, USA-Delibere, b. Contratto USAF-Governo italiano e licenza North American Aviation-Governo italiano-Fiat, year 1956;

Chapter 5

Domestic political stability and external economic equilibrium: the OSP contracts
through the mid- 1950s between the United States and Italy

5.1 Amidst internal political stability and supra-national economic integration: the United States and the F86 off-shore procurement contracts for Italy through the mid-1950s

In chapter four I focused my reconstruction on the bilateral negotiations between Rome and
Washington to start up the assembly of different models of F86 all-weather fighters. In so
doing I aimed, on the one hand, to highlight the American attempt to bypass a multilateral
coordination of rearmament and allocation of the off-shore procurement contracts; on the other, to shed light on the relevance that the nexus between rearmament and productivity played
in the U.S. military aid policies regarding the definition, launch and implementation of the
OSP contracts.

By contrast, this last chapter will focus on the off-shore procurement programs implemented
through the mid-1950s, especially the appropriation of procurement contracts placed with the
Italian aeronautical industry to enable it step up from assembling all-weather fighters to building up a full production source capable of producing and assembling a series of different and
successive models of F86 jet aircraft. I will concentrate on these orders in order to reappraise
the interpretation that has hitherto dominated historical debate on the subject, and argue that
the political turn over in Washington from the Truman Presidency to the Eisenhower Administration, and the arrival in Rome in 1953 of the new American ambassador nominated by the
Republican government, Clare Boothe Luce, marked a significant change in US strategies to
stabilize Italy and to bind the country to the Atlantic Alliance. In fact, most available scholarly reconstructions suggest that under the new ambassador the United States conducted negotiations on the all-weather fighters as leverage to make the Italian governments led by the
Christian Democrats curb the communist anomaly still threatening the Atlantic loyalty of Italy. In particular, I will suggest that by the time the Truman Administration stepped down from
office, the US conception of the Communist rise that identified the left-wing's widespread
popularity across Italian society and among the working class of the Peninsula as stemming
from the country's economic backwardness and comparatively slow economic recovery and
reconstruction compared to other European societies in the aftermath of war, had come of age.
According to this mainstream historiographical view, the new US Administration conducted
negotiations on the OSP contracts to address political objectives, the most important of which

was the curbing of the leftward nation-level trade union CGIL, widely-recognized as being close to the Italian Communist Party and with a loyalty aligned to the Soviet bloc[512]. The scholarly reconstructions on the subject maintain that the new ambassador resorted to the on-going bilateral bargaining on the allocation of OSP to Italy to make the De Gasperi government confront the leftward CGIL and reduce its strength within the Turin-based Fiat plants and most of Northern Italy's mechanical firms[513]. Indeed, it is worth pointing to the fact that any well documented archival research would prove this contention further, and that the U.S. government pursued this position consistently and ever more strongly in the run-up to the general elections scheduled for early summer 1953 as the imminent polls stirred fear in Washington that the Soviet-inspired far left parties might gain a political grip on the country. From the beginning of the 1953, for example, the Mutual Security Agency was to place a package of OSP contracts with the Italian industry in the short term, and in the long run to assign orders to produce a program of all-weather fighters worth up to $150 million to the Italian manufacturers in order to prevent the Christian Democrat party and its allies from suffering a sharp electoral setback[514]. Moreover, the new American Administration consistently continued along this tack following the June 1953 general elections. Indeed, in early 1954 the US ambassador in Rome made her case for a political clean-up in the plants working on the OSP contracts as a precondition to allotting procurements to produce in full the F86 all-weather fighter. In her visit to Washington in January she stressed before her government that «the program has never been firmly approved on military-technical grounds and the Rome Embassy team has not yet approved Fiat for the contract since it has not taken sufficient anti-Communist action in the plants which would be used for the assembly»[515]. Later on in the same year, the head of the Eisenhower Administration's newly established agency for the coordination of US foreign economic assistance programs and military aid, Harold Stassen, pushed this argument further. On the occasion of a meeting with the Italian Finance Minister

---

512 This interpretation is indeed partly proved further through the primary sources we consulted. See in this respect C.Luce to T.Voorhees, 10 February 1954, in NARA, RG84, Rome Embassy, Secret General Records 1953-1955, b. 1, fold. 320.1 Off-Shore Procurement Classified 1953-55;

513 G.G.Migone, Stati Uniti, Fiat, e repressione antioperaia negli anni Cinquanta, in "Rivista di storia contemporanea", n. 3 (1974); P.Bairati, *Valletta*, pp. 252-258; M.Del Pero, American Pressures and Their Containment in Italy During the Ambassadorship of Clare Boothe Luce 1953-1956, in "Diplomatic History", n. 3 (June 2004), pp. 407-439;

514 A.W.Harriman to W.Foster, 1 December 1952, in *FRUS 1952-54*, Vol. 6, *Western Europe and Canada* , Part 2, pp. 1597-1598; A.W.Harriman to W.Foster (Deputy Secretary of Defense, Department of Defense), 'Letter from Mr. Harriman to Mr. Foster on Offshore Procurement in Italy', 23 December 1952, in NARA, RG469, Mission to Italy, Office of the Director, Subject Files (Central Files) 1948-1957, b. 23, fold. 1 (Defense-Production); see also M.Del Pero, *L'alleato scomodo*, p. 177;

515 American Embassy in Rome, Economic Section/USOM, 'Current US Financial Program Issues in Italy', 16 January 1954, in NARA, RG59, Records Relating to the Mutual Security Program, West European Country Files 1952-1956, Lot File 59D448, b. 1;

Ezio Vanoni, Stassen insisted that though over the course of 1953 the Italian economy had showed significant signs of recovery, the persistence of communist strength across Italian society and the influential consensus of the leftward trade unions' strongholds within Fiat and the most important mechanical industries of Northern Italy, was still a constraint on the placing of defense procurement contracts with the Italian industry. The curbing of the red scare was to couple sustained economic growth with political initiatives and means to erode the structure of the Italian communist party across the country and to reduce the CGIL strength in the mechanical industry[516].

This strategy to confront the Communist menace through the coupling of economic growth to raise the living standards with political initiatives to roll back the leftward political parties and trade unions is clearly highlighted and serves to introduce the basic argument of this chapter and my re-appraisal of the mainstream historical view that I briefly outlined above.

In fact, at variance with mainstream interpretations, this chapter aims to offer a balanced view on the American strategies to confront the Communist threat in the country and to stabilize its economic and political outlook through the middle of the decade through the viewpoint of the off-shore procurement contracts that aimed to establish a full production phase in Italy. What ensues from my reconstruction is that the new United States government and the American ambassadorial envoy in Rome changed their interpretation over time of both the nature of Communist rise and the reasons for its successful spread across Italy, as well as their strategies on the most effective and viable way to tame it. It was only for a rather limited period of time, during the first year of Luce ambassadorship in Rome, that the Eisenhower Administration used bilateral negotiations on the OSP contracts to attain political objectives. Soon thereafter both Luce and her government negotiated the implementation of the program to promote sustained economic growth. In this respect, during talks with the Rome Cabinet on the off-shore procurement contracts, the United States once again showed a perception of the Italian communist anomaly as clearly arising from the Italian economy's slow and difficult steps along the path of overcoming the economic restrains typical of postwar reconstruction, as well as poverty based social problems and class conflicts. From roughly the first half of 1954 Washington used multilateral military assistance to pursue two economic objectives with the aim of fighting the red scare in Italy and making the country a stable and fully reliable partner for NATO and the Italian economy a pivotal full production source for the Atlantic Alliance defense needs and security policies: supranational integration of the Italian economy and domestic economic growth. In fact, as I have tried to illustrate in this chapter, in conducting negotiations on the implementation of the OSP contracts to produce the F86 all-weather fighters, the Eisenhower Administration was committed to the twin aim of achieving a series of eco-

---

516 Tasca (US Operation Mission to Italy) to FOA Washington, 'Governor Stassen's Visit to Rome', 29 October 1954, in NARA, RG469, Office of the Deputy Director for Operations (1953-1961), Office of European Operations (1953-1955), Office of the Director, Geographic Files (Central Files) 1953-54, b. 124, fold. Italy-Programs-Economic Development;

nomic targets. Firstly, the redressing of the balance of Italy's foreign exchange equilibrium and the promotion of a high volume of Italian trade exchange through continued trade liberalization and the dismantling of tariff restrictions. Secondly, both Washington and ambassador Luce consistently endorsed a wide range of domestic expansionary economic policies aimed at either raising the average living standard or increasing the number of employed people.

A further argument I will make points to the fact that negotiations, appropriations and the ensuing work on the OSP contracts were at the center of bilateral economic relations between the two countries covering a wide range of issues. This meant that the OSP program was part of bilateral bargaining on the shaping of Italy's move from reconstruction to sustained economic growth, and on the economic assistance initiatives that Washington had committed to with increasing consistence and firmness by the middle of the decade and which would influence and shape this Italian transition from post war recovery to economic take off. Far from underestimating the political leverage underpinning the American guidelines on military assistance, I maintain that Washington's original perception of the nature of communism as a byproduct of economic deprivation, industrial scarcity and social despair was replaced by the idea that a political roll-back was only temporarily worth pursuing and necessary to bind the country to the Atlantic Alliance. Based on my archive research I would argue that even ambassador Luce, usually regarded in the literature as being at the forefront of this fiercely fought strategy to curb the Italian left, assumed this stance only for a rather limited time of period during her ambassadorship in Rome. By the middle of the decade she herself increasingly and firmly supported the implementation of economic aid programs to sustain domestic economic growth, stabilization in the foreign exchange equilibrium, and increasing supranational market integration of the Italian economy within the broader ongoing process of intra-European economic integration. Likewise, I maintain that throughout the first half of the decade the United States conceived the OSP as an economic diplomacy instrument to influence the internal economic policymaking of the Italian governments and to encourage them to adopt some foreign economic and trade policy decisions. I would here contrast the existing literature, by stressing how Washington resorted to bilateral negotiations on the OSP contracts to attain foreign trade liberalization and the dismantling of monopolies and restrictive business practices on the whole. Accordingly, I contend that the Eisenhower Administration drew on all of the OSP-related bilateral diplomatic confrontations with Rome in an attempt to attain a wide range of economic targets all aimed at sustaining Italian economic growth prior to its take off in the late 1950s. Last but not least, I argue that both under the leadership of the Italian Christian democratic statesman De Gasperi through the first half of 1953, and until the middle of the decade, the Italian economic policymakers (the economic ministries, the cohorts of economic technocracies in the Central Bank of Italy and other major Italian economic institution) engaged in negotiations on the OSP contracts to obtain aid for the stabilization of the foreign exchange equilibrium. In addition, they used these negotiations to put pressure on Italy's main European trade partners to adopt wide-ranging trade liberalization in order to improve the assets in the Italian terms of trade. Hence, Italy fought to make the US government use its influence with the British and the French to enable the Italian export industry benefit from fair tariff and quantitative conditions to access these European export markets. On the whole, therefore, my reconstruction in this last chapter clearly indicates that in the framework of bilateral economic relations between the United States and Italy the off-shore procurement contracts were used on both sides to achieve a wide range of much needed outcomes for both the domestic economy and to an even greater extent for foreign trade and monetary issues.

5.2 The economic implications of the all-weather fighter OSP programs economic strategy of the United States toward Italy: the supply side of multilateral rearmament, the Italian terms of trade, and the country's domestic economic expansion

In May 1953, despite the impending general elections in Italy, the deal clinched between the Italian government, the North American Aviation Company and Fiat for the launch of an assembly program which would give the Turin plants as many as 50 F86K all-weather fighters and enable the Italian aeronautical industry to produce all-weather fighter models for NATO was fiercely opposed by several branches of the US government[517]. A year earlier the Rome based representatives of the US government Mutual Security Agency that was to coordinate foreign military assistance, stated that while placing orders in Italy would help prevent the Moscow-inspired left-wing parties from gaining a grip on the electorate «the very fact of providing more work in a country with mass unemployment» meant that the economy did not offer fair conditions: steel prices were still very expensive, the country was highly dependent on foreign supply for most of the required raw and strategic materials, whereas the manufacturers were short of credit liquidity and hampered by a credit crunch that determined high interest rates[518]. These conditions aroused fear among the Americans that a rearmament-induced expansion of the Italian defense industry might lead the Italians to pump money into the money market and head the country towards an inflationary spiral: «a resort to deficit

---

517 'Offshore Procurement of Aircraft in Italy', 11 December 1953, in NARA, RG59, Lot File 58D357, b. 15, fold. 435.03 (OSP 1953-1954); Luce to the Secretary of State, 'F86K project', 2 June 1954, in NARA, RG59, Records of the Office of the Special Assistant for Mutual Security Coordination, Office of the Undersecretary of State 1952-59, Lot File 59D449, b. 25; E.Ortona, *Anni d'America. La diplomazia 1953-1961*, pp. 29-30. Contrary to my own estimates, according to Valerio Castronovo this deal was to allow Fiat to produce as many as 70 F86K all weather fighters (V.Castronovo, *Fiat 1899-1999. Un secolo di storia*, p. 878);
518 Rome Country Team, 'Production Program by Categories', n.d. (but, spring 1952), in NARA, RG469, Mission to Italy, Office of the Director, Subject Files (Central Files) 1948-1957, b. 22, fold. 2 (Defense OSP program: contracts, production);

borrowing at the Bank of Italy»[519] would be likely. These pessimistic economic arguments were repeated over the course of 1953 to oppose a follow-up assembly program for a further 100 F86K jet fighters. On this occasion the MSA and the Embassy in Rome argued that «as to the advisability from the economic point of view of establishing a vast new aircraft industry, pointing to the serious drain on Italy's limited investment funds, the load on the economy as foreign military orders dwindle.»[520]

Notwithstanding this firm opposition in Rome, the Truman Administration worked to place contracts with the Italian aeronautical industry in 1952 and later the Eisenhower Administration strove to start a production program that would enable Italy to work on different models of F86 all-weather fighters. In fact, this new program which started in 1953, offered Italy the chance to step up from assembly to full production over the course of the following two years. A variety of reasons may explain this American decision to permit Italian industry to set up a full production phase to supply the defense needs of NATO and the national air forces of its member states. The literature has pointed to the fact that this US policy aimed to encourage Italy to proceed with foreign trade liberalization and domestic expansionary policies through the implementation of development projects and the institution of agencies such as the internationally-known Agency for the Development of Southern Italy (*Cassa per il Mezzogiorno*), irrespective of the impact on the employment rate[521]. While this argument surely played an important part in the US government's decision to let Italy produce in full the F86 jet fighters[522], several other reasons are worth mentioning. Firstly, as the British Foreign Office underlined in June 1952, the American off-shore purchases of complete aircraft alone would «help to resuscitate the Italian aircraft industry»[523]. Secondly, though that is not pivotal to this chapter's argument, it is worth recalling that the manufacturing situation of the continent pushed the United States in that direction. In fact, by the year 1953 all the other most important European aeronautical and metalworking national industries were at the time working

---

519 P.P.Schaffner to Parker, Memorandum, 'Mission recommendation to SRE regarding position to be taken with Italians in NATO Annual Review', 3 November 1952, in NARA, RG469, Mission to Italy, Office of the Director, Subject Files (Central Files) 1948-1957, b. 26, fold. 2 (Finance 1952-1954);

520 M.P.Arth (DD/P-FOA) to H.Stassen (Director FOA), 'Memorandum: Background on All-Weather Fighters', 1 March 1954, in NARA, RG469, Mission to Italy, Office of the Director, Subject Files (Central Files) 1948-1957 (1954-1957), b. 5, fold. Italy: Defense Production Airplane Fiat F86K Fighters;

521 L.Segreto, *The Importance of the foreign constraint: debates about a new social and economic order in Italy 1945-1955*;

522 In this respect see Department of State, 'Fiscal Year Title I (Europe) Defense Support Program. Supplemental Note. Italy', in NARA, RG59, Lot File 58D357, b. 15, fold. 435.01 Direct Aid 1953-1954;

523 Memorandum by the Secretary of State for Foreign Affairs, 'Aircraft for North Atlantic Treaty Forces: Off-shore Purchases by the United States in Europe', 25 June 1952, in PRO, The Cabinet Papers 1915-1981, CAB/129/53;

at full capacity on the rearmament effort to manufacture in full other jet fighters. In particular, the British firms were committed to produce the Javelin, whereas NATO had placed orders to supply a French type of aircraft named Mystère with the French manufacturers[524]. Considering that German industry was still excluded from industrial cooperation on rearmament[525], and that the production capability of both Belgium and the Netherlands was insufficient to supply other NATO partners[526], both the Secretary of State, Acheson, and his Eisenhower-appointed successor, John Forster Dulles, considered an Italian commitment to serve as a full production source for the Atlantic Alliance as essential.

Though either of these reasons would help explain why the US looked to the Italian economy to form a production source working on the F86 all-weather models, a fair and balanced historical interpretation should also take into account two further motives underpinning that American move to rely on the Italian aircraft industry. Firstly, the United States planned to place a full production chain with Italian industry in order to stimulate a significant expansion of the Italian industrial base conducive to increased employment growth dynamics; secondly, we should consider that such a choice would also tackle the impact of the rearmament effort on the country's balance of payments and its terms of trade. It is therefore worth examining America's changing policy from both these vantage points.

Indeed, in the summer of 1952 the U.S. ambassador to Italy, Bunker, had already made a case to William Draper, then the US special representative in Europe, for placing an off-shore procurement program worth up to $300 million with the Italian metalworking plants. In insisting on this request, the ambassador in Italy had stressed that the appropriation of off-shore procurement contracts might have a political appeal as far as it helped to fight unemployment in the manufacturing sectors involved in the defense effort such as shipbuilding, aeronautics, the truck and car industry and electronics where there were many unemployed workers while the output capacity was significantly unutilized[527]. When the Republicans came to power and ambassador Clare Boothe Luce arrived at the US Embassy in Rome the anti-communist bias

---

524 Pro-memoria for SE Alessandrini 'Collaborazione italo-franco-tedesca nel campo aeronautico', 5 November 1954, in ASMAE, Ambasciata d'Italia a Parigi, 1951-1958 (1954), b. 38, fold. R.11/19-1, s.f. anno 1954 (Collaborazione italo-franco-tedesca nel campo aeronautico);

525 Memorandum by the Secretary of State for Foreign Affairs, 'German Financial Contribution to Defense', 3 May 1952, in PRO, The Cabinet Papers 1915-1981, CAB/129/51;

526 Pro-memoria for SE Alessandrini 'Collaborazione italo-franco-tedesca nel campo aeronautico', 5 November 1954, in ASMAE, Ambasciata d'Italia a Parigi, 1951-1958 (1954), b. 38, fold. R.11/19-1, s.f. anno 1954 (Collaborazione italo-franco-tedesca nel campo aeronautico);

527 E.Bunker to G.Perkins (Assistant Secretary of State for European Affairs, Department of State), 15 August 1952, in NARA, RG469, Mission to Italy, Office of the Director, Subject Files (Central Files) 1948-1957 (1948-54), b. 2, fold. 2 (Aid Negotiations); as regards the rather limited concern of the Rome-based Country Team for the impact of the rearmament program on the Italian balance of payments and the balance deficit H.B.Chenery to C.Parker, 'Background analysis for Aid Negotiations', 17 September 1952, idem;

of the new Administration undoubtedly played an important role in the way the United States negotiated the allotment of the OSP contracts. During the following two years this roll-back stance led the Pentagon, the Department of Defense and the Embassy to discuss and plan the setting up of a «White list» of Italian metalworking firms whose trade union representation made them suitable to work on military procurements[528]. From 1953 through 1954 this American stance, mainly formulated at the Department of Defense and at the US Embassy in Rome, certainly contributed to slowing down the negotiations with Italy on the launch of a full production phase to produce the F86K aircraft across the Peninsula. Indeed, the Department of Defense fiercely opposed the launch of the program[529]. The new ambassador clearly stated «that a nation with a large communist element may not be able to fight effectively against the Kremlin in the event of an emergency».[530] In fact, in early 1954 Luce was convinced that economic and material scarcity was not the source of communist strength: in her meeting with the Eisenhower Administration in Washington she underlined that the persistence of communist strength in a country that had already overcome the immediate post war economic disarray proved that «the idea that economic progress will defeat Communism was simply not true». In line with this perspective, the US Embassy in Rome ventured to suggest that the Eisenhower Administration force Italian firms to fire their entire labor force and re-employ the workers only after a political and trade union clean up[531].

Notwithstanding this roll-back biased diplomatic drive, the new ambassador and the Department of Defense did not prevail on the less orthodox positions that the Department of State took up. As matter of fact, despite the strength of the leftwing and the firm political stance of the Pentagon, the Department of State was successful in its attempt to implement the OSP program in Italy. Thus, in December 1953 the Secretary of State, Dulles, convinced the Department of Defense to accept and to endorse a follow-up program to place as many as 62 all-

---

528 Dulles to the American Embassy in Italy, 26 January 1955, telegram, in NARA, RG56, OASIA, b. 63, fold. Italy/9/52 MSA-FOA Offshore Procurement col. 2; J.Dulles to the American Embassy in Italy, 9 February 1955, telegram, idem;

529 on the Pentagon opposition throughout the fall to a military assistance program for the Italian aeronautics to set up a full production phase to complement the «assembly operation» production lines already underway see L.Ripps to D.Hopkinson, 'Stassen's Meeting with Ambassador Tarchiani of Italy Scheduled for 11 A.M. Tuesday, October 6, 1953', 5 October 1953, in NARA, RG469, Records of the Director (1953-1961), Geographic Files of the Director 1948-1955, b. 11, fold. Italy-commodities-Airplanes;

530 A.Gruenther to C.Luce, 18 December 1953, in DDRS;

531 Memorandum of conversation Luce-Stassen-Tasca-Dulles-Nash, Methods of Reducing Communist Influence in Italy', 2 January 1954, in NARA, RG59, The Secretary and the Undersecretary's Memoranda of Conversation 1953-1964, Lot File 64D199, b. 2; some reference to this meeting held on January 3 can also be found in E.Ortona, Anni d'America. La diplomazia 1953-1961, p. 55;

weather fighters with Italian industry to supply North American Aviation[532]. Besides, as a result of the meetings held in Washington in January 1954, and in line with a policy strongly promoted by the State Department, the Eisenhower Administration decided not to make public the trade union cleaning-up policy that had been proposed[533]. Furthermore, the White House forced the branches and federal Departments involved in implementing the off-shore procurement programs to agree on the principle that this political clean-up was not an objective of multilateral rearmament in itself. Rather, it was a pre-condition to carrying out a rearmament program that Washington considered part of a must-do bilateral agreement on the shaping of Italy's internal economic structure and supranational trade and monetary integration. In fact, under the Eisenhower Administration the allocation of off-shore procurement contracts was on the whole firmly tied to a wider set of economic initiatives at the basis of bilateral economic negotiations between the two countries. Among the others issues at stake, it is worth mentioning the allocation abroad of the American agricultural surplus that in the meantime Washington had placed on the agenda of its foreign economic aid policy; equally important was the ongoing bilateral debate on the scale and scope of Italy's domestic development programs for the Southern areas of the country as well as the undertaking of trade liberalizations to stimulate the inflow of foreign investments and the ratification by Italy of the European Defense Community[534]

Both the OSP and this range of issues were considered by Washington as diplomatic tools that could be used to exert pressure on Rome in order to influence the shaping of Italy's domestic economic growth and foreign economic policy. In particular, throughout its first mandate the Eisenhower Administration showed a consistent concern for both the importance of the foreign exchange equilibrium of the country as a precondition to bring Italy's economy into the Atlantic bloc's trade and monetary area and for influencing the expansion of Italy's domestic mass consumer market.

---

532 'Offshore procurement of aircraft in Italy', 11 December 1953, in NARA, RG59, Lot File 58D357, b. 15, fold. 435.03 OSP 1953-54;

533 The Department of State opposed revealing this decision to the public as this would involve other important NATO allies such as France where communist strength was considerable. On this point see also L.Merchant to General Smith, 'Reply to Mrs. Luce's Letter on OSP, Loan and Assistance Programs in Italy', 25 February 1954, in NARA, RG56, OASIA, b. 15, fold. 435.03 (OSP 1953-54); W.B.Smith to C.B.Luce, 1 March 1954, idem;

534 indeed, the US Embassy in Italy and the FOA Mission to Rome had formulated this proposal for the first time from as early as the beginning of December 1953, see L.Ripps (FOA) to Ringer (FOA), 'Italian Program Problems', 15 December 1953, in NARA, RG59, Lot File 58D357, b. 15, fold. 435.01 Direct Aid 1953-1954; Luce to the Secretary of State, 5 December 1953, in NARA, RG469, Mission to Italy, Office of the Director, Subject Files (Central Files) 1948-1957, b. 22, fold. 4 (Defense: OSP programs Contracts Production 1954); Luce to the Secretary of State, 'OSP Programming', telegram, 7 December 1953, in NARA, RG56, OASIA, b. 63, fold. Italy/9/52 MSA-FOA Off-Shore Procurement Vol. 2);

After taking power the Eisenhower Administration proved to be sensitive to the considerable worsening of the Italian balance of payments. In early 1953, shortly after the new ambassador's arrival in Italy, the US Embassy in Rome which, as we have seen was mostly concerned with problems linked to politics, favored the launch of a financial assistance program worth up to $100 million to help Italy resurrect its foreign exchange equilibrium. According to the economic experts of the Embassy, such a lump sum financial aid by raising «the net increase in gold and dollar reserves would enable Italy to defer for a longer period any deliberalization measures she may feel compelled to take as she runs through her EPU credit»[535].
From the beginning of the same year the Department of State convincingly endorsed the hypothesis of placing the production of a model of all-weather fighters with Italian industry to replace the recently shelved Venom program. In making his case for this decision, Dulles showed his concern for the worsening of Italy's balance of payments against the EPU currency areas. In fact, between 1952 and 1953 Italy's terms of trade against EPU worsened significantly. The EPU was equipped with a monetary device to let its member states transfer some of their own dollar reserves to redress the balance of their terms of trade with the EPU trade areas. According to the Department of State, by resorting to this mechanism Italy ran the risk of deteriorating its terms of trade against the dollar currency area as well[536]. In order to prevent the country from aggravating its balance of payments and even endangering the post war recovery in its foreign exchange equilibrium, the Department of State supported placing offshore procurement contracts in Italy. In fact, given that they would be paid for in US dollars the OSP would enable the country to improve the current account of its balance of payments against the EPU currencies without eroding its dollar reserves. Later, at the end of 1953, the Rome-based economic experts of the State Department argued that a full production phase should be placed with Italy. According to Dulles' Department the country could not afford to

---

535 NARA, RG469, Mission to Italy, Office of the Director, Subject Files (Central Files) 1948-1957 (1948-54), b. 2, fold. 2 (Aid Negotiations-papers);
536 a few months before the foreign exchange equilibrium of Italy ran at the worst level of the period, the State Department pinned this note: «Because of the EPU mechanism, a decline in exports to non-dollar countries, i.e., EPU countries, would also adversely affect Italy's dollar position.» On the one hand, the State Department was inclined to use those funds to stimulate domestic growth investments, on the other the Mutual Security Agency strove to finance and redress the Italian terms of trade. See respectively Department of State, 'State Department Comments on MSA Proposed Fiscal Year 1954 Program for Italy. MSA Aid to Italy in Fiscal Year 1954', 31 October 1952, in NARA, RG59, Office of the Special Assistant for Mutual Security Coordination, Office of the Undersecretary of State 1952-59, Lot File 59D449, b. 25, fold. MAP-Italy (Fiscal Year 1952-54), and Department of State, 'Fiscal Year Title I (Europe) Defense Support Program. Supplemental Note. Italy', n.d., in NARA, RG59, Lot file 58D357, b. 15, fold. 435.01 (Direct Aid 1953-1954); as regards the EPU mechanism to redress the imbalances among its currency area member countries see F.Cotula, J.C.Martinez Oliva, *Stabilità e sviluppo dalla liberazione al miracolo economico*, in F.Cotula, M.De Cecco, G.Toniolo (eds), *La Banca d'Italia. Sintesi della ricerca storica 1893-1960*, Laterza, Roma and Bari, 2003, pp. 429-435;

miss the opportunity of launching a full production phase as this would risk bringing the current account of the Italian balance of payments against the US dollar to the brink of downfall[537]. The Department believed that over the course of 1953 the OSP contracts would be likely to support up to two thirds of the liabilities of the current account of the Italian balance of payments against the US dollar[538]. Hence, by late 1953 the head of FOA was venturing to suggest that by soothing Italian government concerns by shoring up the worsening Italian balance of payments which had remained an issue throughout the post war era, the government of the United States could use negotiations on the OSP programs as a leverage to oblige Italy to adopt expansionary domestic economic policies. Stassen believed that Washington should appropriate OSP contracts in Italy in return for a firm Italian commitment to adopt ‹‹constructive economic policies›› aimed not only at continuing along the path towards trade liberalization, but also at stimulating private foreign investments and launching industrial development projects across the Southern areas of Italy[539]. This approach was widely shared within the Eisenhower Administration: the Secretary of the Treasury himself, George Humphrey, suggested using the ERP-Lira counterpart Funds to finance the imports required to continue a series of industrial development programs in the South[540]. During the first half of 1954 this American stance led Washington to promote a financial assistance package of almost $20 million to finance Italy's import of raw and strategic materials to allow the Italian war material producing industry and its allied firms to work on defense orders. In its bilateral diplomatic relations with Rome the Eisenhower Administration worked hard to make the newly formed Scelba Cabinet sign a deal that would oblige the Italian firms that received these funds to deposit a percentage of their earnings in a government-held counterpart Fund worth up to $15 million which would be used to finance the industrialization of the Southern Italian regions. In June 1954 the two governments signed a bilateral agreement that forced Italy in this direction and eventually resulted in the country starting construction work on much needed infra-

537 M.P.Arth (DD/P-FOA) to Stassen, Memorandum, 'Background on all-weather fighters', 1 March 1954, in NARA, RG469, Office of the Deputy Director for Operations (1953-1961), Office of African and European Operations (1955-1961), Western European Division, Italy Subject File 1950-1956, b. 5, fold. Italy: Defense Production Airplane Fiat F86K Fighters;

538 V.Barnett (Acting Chief, Special Mission to Italy for Economic Cooperation), 'OSP in the Italian economy: Progress Report and Economic Analysis of Fiscal Year 1952 and 1953 contracts', 25 August 1953, in NARA, RG469, Mission to Italy, Office of the Director, Subject Files (Central Files) 1948-1957, b. 22, fold. Defense: OSP Programs Contracts Production 1953;

539 Stassen to the Country Team in Italy, 'Guidance to Italy Country Team on OSP, Counterpart Loans and Assistance, related to Italian Communist Problems', 2 February 1954, telegram, in NARA, RG469, Mission to Italy, Office of the Director, Subject Files (Central Files) 1948-1957 (1954-57), b. 68, fold. Communism-US program;

540 H.Tasca to MSA Washington, 11 December 1953, telegram, in NARA, RG469, Mission to Italy, Office of the Director, Subject Files (Central Files) 1948-1957 (1948-54), b. 2, fold. 2 (Aid Negotiations-papers);

structures and roads[541]. By using bilateral negotiations on the OSP contracts and the military assistance programs to force Italy to adopt expansionary economic policies, the Eisenhower Administration aimed both to raise the average living standards of the working class through a significant leap forward in labor purchasing power, and to stimulate domestic market expansion through the pursuit of job creating economic policies[542]. The 1954 agreement between the two governments is all the more worthy of mention as it sums up the US policy on the OSP contracts through the middle of the decade: the economic experts working at the US Embassy in Rome made it clear that $20 million mutual assistance funds appropriated to Italy were intended both ‹‹to stimulate a more rapid rate of industrial growth in southern and insular Italy›› and ‹‹to assist Italy in meeting the impact of the defense effort on her balance of payments››[543].

Remarkably, between 1954 and 1955 ambassador Luce herself realigned along this growth-oriented approach to military assistance that guided the Department of State foreign policy toward Italy. In early 1952 she suggested that her Administration approve an Economic Development Program. In her view, this Program was to offer financial backing to the Vanoni Plan, a comprehensive development plan which was named after the Italian Finance Minister that drafted it, in order to address the problem of the economic despair that dogged the under-

---

541 H.Stassen to the American Embassy in Italy, 29 January 1955, in NARA, RG469, Mission to Italy, Office of the Director, Subject Files (Central Files) 1948-1957 (1954-57), b. 70, fold. Economic Development South Italy; E.B.Hall (Director, Office of Trade, Investment and Monetary Affairs, FOA) to C.Dillon Glendinning, (Secretary, NAC), 4 January 1955, in NARA, RG56, Nac Papers, Nac Documents and Supplements 1945-1968, b. 26 fold. Nac Documents Vol. 40, N°. 1700-1749; Dunbrow to the Secretary of State, 4 February 1955, telegram, in NARA, RG469, Mission to Italy, Office of the Director, Subject Files (Central Files) 1948-1957, b. 31, fold. 5 (Funds-Lire Correspondence);

542 J.P.McKnight to C.Luce, Office Memorandum 'Answers to Ins Questionnaire to Mr. Henry Tasca', 4 December 1953, in LOC, MD, CBLP, b. 633, fold. 5 (Memoranda: Inter Office October-December 1953);

543 H.Tasca to the Secretary of State, 12 June 1954, telegram, in NARA, RG469, Mission to Italy, Office of the Director, Subject Files (Central Files) 1948-1957 (1954-57), b. 67, fold. Aid Fiscal Year 1954 Counterpart; H.Tasca to FOA Washington, 11 June 1954, telegram, in NARA, RG469, Office of the Deputy Director for Operations (1953-1961), Office of European Operations (1953-55), Office of the Director, Geographic Files (Central Files) 1953-54, b. 122, fold. Italy-Funds-Counterpart; as regards the strategy of using the counterpart funds to finance development projects across the country, see H.Tasca to FOA Washington, 'Fiscal Year Counterpart Financed Loan Program for Southern Italy', 3 May 1954, idem; 'Memorandum on the use which might be made of the Counterpart of Fiscal Year 1954 Defense Support Aid to Italy', idem; on the American belief that rearmament was likely to trigger a deterioration in the Italian balance of payments see also 'Economic analysis of the Italian Reply to the SHAPE Recommendations (Enclosure No. 4 with Ambassador Bunker's letter to Ambassador Draper dated March 6, 1953)', in NARA, RG469, Mission to Italy, Office of the Director, Subject Files (Central Files) 1948-1957, b. 37, fold. 5 (Italian Defense Program 1954);

developed areas of the country[544]. The ambassador's proposal of this economic assistance policy linked it to the objective of matching growth and rearmament on the one side with foreign exchange equilibrium on the other. Accordingly, in spring 1954 she promoted the approval of construction programs to build up a series of NATO military facilities such as military bases and the services they required to be operative. She endorsed this project which over the following three years was to improve the Italian balance of payments' direct and indirect entries for a total sum of over $80 million as a result of foreign investments in the country, maintenance expenses to keep the military bases working and the running expenses of the US forces under operation across the country[545]. By contrast, therefore, it is worth underlining that in 1955 she was still concerned about the political strength of the leftwing trade unions as most of the aeronautical industry was located in the north where the far-left working class movements had their strongholds. Nonetheless, by that time she was clearly committed to securing the appropriations of OSP contracts both to strengthen the loyalty of the country and to sustain its role as a full production source for the Atlantic Alliance[546]. A serious concern that a sudden interruption of economic and military assistance to the country might pave the way for a recession[547], coupled with devising means to prevent the Italian leftwing enterprises from trading with Soviet bloc markets, clearly informed her position[548].

This attempt of the Eisenhower Administration and its ambassador to Italy to target both the development of the Italian aeronautical industry and its allied metalworking firms as a full production source for the Atlantic Alliance, and the promotion of domestic economic growth while avoiding any strain on the balance of payments and the trade balance of the country, combined with the need to stick with the anti-communist foreign policy it had pledged itself to, explain the way in which the F86K OSP programs were implemented through 1955. In fact, in April 1954 ambassador Luce stated before her Italian counterpart a willingness ‹‹to be flexible on present contracts›› and her intention to withhold and re-program the F86K OSP contracts, should the Fiat group be unsuccessful in carrying out a political clean up within its

---

544 Memorandum, 'Discussion at the 237th Meeting of the National Security Council', Thursday, 17 February 1955, in DDEL, Dwight D. Eisenhower Papers, Papers as President of the United States (Ann Whitman File) 1953-1961, NSC Series, b. 6;

545 Luce to Dulles, 18 May 1954, in NARA, RG84, Records of Clare Boothe Luce 1953-56, Top Secret Files, Lot File 64F26, b. 1, fold. Letters 1954;

546 C.Luce to the Secretary of State, 24 May 1954, telegram, in NARA, RG56, OASIA, b. 63, fold. Italy/9/52 MSA-FOA Offshore Procurement Vol. 2;

547 C.Luce to J.Dulles, 15 June 1956, in LOC, MD, CBLP, b. 626, fold. 1 (1956 Dud-Dul, Dulles John Foster);

548 C.B.Elbrick (Western European Division, State Department) to Undersecretary of State, 'OCB Consideration of Outline Plan of Operations with respect to Italy', 24 September 1956, in NARA, RG59, Records Relating to the State Department Participation in the Operations Coordinating Board and the National Security Council 1947-1963, Lot File 62D430, b. 21, fold. Italy;

plants[549]. This proved completely unnecessary as the polls conducted in March 1955 on a closed-shop policy within the Turin plants of the Italian multinational signaled an important set-back for the left. The metalworkers' union, FIOM, which was a fellow-traveler of the CGIL, suffered an historical defeat. Shortly after this turning point, the United States and NATO placed a production program to manufacture a series of F86K all-weather fighters with the Italian automobile giant that would secure orders and working hours to the Italian metal-working and mechanical firms until 1958[550]. In winding up the contract and reporting on it, Luce confirmed her Administration's tendency to be sensitive to the poverty issue that still characterized Italian society: she stated that ‹‹when it could be made clear to the working class that democracy could provide stable employment, they would choose democracy over Communism every time››[551].

This approach to the F86K OSP program for the Italian aeronautical industry was truly con-sistent with the increasing tendency of the Eisenhower Administration to promote sustained internal economic growth in the framework of tightly binding foreign exchange equilibrium. Alongside this foreign economic policy toward the Italian Peninsula it is noteworthy, as a final remark, to mention the different guidelines that Washington, its federal agencies and Europe-based governmental representatives were following by the middle of the decade. Ex-amples of this variety of policies could be firm approval of the launching of an Export-Import Bank loan package by the ambassador in Rome [552], the Department of State's approval to have a commitment from the IBRD to place an industrial development oriented loan pro-gram[553]; not to mention the US National Security Council's move to finance and to channel

549 Memorandum of Conversation Magistrati-Luce, 17 April 1954, in NARA, RG84, Rome Embassy, Secret General Records 1953-1955, b. 1, fold. 320.1 (Off-Shore Procurement Classified 1953-1955);

550 In late 1957, according to the economic advisor of the Italian Embassy in Washington a termina-tion of the F86K production program was likely to spark job losses for as many as 2,000 employees. Memorandum of Conversation G.De Rege-C.H.Harvey (Officer in Charge, Italian-Austrian Affairs, Department of State)-J.D.Crane (Assistant Italian Desk Officer), 'Prospect Facing FIAT Aviation Di-vision', 20 November 1957, in NARA, RG59, Central Files 1955-59, b. 2539, 611.65/11-2057;

551 Memorandum of conversation Dulles-Scelba-Luce-Martino-Jones-Brosio, 30 March 1955, in NARA, RG59, The Secretary's and the Undersecretary's Memoranda of conversation 1953-1964, Lot File 64D199, b. 3 (January 1955-August 1955); Italy's official press release on the meeting Scelba-Martino (Italian foreign Minister)-Dulles-Eisenhower-Humphrey (Secretary for the Treasury)-Stassen-Wilson (Secretary for Defense), 30 March 1955, in AILS, Mario Scelba papers ;

552 G.H.Willis, 'Ambassador Luce on the Italian Program', 7 January 1955, in NARA, RG469, Mis-sion to Italy, Office of the Director, Subject Files (Central Files) 1948-1957, b. 31, fold. 5 (Funds-Lire Correspondence); E.B.Staats (Executive Officer, OCB), Memorandum for J.S.Lay Jr (Executive Sec-retary, National Security Council), 'Progress Report on NSC5411/2 (Italy)', 28 January 1955, top secret, in NARA, RG59, Records relating to the State Department Participation in the Operations Co-ordinating Board and the National Security Council 1947-1963, Lot File 62D430, b. 21, fold. Italy;

553 W.Jones to F.E.Nolting (MSA), 'Fiscal Year '56 Economic Support for Italy', 1 November 1954, in NARA, RG59, Lot File 58D357, b. 16, fold. 435 Aid to Italy 1954; see also L.Merchant to the

governmental and foreign private investments in Southern areas of the country to tackle the increasing shift towards leftwing parties that marked the elections at that time[554].

5.3 Bargaining the burden of Italy's external trade and monetary equilibrium: the OSP contracts and the Italian foreign economic policy objectives

Throughout the book I have highlighted how much importance the US Administrations attached to the impact of the industrial mobilization that the rearmament programs and the placing of military procurement contracts with the Italian industry had on the Italian foreign exchange equilibrium, and particularly its balance of payments. In the previous pages of this chapter I pushed this argument further by focusing on the interest and concerns that the US authorities showed for the worsening of the Italian direct entries against the currency areas of the EPU member states from 1952 through 1953. I underlined that the Americans intended the off-shore procurement contracts to redress the foreign exchange equilibrium of the country against the EPU currency areas as the mutual defense financial appropriations would permit the Italian aeronautical and mechanical industry to import much needed strategic material and instrumental goods and might thus serve to resurrect the Italian balance of payments. This rearmament-related dollar inflow was designed to both ease the strain of the imports on the Italian direct entries' liabilities against the dollar and, as we briefly mentioned, to help recover the Italian Lira's foreign exchange equilibrium against the EPU currencies in line with the EPU financial mechanism that maintained a balance among its member currencies. This American attention stemmed from a long lasting US concern with promoting rearmament and creating self-sufficiency in manufacturing across West European industry in the framework of continued trade exchange and monetary integration among the economies of the Atlantic Alliance. In fact, a thorough reconstruction of the Italian case sheds light on the role that the national economic policymakers played in pushing the American authorities further in this direction. In other words, in striking contrast with what the literature on the subject has so far maintained, I would argue that just as the US authorities used bilateral negotiations on the OSP contracts to influence Italy's foreign economic policy and domestic expansionary initia-

---

Rome Embassy, n.d., *idem*; L.Merchant to C.Luce, 9 December 1954, idem; J.Dulles to American Embassy in Italy, 10 December 1954, telegram, in NARA, RG469, Office of the Deputy Director for Operations (1953-1961), Office of European Operations (1953-1955), Office of the Director, Geographic Files (Central Files) 1953-55, 123, fold. Italy-Funds-Program 1954;

554 'Progress Report on NSC5411/2. United States Policy toward Italy', 26 January 1955, in NARA, RG59, Records Relating to the State Department Participation in the Operations Coordinating Board and the National Security Council 1947-1963, Lot File 62D430, b. 21, fold. Italy, p. 4;

tives so the Italian counterparts engaged in these negotiations to improve the country's balance of payments and terms of trade, with particular reference to the imbalance that put pressure on the external equilibrium of Rome against the other European currencies. This perspective is clearly at odds with the literature on the subject, that has authoritatively stressed that after 1951 Italy undertook the process of trade liberalization toward its European partners and subsequently threatened to withdraw from it in order to obtain as many OSP contracts as possible[555]. This chapter will therefore worth briefly follow the economic diplomacy initiatives that the Rome Cabinet put on the table both at a bilateral level and at multilateral talks such as the international economic institutions' periodical meetings to negotiate the level of trade liberalization.

The issue of trade liberalization specifically pertained to the Italian Lira's terms of trade and balance of payments equilibrium against the French Franc and British Pound. In this respect, it is worth going back to the Korean War and its impact on the international monetary system. From 1950 to 1951 Italy's traditional scarcity in raw and strategic material was the main cause for both the sharp worsening in its terms of trade against the US dollar and the skyrocketing inflation rate it suffered as a result of importing overpriced raw materials. By contrast, during the conflict in Far East Asia, the current account of the Italian balance of payments against the British and the French currencies had steadily improved. A significant rise in the export of the Italian low capital intensive manufacturing sectors, dominated by the textile industry, toward the raw and strategic material supplying backward economies belonging to the French and the British currency areas, triggered these dynamics[556]. As a result, when in late 1951 the Italian Minister for Foreign Trade, Ugo La Malfa, launched an unprecedented program of trade liberalizations, the country was, on the one hand, in deficit toward the dollar; on the other hand, its exchange equilibrium toward the United Kingdom and France, as well as their currency trade areas at large, saw a steady upward trend[557]. In this context, the firm commitment by the Italian Minister for Foreign Trade to venture on trade liberalization policies was intended to prevent the British and the French from adopting currency devaluation or any measures to raise protectionist tariffs or quota restrictions that they might be tempted to

---

555 L.Segreto, *L'Italia nel sistema economico internazionale. Attori e politiche tra anni cinquanta e sessanta*, in L.Tosi (ed.), *Politica ed economia nelle relazioni internazionali dell'Italia del secondo dopoguerra*, p. 185;

556 R.Gualtieri, *La politica economica del centrismo e il quadro internazionale*, pp. 105-106; D.Menichella, *Considerazioni finali all'assemblea della Banca d'Italia*. 1951, 31 May 1952, in F.Cotula, C.O.Gelsomino, A.Gigliobianco (eds), Donato Menichella. *Stabilità e sviluppo dell'economia italiana 1946-1960*, pp. 131-132;

557 'Briefing Paper' for Mr Bruce Annual Meeting of IMF and IBRD, 26 August 1952, in NARA, RG59, Lot File 58D357, b. 12, fold. 101.10 (Position Papers 1952-54); see also the testimony of G.Carli, *Cinquant'anni di vita italiana*, Laterza, p. 115;

use to sustain their terms of trade toward the Italian economy[558]. To this end, Italy adopted a comprehensive program of trade liberalizations that coupled a sharp cutting of quantitative restrictions with a 10 per cent reduction of import duties and the concession of incentives to stimulate a wide range of importers from the EPU markets[559].

Shortly thereafter, however, both the governments of London and France reduced their import quotas to protect both domestic growth and their reserves from imported inflation, in clear contrast with the Italian trade liberalization initiatives[560].

All of this clearly explains the huge upset in the Italian balance of payments against the EPU area: from January 1952 through December 1952 Italy experienced a sharp deterioration of its sound credit position. In fact, over this period it passed from a credit position of close to $250 million to a debit of nearly $95 million[561]. This imbalance was the result not only of the British and French severe protectionist measures, but also of a wide range of trade and monetary dynamics. Mostly, over the course of 1952 the Italian exporters experienced a slowing down of exports toward France and the United Kingdom which was due to a substantial reduction in the Italian textile and garment industry's penetration of foreign markets. The slowing down in the price hike on the British and French internal markets, coupled with a downfall in the demand for textile and labor intensive goods on the part of the developing countries that supplied raw materials triggered by the worldwide recession that followed the Korean War, explain the decrease in exports that hit the Italian textile industry during 1952[562]. Moreover, the traditional lack of governmental incentives such as tax exemptions to promote competitiveness on foreign markets further depressed the Italian export drive[563], and in turn led the Italian

---

558 prior to the founding of the EPU in 1950, which coincided with the Italian decision to accrue its reserves in US dollars, Italy had put aside a share of its reserves in British Pounds. In this context, a British currency devaluation was likely to hit the Italian reserves in British Pounds. On this point L.Mechi, *L'Europa di Ugo La Malfa*, pp.52-53; G.Carli, *Cinquant'anni di vita italiana*, p. 116;

559 B.Bottiglieri, *La politica economica dell'Italia centrista*, pp. 158-159; F.Cotula-J.C.Martinez Oliva, *Stabilità e sviluppo dalla liberazione al 'miracolo economico'*, in F.Cotula, M.De Cecco, G.Toniolo (eds), *La Banca d'Italia. Sintesi della ricerca storica*, Laterza, Roma-Bari 2003, p. 434;

560 *Nuove restrizioni annunciate dal Cancelliere dello Scacchiere*, in "Corriere della Sera", 8 November 1951; *Il drenaggio delle riserve britanniche e le misure governative per frenarlo*, in "Il Sole", 8 November 1951;

561 MSA, Office of the Assistant Director for Europe, 'Italy', 6 February 1953, in NARA, RG469, Mission to Italy, Office of the Director, Subject Files (Central Files) 1948-1957, b. 25, fold. 6 (Evaluation Team), p. 7;

562 'The Italian Balance of Payments. Position and Prospects', n.d. (but probably 1953), in ACS, Ministero delle Finanze, Gab., Ufficio Paesi Esteri, b. 13, p. 10;

563 M.L.Cavalcanti, *La politica commerciale italiana 1945-1952. Uomini e fatti*, Esi, Napoli, 1984;

business community to call upon the government to sustain their exports on foreign markets[564].

Though the worsening of the Italian balance of payments stemmed from such a wide-ranging set of causes, at an international level the economic ministers of the De Gasperi Cabinet argued strongly that, in fact, France and the United Kingdom's unfair protectionist trade policies toward the Italian importers were the main cause for the continuing deterioration of the Italian terms of trade against the EPU currency areas. From 1952 to 1953 they struggled to make the OSP contracts part of a bilateral negotiation with the United States to set up different trade arrangements among the Atlantic bloc currencies.

In early 1952 the Italian economic ministers brought this sudden deterioration in the Italian foreign exchange equilibrium before the attention of the United States government. Furthermore, they struggled to capture the attention of Italy's western bloc allies at international gatherings and at the annual meetings of Washington-backed international economic institutions such as the International Monetary Fund or the Organization for European Economic Cooperation. In late Winter 1952, during a conversation with the head of the ECA Mission to Rome Dayton, the Italian Treasury Minister, Pella, stated that «Italy should not be penalized for its achievements in liberalizing trade and expanding exports», and called for a dollar-currency financial assistance package aimed both at funding the ordinary balance sheet of the Italian Ministry for Defense, and easing off the pressure of the rearmament program on the current account of the Italian balance of payments against the dollar markets. Throughout the following months, the increasingly tricky situation of the Italian balance of payments came to dominate the Rome government's foreign economic diplomacy even further: indeed, the Italians repeatedly linked the concession by the United States and NATO of that slice of dollar-currency financial aid to the negotiations on the OSP contracts. In August 1952, the Italian Minister for Foreign Trade, La Malfa, expressed his utmost concern to the US Acting Secretary of State, Bruce, for the deterioration of the Italian external equilibrium. In particular, the balance of payments was expected to collapse by spring 1953[565]. During that meeting, the Italian politician affirmed his hope «that Italy would be able to avoid modifying its trade policies». Despite this statement, for the first time he started airing the idea of raising some tariff

---

564 as regards the debate on the introduction of securities on credits to exports see Campilli to La Malfa, 1 July 1952, in ACS, ULM, b. 18, fold. 1, s.f. Garanzie crediti alle esportazioni; as regards the calls for the introduction of tax incentives and exemptions on the export industry and governmental policies in support of the Italian export drive in 1952 see for example 'Relazioni Fiat e Montecatini', 24 April 1953, in ACS, ULM, b. 18 fold. 2, e G.Carli, *Aspetti della crisi della bilancia italiana dei pagamenti e provvedimenti per attenuarla*, in "Moneta e Credito", n. 22 (1953);

565 see for example L.Segreto, *L'Italia nel sistema economico internazionale. Attori e politiche tra anni cinquanta e sessanta*, pp. 184-185; L.Mechi, *L'Europa di Ugo La Malfa*, introduction and pp. 52-59; S.Battilossi, *L'Italia nel sistema economico internazionale*, pp. 318-327; P.Alessandrini, *L'economia italiana dalla ricostruzione allo Sme*, in "Rassegna economica", n. 1 (1983);

barriers on goods imported from the EPU markets[566]. La Malfa reiterated his argument one month later, when he asked the United States to take action either to pressurize London and Paris to reduce their tariffs and quota restrictions, or to let the Italian manufacturers increase their exports toward the US dollar currency markets, first and foremost the US consumer markets[567]. Throughout the fall of 1952 the Italian Minister repeatedly expressed to the Americans the idea of retaliation against the British and the French which would take the form of withdrawal from trade liberalizations[568]. This threat was reiterated into the spring of 1953 not only to the United States but also to France and the United Kingdom[569]. This Italian position was maintained even as the United States showed an increasing commitment to enhance internal industrial investment and to force the Italian government and business community to undertake domestic expansionary policies. Against this background the US government conceived the appropriation of OSP contracts as a way to stimulate domestic expansion. According to the Americans the off-shore procurements were to lever both the standard of livings and the employment rate in the framework of a comprehensive domestic development project to shift the Italian economy from material reconstruction to sustained industrialization and

---

566 J.C.Bonbright to the Acting Secretary, 'Meeting with Italian Cabinet Ministers at 4.00 p.m. today', 29 August 1952, in NARA, RG59, Lot File 58D357, b. 12, fold. 101.10 (Position Papers 1952-54); Memorandum of Conversation Pella-La Malfa-Magistrati-Bruce-Knight-Tesoro, 'Italy's Economic Problems', 29 August 1952, in NARA, RG469, Mission to Italy, Office of the Director, Subject Files (Central Files) 1948-1957, b. 36, fold. 6 (Italy Economic Problems); for these meetings with the Undersecretary Bruce and the MSA see also respectively Memorandum of Conversation La Malfa-Pella-Bruce, 29 August 1952, in NARA, RG59, Conference Files, Lot File 59D95, CF120, and Memorandum of conversation Pella-La Malfa-MSA officials, 29 August 1952, in NARA, RG59, Central Files 1950-54, 865.00/-2952;

567 M.Magistrati, 'Appunto del direttore generale della Cooperazione internazionale del Ministero degli Affari Esteri sulla visita dei ministri Pella e La Malfa negli Stati Uniti', 25 September 1952, in ACS, ULM, b. 20;

568 A.Tarchiani to Ministero Affari Esteri, 'Studi ed orientamenti politica estera economica Stati Uniti. Missione in Europa del Ministro Sawyer', 27 October 1952, in ACS, PCM, Gab., 1951-54, b. 4-12; Zoppi (Segretario Generale Ministero MAE) to MCE, Gab., 'Missione in Italia del Ministro del Commercio degli Stati Uniti Charles Sawyer', 11 November 1952, idem; 'Riunione del 18 novembre 1952 in occasione della visita del Ministro Sawyer del Dipartimento del Commercio americano. Dichiarazioni del Governatore della Banca d'Italia', November 1952, in ASBI, Fondo Studi, pratt., n. 338, fold. 11; 'Appunti del dr. Menichella per Sawyer', 21 November 1952, idem; 'Visit of Mr. Sawyer to Europe', 13 November 1952, in ASCE, OEEC Papers, Council Minutes, File OEEC 35.34; *Colloquio La Malfa-Sawyer*, in "Corriere della Sera", 19 November 1952; see also L.Mechi, *L'Europa di Ugo La Malfa*, p. 74;

569 A.Corrias (Ministero Affari Esteri, DGAE), 'Appunto per S.E. il ministro', 21 September 1953, in ASMAE, DGAP, Ufficio I 1950/1957, b. 216 (politica estera americana in funzione economica);

expanding domestic aggregate demand[570]. On the other hand, the American policymakers underestimated the on-going deterioration in the Italian foreign exchange equilibrium. Thus, for example, in early August 1952 the US Special Representative in Europe stated that regardless of the figures «there is no urgent need for aid on balance of payments grounds»[571].

With the beginning of the New Year and the start of Eisenhower's Republican Administration, and as a result of continued Italian insistence, Washington proved to be more receptive toward the issue of the imbalances that shook Italy's balance of payments and supra-national market integration. In fact, after further urging by the Italian Minister, Pella, who underlined for the umpteenth time that Italy's monetary and foreign exchange equilibrium was a must-do, essential requirement for his country's full commitment to carry on domestic expansionary economic policies and investment programs[572], the new US government showed signs of increasing attention to the problem and a willingness to tailor trade policy to provide the Italian exporters with much-needed assistance in order to recover a fair share of the intra-European trade exchanges in consumer goods[573]. In April 1953 the initial reaction by the De Gasperi Cabinet to this American focus on the Italian foreign monetary issue was to reassure its US counterpart as regards its commitment to maintain the trade liberalization measures previously adopted[574]. However, a few months later, in the summer of 1953 when the long era of De Gasperi-led coalition governments came to an end, the new monetary and budget- minded Cabinet headed by Pella reiterated the Italian threat to abandon the country's trade liberaliza-

---

570 J.C.Bonbright to the Acting Secretary, 'Meeting with Italian Cabinet Ministers at 4 p.m. today', 29 August 1952, in NARA, RG59, Lot File 58D357, b. 12, fold. 101.10 (Position Papers 1952-54); H.B.Chenery, 'A Proposed Action Program for Italy. Summary of Country Team Recommendations given in Objectives of US Aid to Italy in 1952/53', 1 August 1952, in NARA, RG469, Mission to Italy, Office of the Director, Subject Files (Central Files) 1948-1957, b. 17, fold. 3 (Conferences. Chiefs of Missions);

571 Office of the United States Special Representative in Europe, 'Supplemental Agenda book for item 7. Agenda for MSA Mission chiefs conference', 2 August 1952, in NARA, RG469, Mission to Italy, Office of the Director, Subject Files (Central Files) 1948-1957, b. 17, fold. 3 (Conferences. Chiefs of Missions);

572 Memorandum of conversation De Gasperi-Pacciardi-Pella-La Malfa-Dulles-Stassen-Bunker-Parker, 31 January 1953, in NARA, RG59, The Secretary's and the Undersecretary's Memoranda of conversation 1953-1964, Lot File 64D199, b. 1; on the Truman Administration's insistence on making the Italians boost domestic investments see for example Memorandum of conversation E.Bunker-A.De Gasperi, 5 September 1952, in *FRUS 1952-54*, Vol. 6, *Western Europe and Canada* , Part 2, p. 1594;

573 A.Tarchiani to A.De Gasperi, 'aiuti americani', 27 February 1953, in ACS, ULM, b. 18, fold. 2, s.f. rapporti economico-politici Italia-Usa;

574 Parker (MSA Rome) to the Secretary of State, 13 April 1953, telegram, in NARA, RG469, Mission to Italy, Office of the Director, Subject Files (Central Files) 1948-1957 (1948-54), b. 2, fold. 2 (Aid Negotiations-papers);

tions against the EPU partners[575]. Indeed, not only did Italy threaten to abandon its trade liberalizations but Pella also aired the idea of raising protectionist policies against the US dollar currency markets too. In particular, during a fall gathering of the International Monetary Fund, the Italian government made the point that trade discriminations and barriers against the dollar-currency markets might be used as a successful financial device to finance the sharp Italian imbalances against the EPU currencies without withdrawing from its trade liberalizations toward the EPU partners[576]. Eventually, in late fall Italy threatened a severe narrowing of its market openness to the American and EPU-member European markets to reposition its import flows toward non-western supplying markets[577]. Indeed, it is worth pointing to the fact that by the end of 1953 the weakening of Italy's position within the EPU induced the government of Rome to intensify its trade exchanges and partnership with the Soviet bloc markets[578]. The new US Administration's move to search for a balance between putting pressure on the Italians to make them undertake the long-awaited domestic expansionary policies, and providing Rome with dollar-currency financial assistance to improve the country's foreign exchange equilibrium, should therefore be placed against the background of this Italian counter reaction.

In the framework of this broad set of economic diplomacy relations between the two countries, the bilateral negotiations on the off-shore procurement contracts turned out to be used as a tool by both parties to achieve their respective foreign economic policy objectives, whether domestic expansionary policies or balance of payments equilibrium. In fact, on several occasions the centrist Italian governments linked their threat to withdraw from liberalization deliberately to lure as many OSP contracts as possible from NATO[579].

---

575 E.L.Ripps to Stassen, 'Meeting with Ambassador Tarchiani of Italy Scheduled for 11 A.M. Tuesday, 6/10/1953', 5 October 1953, in NARA, RG469, Records of the Directors (1953-1961), Geographic Files of the Director 1948-1955, b. 11, fold. Italy-commodities-Airplanes); ASCE, OEEC papers, Council Minutes for 1953; 'The Italian Balance of Payments. Positions and Prospects', n.d. (but, 1953), in ACS, Ministero delle Finanze, Gab., Ufficio Paesi Esteri, b. 13; see also Ambasciata italiana a Washington to MAE, DGCI, 'Bilancia dei pagamenti e aiuti economici americani', 18 November 1953, in ACS, Ministero delle Finanze, Gab., Ufficio Paesi Esteri, b. 13;
576 NAC, NAC Staff Committee, Minutes of Meetings, Meeting No. 400, 1 October 1953, in NARA, RG56, NAC papers, NAC Staff Committee papers, Minutes of Meetings 1945-1959, b. 2;
577 Ambasciata italiana a Washington to MAE, DCGI, 'Bilancia dei pagamenti e aiuti economici americani', 18 November 1953, in ACS, Ministero delle Finanze, Gab., Ufficio Paesi Esteri, b. 13;
578 Mutual Security Agency, 'Title I (Europe) Defense Support. Analysis of Effects of Assumed Expenditure Limitations. Italy', 14 March 1953, in NARA, RG469, Records of the Directors (1953-1961), Geographic Files of the Director 1948-1955, (1953-55), b. 11, fold. Italy;
579 In this regard see for example D. Menichella, *Discorso all'assemblea dell'Associazione Bancaria italiana*, in "Bancaria", n. 11 (1952), pp. 1136-49;

Conclusions

In the period after the birth of the Atlantic Alliance, and following the shift from material re-construction to the steady economic growth in Western Europe of the mid-1950s, both the governments of the United States and the various branches of NATO that were involved in the rearmament-induced industrial mobilization, approached the economic implications of this industrial effort in two ways. On the one hand, they stressed its impact on internal economic growth in each West European economy; on the other, they were aware that with the ending of the European Recovery Program the rearmament effort was to have serious implications on the balance of payments of the whole European economy. On the whole, most cabinet-level federal agencies in Washington, as well as the structures in Brussels that coordinated the in-dustrial effort at NATO level, offered a very consistent and tidy twofold policy guideline: from the Washington-based *National Advisory Council on International Monetary and Fi-nancial Problems* to the *Temporary Council Committee* (TCC) of NATO, from the central *Mutual Security Agency* operating in the United States to its national Missions operating across Western Europe, not to mention the US Treasury Department, the economic implica-tions of rearmament were regarded as an opportunity to stabilize the European economies and favor their integration into the broader post World War II international economic system with tight monetary and trade integration among the Western bloc economies[580].

The interpretation I offer in this work suggests that fears that rearmament might imperil the European economies and drive them towards sharp economic downturns were, in fact, super-seded by this perspective.

This new outlook on the connection between rearmament and growth goes back to the idea, as the TCC put it in 1951, that «the prime requisite for carrying out defense program, and at same time maintaining economic strength, is a satisfactory rate of general economic expan-sion». At the same time, however, this overall economic growth could not be achieved with-

---

580 According to the US government the OSP were an instrument to fill up the so called 'dollar gap' in Western Europe, in turn a much needed condition on the way «towards multilateral NATO objec-tives». In this regard, see Mutual Security Agency, 'Competitive Bidding and the Price Problem in Offshore Procurement', 2 April 1953, in NARA, RG469, Mission to Italy, Office of the Director, Sub-ject Files (Central Files) 1948-1957, b. 22, fold. 3 (Defense OSP Program Contracts-Production 1953); V.Barnett (MSA Rome) to ECA-MSA Washington, 9 June 1952, idem, fold. 5 (Defense : Procure-ment); Nac Meeting n.° 190, 13 March 1952, in NARA, RG56, Nac papers, Nac Minutes, b. 2; US Special Representative in Europe (SRE)-Treasury Department, 'Restoring Economic Equilibrium in the North Atlantic Community', 19 January 1953, in NARA, RG56, Nac Subject File 1946-1953, b. 29;

out guaranteeing the minimum conditions of economic growth that rearmament would induce and sustain[581].

Therefore, the government of Washington saw the creation of a truly balanced and integrated intra-European trade and currency market and the beginning of currency convertibility, as the two pre-conditions necessary for achieving rearmament programs in most West European member states of NATO. These were required circumstances for ensuring the much needed coordination among economies as diverse in terms of raw materials, industrial infrastructures and manpower as were those of Western Europe. Italy is an exemplary national case study when discussing this effort to balance domestic economic growth and external trade and monetary equilibrium as its involvement in the rearmament programs, which aimed to exploit Italian manufacturing capacity, stimulated an expansion in its domestic aggregate demand for durables and civilian consumer goods. The financial aid offered by the military assistance programs aimed to ease pressure on the Italian trade and balance of payments which had been induced by the increase in imports required to meet a steady rise in civilian demand boosted by war mobilization. Had the imbalances in the trade and monetary equilibrium not been addressed through external aid, either a rise in domestic aggregate demand exceeding the rate of industrial growth, or a steady intervention on the discount rate would have set off leapfrogging inflation. In the majority of West European countries this aid was granted in a situation where the restructuring of reserves and monetary stability was already underway.

The solution to these problems that NATO chose was to organize and distribute off-shore procurement contracts rewarded in US dollars and distributed to most of its European partners. There was an exchange between the West European economies of the NATO member states and the Federal Republic of Germany on the one side, and the American economy on the other, of raw, scarce and strategic material for investment and instrumental goods, as well as machine tools, spare parts and end-item weapons. In this framework, each manufacturing economy supplied either its own national defense system or the military of other member states of NATO. At the same time, the Atlantic Alliance mediated between its member states to negotiate deals on both force requirements, and the allotment of the off-shore contracts, as well as mutual exchange in raw material or processed goods.

Therefore, the OSP were designed to conciliate national economic growth and supranational economic integration on three levels: manufacturing, trade and payments.

The adoption of the off-shore procurement programs targeted all three levels at the same time. As a matter of fact, the OSP aimed firstly to improve coordination and rationalization of industrial capacity, manufacturing infrastructures and manpower by transferring raw material, semi-manufactured goods, armament components, and military end-items from one Western

---

581 P.Porter to Eca Rome, telegram, 21 December 1951, in NARA, RG469, Mission to Italy, Office of the Director , Subject files (Central files) 1948-1957, b. 23, fold. 3 (TCC);

bloc economy to another according to their military position and production requirements[582]. Secondly, a common budgetary fund was set up to finance this multilateral cooperation in trade and manufacturing and every NATO member state contributed to it in proportion to their national income. The goal of this common fund was to finance the industrial mobilization of the European economies involved in the rearmament process without impairing their internal monetary stability and balance of payments equilibrium. At the same time, this financial mechanism removed possible long-term hurdles to the supranational industrial and trade integration process caused by the money supply. Thus, by promoting exchange and payments, the multilateral setting of the Atlantic Alliance defense production programs helped the European economies to proceed beyond the bilateral trade system set up in Europe in the aftermath of World War II.

The Italian economy is a remarkable case in point due to its post war conditions. Its real economy suffered from scarcity in raw materials, oversupply of labor and underutilized industrial capacity and manufacturing infrastructures, while its monetary and financial situation was characterized by a very restricted internal money market and difficulties linked to the recovery of both its internal monetary and currency stability and its balance of payments equilibrium. Italy is therefore an ideal case study for investigating and understanding to what extent the twofold aims of domestic economic development and foreign exchange equilibrium were compatible against the backdrop of international economic integration of the Western bloc European states driven by the US military assistance programs under the aegis of NATO. The military assistance in Italy had a truly transversal scope, involving both defense security policies and foreign and internal economic policies, and marked by the well recognized anticommunist bias typical of US policies toward Western Europe in the early Cold War years. There can be no doubt, therefore, of the value of research into the defense and security policies implemented from the birth of the Atlantic Alliance to the mid-1950s. This analysis allows us to reconstruct Washington's complex and contradictory involvement in Italy during this turbulent period of bi-polar confrontation, and to examine the reactions of the Italian ruling class, forced to alternate between anti-communist policies and attempts to broaden social inclusion to bring the Italian working class into the pro-western and market-oriented mainstream of the Italian Republic.

These book-end conclusions aim to sum up the principal results of my research, which was based on a historical thesis proceeding along the three lines of investigation I set out at the very beginning of this work. Firstly, a close attention to the different ways in which domestic economic developments were run in Western Europe at government-level economic policymaking, and the US government intervention to influence and shape them through its foreign economic and assistance programs after the end of the Marshall Plan. Secondly, a step-by-

---

582 according to the long standing transatlantic debate we have been discussing in these pages, this wide-ranging coordination in production and exchange was likely to involve not only strategic material, investment goods, weapons and the like, further as also the European labor force.

step examination of the changing dynamics of economic diplomacy between the United States and Italy over the time period considered. Lastly, I explored the variety of economic policy options that were the subject of lengthy debate among the Italian political elites and economic technocracies over these years, as well as the economic cultures they stemmed from. These debates are of especial interest given that the so-called Italian centrism, from the beginning of the first legislature through the mid-1950s, provides an excellent showcase for the ambivalent stance of most West European democracies which had to accommodate transatlantic bonds with European integration.

It may be worthwhile to start with some remarks on the changing nature of bilateral economic relations between Rome and Washington due to their relevancy to the historical reconstruction developed in this book.

Firstly, both throughout the bilateral negotiations on U.S. military assistance to Italy and later when the military assistance programs took place under the aegis of NATO, the De Gasperi governments maintained the monetarist approach that had characterized post war Italian management of the economic appropriations granted under the European Recovery Programs, and in particular the so called *counterpart funds*. This orthodox Italian monetary policy continued into the new decade as the Rome governments strove to direct the currency from US financial aid, and the counterpart funds it generated, to ease the pressure of rearmament on the public finances of Italy and on the liabilities of the Italian Defense Ministry. This approach dominated Italian economic policy when managing both procurement contracts for the production of military end-items for the Italian Army and those destined for other countries involved in the OSP, and when managing the dollar payments and revenues that Italy earned as a manufacturing supply economy for its Atlantic partners as part of the off-shore procurement programs.

Secondly, it is important to pay close attention to the impact of rearmament on Italy's balance of payments and foreign trade as this enables us to reconsider the role of the off-shore procurement contracts in the economic relations between Italy and the United States. Most studies on the subject hold that in the early 1950s the Italian governments considered the OSP as a mere means to bargain Italy's trade liberalizations before its Western allies[583]. By contrast, I would argue that the negotiations between Italy and the United States on the OSP, as influenced by the positioning of the Italian Lira against the dollar currency area and the currencies of the European Payments Union, lead to different conclusions. I would contend that both Rome and Washington regarded the OSP as just one of many bargaining instruments at hand to be used to alter their bilateral economic and political relations. In fact, both countries placed the off-shore procurement contracts in the broader context of the international economic diplomacy of the early Cold War years. Both Italy and the United States resorted to this use of the OSP given that the Italian economy was a crucial player in the economic Cold War

---

583 So far, the main reference in the literature is still L.Segreto, *L'Italia nel sistema economico internazionale. Attori e politiche tra anni cinquanta e sessanta*, p. 185;

between the Western countries and the Soviet bloc when their respective spheres of economic influence were drawn up across Europe. The US Administrations used the OSP to contain the Italian trade deals with the Soviet dominated economies of Eastern Europe. Italy, on the other hand, exploited the negotiations on these monetary contracts to improve its position and bargaining power in the intra-European trade integration process. Since Italy had suffered from a worsening debt position within EPU after the outbreak of the Korean War as a result of French and British restrictive trade policies against the Lira, Rome reacted with the twofold threat of expansion of its trade partnership with the Soviet bloc, and a reduction of the recently adopted liberalization of trade toward the would-be European common market economies. If we consider the situation in Italy to further analyze the international economic integration driven by NATO's rearmament programs, as used to influence the Italian governments' domestic economic policies and the prospective material take-off of the late 1950s, it is clear that our study must go beyond Italian economic policies alone. While we must indeed reflect on the country's economic policy we must also investigate the industrial policies that were implemented to modernize the Italian economy and encourage the access of its manufacturing system to the interdependent world economy of the post World War II era, as well as integrating its processed goods in the international trade system. This theme involves consideration of US strategies to influence the process of supranational economic integration through the imposition of international constraints.

The 1951 Mutual Security Act, thanks to which a multilateral military assistance program such as the OSP became law, later linked the implementation of coordinated defense policies at NATO level to market-oriented and free enterprise-centered internal economic developments. By law the US military assistance was closely bound to a significant reduction in restrictive business practices and a significant advance in industrial productivity based on market competition among firms, rather than on nominal wage cuts and significant reductions in labor purchasing power. In this respect, the American strategy toward Italy was implemented in most West European economies. The attention that from time to time this book devoted to the impact that the rearmament programs had on the process of industrial modernization, whether on the supply or on the consumption side of the production chain, revolves around this broader research perspective. The issue of industrial and economic modernization at large is a recurrent theme in the military assistance programs involving the Italian mechanical and aeronautical firms. In this respect, the combination of military rearmament and industrial productivity led the American initiatives to promote and finance the off-shore procurement programs[584].

---

584 'Memorandum of understanding between the Government of the United States and the Government of Italy relating to Offshore procurement', in NARA, RG84, Rome Embassy, Secret General Records 1953-1954, b. 1, fold. 320.1; V.Barnett to the Italian Government, 30 March 1953, in ACS, PCM, CIR, b. 77; Nac Meeting n. 188, 23 January 1952, in NARA, RG56, Nac papers, Nac Minutes, b. 2, fold.. Nac Minutes 188-197 (1952);

Although the involvement of the aeronautical industry in the ERP assistance programs was marginal, a monographic work on the role of this sector is of interest given that the US government used the OSP to reshape the Italian economy according to the principles of free trade and market competition and to demolish a highly monopolistic sector such as the Italian aeronautical industry of the early 1950s, when the Italian state shareholding system owned one fourth of the available manufacturing capacity. The American struggle to introduce a cost-cutting industrial policy in Italy involved both a constant fight against restrictive business practices, and a reorganization of the production chain to raise industrial productivity and increase price competitiveness. In this respect, it is worth stressing how the American authorities in Europe aimed to introduce the so-called productivity drive both in the industries producing durables and in the heavy processing firms working on investment and instrumental goods. Furthermore, as the example of Fiat illustrates, the introduction of new production methods came with a rise in technological added value which aimed to reshape the Italian mechanical sector and make it more capital intensive. For the Americans a competitive Italian manufacturing industry had to be based on technological advance rather than on cost-cutting wage policies[585].

This close interplay between rearmament and productivity took place against the overall American move to use the early military assistance programs to modernize the industrial system and to stabilize its labor market according to a demand-supporting economic strategy. Throughout the first two years, the military aid programs were never intended to expand the industrial base and to reduce the employment rate, rather the opposite was true. During these early phases the American plans were to restore pre war levels of industrial activity and employment rates either by resurrecting the existing industrial capacity or by cutting production costs and raising industrial productivity. A redistributive fiscal policy that aimed to increase the purchasing power of the low-income wage earners was to complement this strategy. Accordingly, between the Mutual Defense Assistance Programs and the early OSP programs, the United States' government worked hard to make the US Congress pass laws to finance low capital intensive and labor intensive procurement contracts to repair weapons and to produce components, machine tools and spare parts, as well as to introduce production standardizations according to the American production models. Therefore, these early OSP contracts were to benefit the low technological added value and high labor intensive manufacturing sectors.

When the all-weather fighters went into production in 1953 the American demand-supporting economic strategy shifted to a demand-expanding policy. From that year onwards the aim of

---

585 On the whole, from the post war reconstruction through the eruption of Korean War, the Italian industrial system based its export and competitiveness on fiercely cost cutting wage policies and low growth rate in terms of domestic aggregate demand and civilian consumption. In Italy this policy was the hallmark of post war industrial relations clearly bound to foreign trade and export policies by far still based on the labor intensive and low capital intensive manufacturing sectors.

the OSP was to expand the Italian industrial base while introducing moves to cool off the financial impact of this expanding level of industrial activity on Italy's imports and on the balance of payments equilibrium. With the F86K production program Italy became a fully-fledged production source for the Atlantic community, clearly illustrating America's new demand-expanding policy to sustain the Italian economy. Henceforth, the allotment of OSP contracts to supply other NATO member states with instrumental goods, military spare parts or end items, which led Italy to supply the West Germany after its full admission to the Atlantic Alliance, was to be part of the American strategy to promote a clear-cut model of economic growth in Italy. In American eyes, the best path to economic advance was to combine a reduction in the unemployment rate and follow-up expansion in the internal aggregate demand for civilian consumption without impairing the country's monetary stability and foreign trade equilibrium, which was deemed necessary to achieve the supranational integration of Italy in the international economy.

Between 1953 and 1955 this American strategy to re-shape the Italian economy was increasingly interwoven with the well-known US initiatives to contain the Italian Communist party and the working class movement that were undertaken by the Eisenhower Administration and its ambassador to Italy, Clare Boothe Luce. This work argues that under the ambassadorship of Clare Boothe Luce the earlier strategy to fight the red scare through a wide-reaching call for a broad social inclusion based on steadily rising living standards and economic aid programs germane to the ERP, was only temporarily left aside and overshadowed. The former approach to fighting the communist threat by addressing the poverty-biased issue gave way to an anti-communist political bias which aimed to pursue a policy of exclusion that would segregate the Italian left-wing trade union movement in the workplace and downgrade the Italian Communist Party to a political minority by pushing it out of the national government. This American policy, which has been amply studied in the literature, was only temporarily pursued by the United States for three reasons. Firstly, we must remember that the Eisenhower Administration inherited from its predecessor the idea that the international security policies of NATO and the national economic policies of its member states were bound together. Secondly, by 1954 Clare Luce herself had realized that consistent American support for mid-term economic growth and an expansionary policy was indispensable if Italy were to be a loyal and stable partner of NATO[586]. Lastly, Italy's role in the Atlantic Alliance's multilateral produc-

---

586 The US Embassy in Rome pushed forward this policy between 1955 and 1956, when it came to term with the changing nature of USSR strategy to bring Italy into its own sphere of influence, increasingly based on offers to strengthen economic and trade ties with Rome. In this respect see J.Jernegan to the Secretary of State, 17 July 1956, telegram, in NARA, RG56, OASIA, b. 63, fold. Italy MSA/FOA General 1952-59; C.Luce to J.Dulles, 10 October 1956, in NARA, RG59, Central Files 1955-1959, b. 2539, 611.65/10-1056. Furthermore, as this books outlines in the very last chapter, the US Embassy came up with this diplomatic drift on the occasion of those development and growth programs -the most known of whom being the Piano Vanoni- that Italy formulated and brought before

tion programs as a manufacturing supply economy triggered this shift in American policy. Nevertheless, it is worth stressing that wide-ranging studies on the international aid programs backed by Washington are necessary to complete our understanding of the nature and meaning of the United States strategy in Italy as it switched between the so-called anti-communist containment policies and forward-looking expansionary initiatives, in order to complement the research in this book on the off-shore procurement contracts. In fact, further support for my arguments on the shift in American strategies to stabilize the country and contain the red scare by the mid-1950s could come from an exploration of the credit lines that the IBRD granted to Italy and its *Cassa per il Mezzogiorno* (Fund for the South - the government-run agency set up in 1950 to promote and to finance industrial development in the Southern Italian regions). Moreover, it might be helpful to investigate the Export Import Bank loans to Italy at the time. The Eximbank had provided Rome with financial aid packages from as early as 1950, but they became significant only at the middle of the decade, when the country was the recipient of extraordinary appropriations[587]. Furthermore, it is worth reconstructing the way in which the counterpart funds that accrued after 1953 were used to stimulate the Italian economy[588].

It is worth reviewing a summary of the much debated, twofold alternative for the harmonization of domestic economic policies and the supranational integration of the Italian economy as it regards the third line of investigation I adopted. The debate over the strengthening of transatlantic ties and the perspective offered by the European economic integration process caused clashes and re-alignment among the Italian political and economic elites. All nation-level Italian economic policy makers and technocrats involved in the bilateral and multilateral negotiations on the military assistance programs had a pro-transatlantic view and were inclined to

---

the OEEC by the middle of the decade. On this see C.Luce to FOA, 22 December 1954, telegram, idem; M.Brosio to Ministero degli Esteri, 'Rapporti economici Italia-USA', 6 September 1956, in ACS, Ministero del Tesoro, Gab., Affari Generali 1948-1964, b. 52; Memorandum of Meeting Dulles-Hoover-Stassen-Nolting, 'Aid Problems for Fiscal Year 1956', 18 January 1955, in NARA, The Secretary's and the Undersecretary's Memoranda of Conversation 1953-1964, Lot File 64D199, b. 3; 587 IBRD, Press Release n. 402, '70$ Million Italian Loan', 1 June 1955, in NARA, RG469, Mission to Italy, Food and Agriculture Division, Agricultural Reports 1949-1956, b. 2; 'Proposed Export-Import Bank $10 Million Loan in Italy', in Nac Meeting n. 494, 4 September 1956, in NARA, RG56, NAC papers, NAC Staff Committee papers, Minutes of Meetings 1945-1959, b. 3; 'Proposed International Bank Loan of Approximately $75 Million to Italy', in Nac Meeting n. 497, 9 October 1956, idem; S.Van Dyke to D.A.Fitzgerald, 'ICA/State Controversy Regarding the OCB Outline Plan of Operations for Italy', 30 August 1956, in NARA, RG469, Office of the Deputy Director for Operations (1953-1961), Office of African and European Operations (1955-1961), Western Europe Division, Italy Subject Files 1950-56, b. 10, fasc. Italy OCB Fiscal Year 1956; 588 since 1954 thereafter, according to the Agricultural Trade and Development Assistance Act, the selling of American agricultural surplus increasingly accounted for the total amount of counterpart funds available to Italy. For a first overview of this theme see C.Villani, *Il Prezzo della stabilità*,

strengthen Italy's bonds with the dollar currency area and its commodity markets. This perspective reunified both the Italian representatives on the executive boards of NATO, who were working on the industrial and financial implications of rearmament, and the country's ambassadors at the annual meetings and summits of the IMF and the other international financial institutions. Accordingly, leading Italian policymakers such as Giuseppe Pella and Ezio Vanoni, Massimo Magistrati and Piero Malvestiti, not to mention the key figure of Giovanni Malagodi, all of whom differed considerably as regards economic culture and political background, shared this pro-dollar approach to the opening up of the Italian economy to the international trade and in favor of monetary integration process. One of the principal aims of these policymakers was to redress the Italian balance of payments against the other West European currency areas, a parameter that had seen both ups and downs over the period examined in this book. The policymakers held the view that this goal should be fostered in conjunction with an ever stronger trade partnership with the commodity markets anchored to the US dollar. By contrast, the Italian ruling class involved in the early steps of leading European economic institutions like the OEEC and the European Payments Union championed the alternative offered by the European economic integration process. Both Guido Carli and the midsized Italian export-oriented firms, which included the bulk of Italy's low capital-intensive and high labor-intensive manufacturing sectors, considered the military procurement contracts of NATO as a fly-wheel to a European trade integration process and political partnership between Italy and the United States.

These two options would have a very different and asymmetric impact on the Italian trade and monetary policies, as the off-shore procurement programs channeled financial aid in US dollars, military spare parts and end-items to increase the inflow of dollars and to significantly reduce the offsetting of trade and payments in European currencies. In the framework of this engineering to couple currency stability and trade exchange through the military assistance programs, Italy came up with two answers. The case for a partnership with the dollar area was strengthened by the worsening of Italy's current account in the balance of payments against the European currency markets, which had been generated by the choice to ease quantitative and quota trade restrictions after fall 1951, together with the financial aid in US dollars granted by the military assistance programs to cover rearmament-related imports. This led to a striking imbalance in the current account of Italy's balance of payments against the dollar markets and the West European partners currency areas respectively. The Italian policymakers planned to achieve this dollar-pegged strategy to bring Italy into the post war international economy in two steps: firstly, Italy was to increase its imports of raw and strategic materials, and then to become the demand market for American military spare parts, end-items, and investment goods. In the eyes of the Italian Christian Democratic elites and the economic technocracies this monetary and trade option would come with a relatively cheap technological update from the dollar currency areas. In this case, the military assistance programs provided the Italian economy with funds to be used to finance technological imports from the US market. This strategy was pushed forward through the early 1960s, when in the American eyes the Italian import of technological hardware was to help resurrect the US balance of payments from its shrinking imbalance[589]. The Italian governments saw this tight trade and monetary partnership with the dollar markets as a required choice to effect the reorganization of Italian manufacturing and ensure competitive price bidding on the international trade market. I thus analyzed the military assistance programs implemented through the early 1950s in order to pursue this line of interpretation on the industrial modernization of the Italian mechanical manufacturing system that received orders from the aeronautical industry. My study on these military procurements involved the economic policy issues related to the approach of integrating Italy in the international economy through rearmament. Accordingly, this book tackled issues such as fiscal policy, monetary policy, or the credit policy that was undertaken to stimulate domestic investments in the manufacturing sectors that were producing military procurements. Again, it is within this interpretative framework that I focused on the social and labor policies that were promoted to stabilize the Italian economy and keep the Italian industrial output stable and continuous.

The Italian political and economic policymakers tried to cope with the economic implications of rearmament on Italy by means of a second option that aimed to integrate the Italian economy into the European trade markets and currency areas. This approach was strongly backed by the United States authorities and eventually prevailed. It is worth investigating this option not only because it was the one that prevailed, but also because it is important in two different ways. Firstly, the integration of the Italian economy in the European market improved the Italian balance of trade; secondly, its contribution to the resurrection of the Italian balance of payments was intended to provide the Italian manufacturing firms with monetary liquidity either to finance domestic industrial investments, or to import raw, strategic and scarce materials. Furthermore, in the eyes of the Italian entrepreneurs and economic elites, the integration of the Italian economy within the European context was to strengthen the Italian Lira and the Italian manufacturing system in the international economy through its close trade partnership with the economy of the Federal Republic of Germany[590].

---

589 Memorandum for the President, 'Report on Measures to improve e the balance of payments', 1961, in HSTPL, Papers of Dean Acheson, accessed on DDRS;
590 for a detailed reconstruction of this entrepreneurial strategy see F.Petrini, *Il liberismo a una dimensione*, pp. 300 ff.;

ARCHIVAL SOURCES

Dwight D.Eisenhower Presidential Library, Abilene, Kansas, USA

J.F.Dulles Papers 1951-1959, Subject Series

Dwight D. Eisenhower Papers, Papers as President of the United States (Ann Whitman File) 1953-1961, NSC Series

White House Office, Office of the Special Assistant for National Security Affairs (Robert Cutler, Dillon Anderson and Gordon Gray), Records 1952-1961, NSC Series

H.S. Truman Presidential Library, Independence, Mo. , USA

Papers of Dean Acheson

Records of the Psychological Strategic Board

President's Secretary's Files

NATO Collection, North Atlantic Council

Development and Ratification of NATO Collection

Oral History Interviews:

Richard M. Bissell oral interview
John W. Snyder oral interview
Averell Harriman oral interview
John Ohly oral interview
Paul Hoffman oral interview
Milton Katz oral interview

Columbia University, Butler Library, Rare Books and Manuscripts Division, New York City
papers of A.Harriman

Digital National Security Archive. The Documents that made US Policy (http://nsarchive.chadwyck.com/marketing/index.jsp);

The Library of Congress, Manuscript Division, Washington DC, USA

Paul Nitze Papers, Subject Files 1942-1989

Clare Boothe Luce Papers

National Archives and Records Administration (NARA), College Park , Maryland (Md), USA

Record Group 43, Records of International Conferences

Commissions and Expositions, Records of International Meetings on Post war Policy 1945-1955, Records Relating to the North Atlantic Council (NAC), Records concerning the seventh session of NAC

Record Group 56, General Records of the Department of the Treasury

Papers of the National Advisory Council on International Monetary and Financial Problems (NAC):

-NAC Papers, NAC Minutes

-NAC Staff Committee Minutes 1945-59

-NAC papers, NAC Staff Committee papers, Minutes of Meetings 1945-1959

-NAC Papers, Nac Documents and Supplements 1945-1968

Records of the Office of the Assistant Secretary for International Affairs 1934-1974 (OASIA)

Record Group 59, General Records of the Department of State

-Central files 1950-54

-Central Files 1955-59

-Records of the Office of the Special Assistant for Mutual Security Coordination, Office of the Undersecretary of State 1952-59

-Records of the Office of the Special Assistant for Mutual Security Coordination, Office of the Undersecretary of State 1952-59, Lot File 59D449

-Lot File 52-26, Records of the Mutual Defense Assistance Program, Subject File relating to Program Management (Bell Rowe File) 1949-1952

-The Secretary and the Undersecretary's Memoranda of Conversation 1953-1964, Lot File 64D199

-Records Relating to the State Department Participation in the Operations Coordinating Board and the National Security Council 1947-1963, Lot File 62D430

-Records Relating to the Mutual Security Program, West European Country Files 1952-1956, Lot File 59D448

-Lot File 58D357

Record Group 84, Foreign Service Posts of the Department of State

-Rome Embassy, Secret General Records 1953-55

-Records of Clare Boothe Luce 1953-56, Top Secret Files, Lot File 64F26

Record Group 273, Records of the National Security Council

-National Security Council Policy Papers

Record Group 330, Records of the Office of the Secretary of Defense

-Country Files (CAIN) 1950-1955;

Record Group 469, General Records of the United States Foreign Assistance Agencies (1948-1961)

-Mission to Italy, Office of the Director, Subject Files (Central Files) 1948-57

-Mission to Italy, Food and Agriculture Division, Agricultural Reports 1949-1956

-Office of the Deputy Director for Operations (1953-1961), Office of African and European Operations (1955-1961), Western European Division, Italy Subject File 1950-1956

-Office of the Deputy Director for Operations (1953-1961), Office of European Operations (1953-1955), Italy Division, Decimal File 1948-1954

-Office of the Deputy Director for Operations (1953-1961), Office of European Operations (1953-1955), Office of the Director, Geographic Files (Central Files) 1953-54

-Records of the Directors (1953-1961), Geographic Files of the Director 1948-1955

-Records of the Directors (1953-1961), Geographic Files of the Director 1948-1955, (1953-55)

-Deputy to the Director, Subject Files of Glen A.Lloyd, Deputy to the Director 1953-55

-Mission Files, Finance and Program Review Division, Military Production Files

Historical Archives of the European Communities, Firenze, Italy

-Ivan Matteo Lombardo Papers

-OEEC Papers, Council Minutes

The National Archives of the United Kingdom, Kew, Richmond, Surrey, United Kingdom

-The Cabinet Papers 1915-1981

Historical Archive of the Italian Foreign Office, Roma, Italy

-Direzione Generale Affari Politici

-Ambasciata d'Italia a Parigi, 1951-1958 (1954)

-Fondo Cassaforte

Fiat Historical Archive, Torino, Italy

-Minutes of the board of directors

-USA-Delibere

Historical Archive of the Luigi Sturzo Institute, Roma, Italy

-Mario Scelba Papers

Historical Archive of the Italian Employer's Federation, Roma, Italy

-Fondo CED

-Fondo Comitati Permanenti

National Archives of Italy, Roma, Italy

-Presidenza del Consiglio dei Ministri, Gab., 1951-1954

-Presidenza del Consiglio dei Ministri, Comitato Interministeriale per la Ricostruzione

-Ministero delle Finanze, Gab.

-Ministero del Commercio con l'Estero, Direzione Generale Importazioni e Esportazioni

-Ministero del Tesoro, Direzione Generale del Tesoro, Ispettorato Generale per i rapporti con l'estero

-Ministero del Tesoro, Gab., Affari Generali 1948-1964

-Ministero dell'Industria, del commercio e dell'Artigianato, Segreteria Campilli

-Ministero Bilancio e Programmazione economica, Gab., Archivio Generale

-Archivio Storico IRI, Numerazione rossa, Finmeccanica varie

-Archivio Storico IRI, numerazione nera, Siderurgia

-Archivio Storico IRI, Numerazione rossa (pratiche societarie)

-Ministero dell'Aeronautica, Segretariato Generale, Archivio Generale
Ugo La Malfa Papers

Historical Archives of the Central Bank of Italy

Carte Caffè, Fondo Studi

Historical Archive of the National Institute for Industrial Reconstruction, Roma, Italy

Ufficio Tecnico Centrale (IRI Roma)

PRINTED SOURCES

Declassified Documents and Reference System, Farmington Hills (MI), 2008-2010

Foreign Relations of the United States, Government Printing Office, Washington, DC:

FRUS, 1944, Vol. 3, *The British Commonwealth and Europe*, 1965;

FRUS 1945, Vol. 1, *The Conference of Berlin (The Potsdam Conference)*, 1960;

FRUS, 1945, Vol. 4, *Europe*, 1945;

FRUS, 1946, Vol. 5, *The British Commonwealth, Western and Central Europe*, 1969;

FRUS, 1947, Vol. 3, *The British Commonwealth, Europe*, 1947;

FRUS 1948, Vol. 1: *General: United Nations*, part 2, 1976;

FRUS 1949, Vol. 1, *National Security Affairs: Foreign Economic Policy,* 1976;

FRUS, 1949, Vol. 3, *Council of Foreign Ministers, Germany and Austria*, 1949;

FRUS 1949, Vol. 4, *Western Europe*, 1975;

FRUS 1950, Vol. 1, *National Security Affairs: Foreign Economic Policy,* 1977;

FRUS 1950, Vol. 3, *Western Europe*, 1977;

FRUS, 1951, Vol. 1, *National Security Affairs, Foreign Economic Policy*, 1980;

FRUS 1951, Vol. 4, *Europe: Political and Economic Relations*, 1985;

FRUS, 1952-54, Vol. 6, *Western Europe and Canada*, Part 2, 1986;

Documents on British Policy Overseas, Her Majesty's Stationery Office, London 1989

Series II, vol. III, *German Rearmament September-December 1950*;

OTHER PRINTED SOURCES

G.Antonazzi (ed.), *Carteggio Sturzo-De Gasperi 1920-1953*, Morcelliana, Brescia 1999

Banca d'Italia, *Relazione annuale per l'anno 1951*, Banca d'Italia, Roma 1952;

Carteggio Sturzo-Scelba 1923-1956, Istituto Luigi Sturzo, Roma 1994;

F.Cotula, C.O. Gelsomino, A.Gigliobianco, (eds), *Donato Menichella: Stabilità e sviluppo dell'economia italiana, 1946-1960*. Vol. 2, *Considerazioni finali all'assemblea della Banca d'Italia*, Laterza, Roma and Bari, 1997;

M.R.De Gasperi (ed.), *De Gasperi scrive. Corrispondenza con capi di stato cardinali uomini politici giornalisti diplomatici*, Morcelliana, Brescia 1974;

Department of Commerce, "Survey of Current Business",

Documents on American Foreign Relations, Vol. 4, *July 1943-June 1944*, the World Peace Foundation and Princeton University Press, Princeton (NJ), 1976;

Documents on American Foreign Relations, vol. 7, The World Peace Foundation and Princeton University Press, Princeton (NJ), 1976;

D.Folliot, *Documents on International Affairs*, 1951;

Gordon Gray, *Report to the President on Foreign Economic Policies*, Washington DC, 1950;

Guido Carli e le istituzioni economiche internazionali, in *Scritti e discorsi di Guido Carli*, Bollati Boringhieri,Torino, 2009;

P. Malvestiti, *Lettere al presidente. Carteggio De Gasperi-Malvestiti 1948-1953*, Bonetti, Milano, 1964;

G.Pella, *OCSE. Dalla cooperazione europea alla cooperazione euro-americana*, Banco di Roma, Roma, 1961;

Public Papers of the United States. Harry S.Truman (http://www.trumanlibrary.org/publicpapers/index.php);

G.Rochat (ed.), *Atti del Comando generale del Corpo Volontari della libertà (gennaio 1944-aprile 1945)*, FrancoAngeli, Milano, 1972;

Harry S.Truman, *Report to Congress on the Mutual Defense Assistance Program*, Washington D.C., 1950-52;

US Department of Commerce, *Markets after the Defense Expansion*, Washington D.C., 1952;

US Congress, Senate, Committee on Appropriations, Special Subcommittee on Foreign Economic Cooperation, *Analysis of the Gray Report*, 82d Cong., 1st session, 1951, Washington D.C., 1951;

U.S. Congress, Senate, Committee on Appropriations, Special Subcommittee on Foreign Economic Cooperation, *Analysis of the Gray Report*, 82d Cong., 1st session, 1951, Washington D.C., 1951;

Verbali del Consiglio dei Ministri, luglio 1943-maggio 1948, Vol. 7, tome 1, *Governo De Gasperi 13/7/1946-2/2/1947*, Presidenza del Consiglio dei Ministri, Roma 1997;

MEMOIRS

D.Acheson, *Present at the Creation: My Years in the State Department*, Norton & Co, New York, 1987;

G.Carli, *Cinquant'anni di vita italiana*, Laterza, Roma and Bari, 1993;

C.Sforza, *Cinque anni a Palazzo Chigi: La politica estera italiana dal 1947 al 1951*, Atlante, Roma, 1952;

Lord Ismay, *NATO: The First Five Years, 1949-1954*, Paris, 1954;

H.Macmillan, *Memoirs*, Vol. 2, *the Blast of War*, London, Macmillan 1967;

P.H.Nitze, *From Hiroshima to Glasnost: At the Center of the Decision: A Memoir*, Weidenfeld, New York, 1989;

H.S.Truman, *Memoirs*, vol. 2, *Years of Trial and Hope*, Doubleday & Co., New York, 1955;

Scritti e discorsi di Guido Carli, Vol. 2, *Guido Carli e le istituzioni economiche internazionali*, edited by G.Di Taranto, Bollati Boringhieri, Torino, 2009;

Newspapers and periodicals

"Bancaria"

"Corriere della Sera"

"Fortune"

"Il mondo"

"Il Sole"

"Moneta e credito"

"The Journal of Commerce"

"The New York Times"

Abbreviations

The following abbreviations are used throughout this book and the footnotes

ACS= Archivio Centrale dello Stato, Roma (National Archives of Italy)

AILS= Archivio Storico Istituto Luigi Sturzo, Roma (Historical Archive of the Luigi Sturzo Institute)

AMP= Additional Military Productions

ARAR= Azienda per il Rilievo e l'Alienazione dei Residuati Bellici

ASBI= Archivio Storico Banca d'Italia, Roma (Historical Archives of the Central Bank of Italy)

ASC= Archivio Storico Confindustria, Roma (Historical Archive of the Italian Employer's Federation)

ASCE= Archivi Storici delle Comunità Europee, Firenze (Historical Archives of the European Communities)

ASF= Archivio Storico Fiat, Torino (Fiat Historical Archive)

ASIRI=Archivio Storico Istituto per la Ricostruzione Industriale, Roma (Historical Archive of the National Institute for Industrial Reconstruction)

ASMAE= Archivio Storico del Ministero Affari Esteri, Roma (Historical Archive of the Italian Foreign Office)

b. = box

CAB= Cabinet papers

Caffè= Historical Archives of the Central Bank of Italy, Federico Caffè papers

Cassaforte= Historical Archive of the Italian Foreign Office, Cassaforte series

CBLP= Clare Boothe Luce Papers

CED= Comunità Europea di Difesa (European Defense Community)

CGIL= Confederazione Generale Italiana del Lavoro

CIR= Comitato Interministeriale per la Ricostruzione

CU= Columbia University, New York City, USA

DBPO= Documents on British Policy Overseas, London, UK

DDEL= Dwight D.Eisenhower Presidential Library, Abilene, Kansas, USA

DDRS= Declassified Documents and Reference System, Gale, Farmington Hills, Michigan 2008

DEFC= Defense Economic and Financial Committee

DELTEC= Delegazione Tecnica Italiana a Washington

DG= Direzione Generale

DGAE= Direzione Generale Affari Economici

DGAP= Direzione Generale Affari Politici

DGCE= Direzione Generale Cooperazione Economica

DGCI= Direzione Generale Cooperazione Internazionale

DPB= Defense Production Board

ECA= Economic Cooperation Administration

EPU= European Payments Union

ERP= European Recovery Program

FAAC= Foreign Assistance Correlation Committee

FEB= Financial and Economic Board

Fiat= Fabbrica Italiana Automobili Torino

FIOM= Federazione Impiegati e Operai Metallurgici

FOA= Foreign Operations Administration

Fold.= folder

FRUS= Foreign Relations of the United States

GAB= Gabinetto

GATT= General Agreement on Tariffs and Trade

GDP= Gross Domestic Product

GNP= Gross National Product

HPPP= High Priority Production Programs

HSTPL= H.S. Truman Presidential Library, Independence, Mo., USA

IBRD= International Bank for Reconstruction and Development

IMF= International Monetary Fund

IMI=Istituto Mobiliare Italiano

IML= Ivan Matteo Lombardo Papers

IRFE=Ispettorato Generale per i Rapporti con l'Estero

IRI= Istituto per la Ricostruzione Industriale

JCS= Joint Chiefs of Staff

LOC=Library of Congress, Washington DC, USA

MAAG= Military Assistant Advisory Group

MAE= Ministero Affari Esteri, Roma (Italian Foreign Office)

MCE= Ministero per il Commercio con l'Estero (Italian Ministry for Foreign Trade)

MD= Columbia University, Butler Library, Rare Books and Manuscripts Division

MDAA=Mutual Defense Assistance Act

MDAP= Mutual Defense Assistance Program

MICA= Ministero dell'Industria Commercio e Artigianato

MSA= Mutual Security Agency

MSP= Mutual Security Program

MTDP= Mid Term Defense Program

n.a.= no author

n.d.= no date

NAC= National Advisory Council on International Monetary and Financial Problems

NATO= North Atlantic Treaty Organization

NSC= National Security Council

OA= Organizzazione Patto Atlantico

OASIA= Records of the Office of the Assistant Secretary for International Affairs

OCSE= Organizzazione per la Cooperazione e lo Sviluppo Economico

OECE= Organizzazione Europea per la Cooperazione Economica

OEEC= Organization for European Economic Cooperation

OSP=Off-shore procurements program

PCM=Presidenza del Consiglio dei Ministri

Pratt.=Pratiche

PRO= The National Archives UK, Kew, Richmond, Surrey, United Kingdom

RFT= Repubblica Federale Tedesca

s.f.= sub folder

SRE= United States Special Representative in Europe

TCC=Temporary Council Committee

ULM= Ugo La Malfa Papers

USAF= United States Air Forces

USSR= Union of Soviet Socialist Republics

Index

214

Arbeit, Bildung & Gesellschaft
Labour, Education & Society

Herausgegeben von Prof. Dr. György Széll, Prof. Dr. Heinz Sünker,
Dr. Anne Inga Hilsen und Dr. Francesco Garibaldo

Bd.   22   Christoph Sänger: Anna Siemsen – Bildung und Literatur. 2011.

Bd.   23   Nam-Kook Kim: Deliberative Multiculturalism in Britain. A Response to Devolution, European Integration, and Multicultural Challenges. 2011.

Bd.   24   Mirella Baglioni / Bernd Brandl (eds.): Changing Labour Relations. Between Path Dependency and Global Trends. 2011.

Bd.   25   Rüdiger Kühr: Japan`s Transnational Environmental Policies. The Case of Environmental Technology Transfer to Newly Industrializing Countries. 2011.

Bd.   26   Francesco Garibaldo / Dinghong Yi (eds.): Labour and Sustainable Development. North-South Perspectives. 2012.

Bd.   27   Francesco Garibaldo / Mirella Baglioni / Catherine Casey / Volker Telljohann (eds.): Workers, Citizens, Governance. Socio-Cultural Innovation at Work. 2012.

Bd.   28   Simone Selva: Supra-National Integration and Domestic Economic Growth. The United States and Italy in the Western Bloc Rearmament Programs 1945-1955. Translation by Filippo del Lucchese, revision by Simone Selva. 2012.

www.peterlang.de